The Teaching for Social Justice Series

William Ayers—Series Editor
Therese Quinn—Associate Series Editor

Pedagogy of the Poor:
Building the Movement to End Poverty
WILLIE BAPTIST AND JAN REHMANN

Grow Your Own Teachers:
Grassroots Change for Teacher Education
ELIZABETH A. SKINNER, MARIA TERESA
GARRETÓN, AND BRIAN D. SCHULTZ, EDITORS

Girl Time: Literacy, Justice,
and the School-to-Prison Pipeline
MAISHA T. WINN

Holler If You Hear Me: The Education of a
Teacher and His Students, Second Edition
GREGORY MICHIE

Controversies in the Classroom:
A Radical Teacher Reader
JOSEPH ENTIN, ROBERT C. ROSEN, AND
LEONARD VOGT, EDITORS

Spectacular Things Happen Along the Way:
Lessons from an Urban Classroom
BRIAN D. SCHULTZ

The Seduction of Common Sense: How the Right
Has Framed the Debate on America's Schools
KEVIN K. KUMASHIRO

Teach Freedom: Education for Liberation
in the African-American Tradition
CHARLES M. PAYNE AND
CAROL SILLS STRICKLAND, EDITORS

Social Studies for Social Justice: Teaching
Strategies for the Elementary Classroom
RAHIMA C. WADE

Pledging Allegiance:
The Politics of Patriotism in America's Schools
JOEL WESTHEIMER, EDITOR

See You When We Get There:
Teaching for Change in Urban Schools
GREGORY MICHIE

Echoes of Brown: Youth Documenting
and Performing the Legacy of *Brown v.
Board of Education*
MICHELLE FINE

Writing in the Asylum:
Student Poets in City Schools
JENNIFER MCCORMICK

Teaching the Personal and the Political:
Essays on Hope and Justice
WILLIAM AYERS

Teaching Science for Social Justice
ANGELA CALABRESE BARTON, WITH
JASON L. ERMER, TANAHIA A. BURKETT,
AND MARGERY D. OSBORNE

Putting the Children First:
The Changing Face of Newark's Public Schools
JONATHAN G. SILIN AND
CAROL LIPPMAN, EDITORS

Refusing Racism:
White Allies and the Struggle for Civil Rights
CYNTHIA STOKES BROWN

A School of Our Own: Parents, Power, and
Community at the East Harlem Block Schools
TOM RODERICK

The White Architects of Black Education:
Ideology and Power in America, 1865–1954
WILLIAM WATKINS

The Public Assault on America's Children:
Poverty, Violence, and Juvenile Injustice
VALERIE POLAKOW, EDITOR

Construction Sites: Excavating Race, Class, and
Gender Among Urban Youths
LOIS WEIS AND
MICHELLE FINE, EDITORS

Walking the Color Line:
The Art and Practice of Anti-Racist Teaching
MARK PERRY

A Simple Justice: The Challenge of Small Schools
WILLIAM AYERS, MICHAEL KLONSKY, and
GABRIELLE H. LYON, EDITORS

Teaching for Social Justice:
A Democracy and Education Reader
W

D0775837

Pedagogy of the Poor

BUILDING THE MOVEMENT TO END POVERTY

Willie Baptist
Jan Rehmann

Teachers College
Columbia University
New York and London

Published by Teachers College Press, 1234 Amsterdam Avenue, New York, New York, 10027

Library of Congress Cataloging-in-Publication Data

Baptist, Willie.
    Pedagogy of the poor : building the movement to end poverty / Willie Baptist and Jan Rehmann.
        p. cm. — (The teaching for social justice series)
    Includes bibliographical references and index.
        ISBN 978-0-8077-5228-9 (pbk. : alk. paper) — ISBN 978-0-8077-5229-6 (hardcover : alk. paper) 1. Baptist, Willie. 2. Poverty—California—Los Angeles. 3. Marginality, Social—California—Los Angeles. 4. Social justice—California—Los Angeles. I. Rehmann, Jan. II. Title.
    HC108.L55B37 2011
    362.5092—dc22
    [B]
                                                                                    2011013345

ISBN 978-0-8077-5228-9 (paperback)
ISBN 978-0-8077-5229-6 (hardcover)

Printed on acid-free paper

Manufactured in the United States of America

18 17 16 15 14 13 12 11   8 7 6 5 4 3 2 1

Contents

Series Foreword

Schools serve society; society is reflected in its schools. Schools are in fact microcosms of the societies in which they're embedded, and every school is both mirror of and window into a specific social order. If one understands the schools, one can see the whole of society; if one fully grasps the intricacies of society, one will know something about how its schools are organized.

In a totalitarian society schools are built for obedience and conformity; in a kingdom, schools teach fealty and loyalty to the crown; under apartheid, schools inculcate that privilege and oppressions are distributed along the color line. These schools might be "excellent" by some measures, but whatever else is taught—math or music, literature or science—the insistent curriculum under all else is the big lessons of how to function here and now: German schools in the middle of the 20th century produced excellent scientists and athletes and artists and intellectuals, and they also produced obedience and conformity, moral blindness and easy agreement, obtuse patriotism, and a willingness to give orders that led to furnaces.

In an authentic democracy, schools would aim for something entirely different: a commitment to free inquiry, questioning, and participation; a push for access and equity and simple fairness; a curriculum that encouraged independent thought and judgment; a standard of full recognition of the humanity of each individual. In other words, schools in a vibrant democracy would put the highest priority on the creation of free people geared toward enlightenment and liberation.

When the aim of education is the absorption of facts, learning becomes exclusively and exhaustively selfish, and there is no obvious social motive for learning. The measure of success is always a competitive one—it's about comparing results and sorting people into winners and losers. People are turned against one another, and every difference becomes a potential deficit. Getting ahead of others is the primary goal in such places, and mutual assistance, which can be so natural, is severely restricted or banned. On the other hand, where active work is the order of the day, helping others is not a form of charity, something that impoverishes both recipient and benefactor.

Rather, a spirit of open communication, interchange, and analysis becomes commonplace, and there's a recognition that the people you're trying to help know better. Of course, in these places there is a certain natural disorder, a certain amount of anarchy and chaos, as there is in any busy workshop. But there is a deeper discipline at work, the discipline of getting things done and learning through life, and there is an appreciation of knowledge as an inherently public good—something that can be reproduced at little or no cost, and unlike commodities, when it is given away, no one has any less of it. In a flourishing democracy, knowledge would be shared without any reservation or restrictions whatsoever.

The education we're accustomed to is simply a caricature—it's neither authentically nor primarily about full human development. Why, for example, is education thought of as only kindergarten through 12th grade, or kindergarten through university? Why does education occur only early in life? Why is there a point in our lives when we no longer think we need education? Why, again, is there a hierarchy of teacher over students? Why are there grades and grade levels? Why does attendance matter? Why is punctuality valuable? Why, indeed, do we think of a productive and a service sector in our society, with education designated as a service activity? Why is education separate from production?

The development of free people in a free society—this is the central goal of teaching for social justice. This means teaching toward freedom and democracy, and it's based on a common faith in the incalculable value of every human being; it assumes that the fullest development of all is the condition for the full development of each, and, conversely, that the fullest development of each is the condition for the full development of all. One traditional way of expressing this ideal is this: Whatever the wisest and most privileged parents in a democracy want for their kids becomes the standard for what we as a community want for all of our children.

The democratic ideal has policy implications, of course, but is deeply implicated as well in questions of teaching and curriculum. We expect schools in a democratic society to be defined by a spirit of cooperation, inclusion, and full participation, places that honor diversity while building unity. Schools in a democracy resist the overspecialization of human activity, the separation of the intellectual from the manual, the head from the hand, and the heart from the brain, the creative, and the functional. The standard is fluidity of function, the variation of work and capacity, the mobilization of intelligence and creativity and initiative and work in all directions.

While many of us long for teaching as something transcendent and powerful and free, we find ourselves too often locked in situations that reduce teaching to a kind of glorified clerking, passing along a curriculum of received wisdom and predigested bits of information. A fundamental choice and challenge for teachers, then, is this: to acquiesce to the machinery of control, or to take a stand with our students in a search for meaning and a journey of transformation. To teach obedience and conformity, or to teach its polar opposite: initiative and imagination, curiosity and questioning, the capacity to name the world; to identify the obstacles to your full humanity; and the courage to act upon whatever the known demands. On the side of a liberating and humanizing education is a pedagogy of questioning, an approach that opens rather than closes the prosy process of thinking, comparing, reasoning, perspective-taking, and dialogue. It demands something upending and revolutionary from students and teachers alike: Repudiate your place in the pecking order, it urges, remove that distorted, congenial mask of compliance. *You must change.*

A generous approach to teaching grounds itself in cherishing happiness, respecting reason, and—fundamentally—honoring each human life as sacred and not duplicable. Clarity about classrooms is not based on being able to answer every dilemma or challenge or conundrum that presents itself, but flows rather from seeing classroom life as a work-in-progress—contingent, dynamic, in-the-making, unfinished, always reaching for something more. The ethical core of teaching is about creating hope in students. Because the future is unknown, optimism is simply dreaming, pessimism merely a dreary turn of mind. Hopefulness, on the other hand, is a political and moral choice based on the fact that history is still in-the-making, each of us necessarily a work-in-progress, and the future entirely unknown and unknowable. Teaching for social justice provides images of possibility—*It can all change!*—and in that way rekindles hope.

A robust, humanistic education for today can draw on the diverse threads spun by our freedom-seeking foremothers and forefathers. We begin by embracing the importance of dialogue with one another, and dialogue, as well, with a rich and varied past and a dynamic, unfolding future. Dialogue is both the most hopeful and the most dangerous pedagogical practice, for in dialogue our own dogmas and certainties must be held in abeyance, must be subject to scrutiny, and there will be, to be sure, inevitable mistakes and misunderstandings. But the promise remains that if we unlock the wisdom in the room, if we face one another without masks and as the best we can be, we each might contribute a bit, and we each might learn something powerful and new.

The core lessons of a liberating education—an education for participation, engagement, and democracy—are these: Each human being is unique and of incalculable value, and we each have a mind of our own; we are all works-in-progress swimming through a dynamic history in-the-making toward an uncertain and indeterminate shore; we can choose to join with others and act on our own judgments and in our own freedom; human enlightenment and liberation are always the result of thoughtful action.

There are a series of contradictions in these propositions that must somehow be embraced, and not fled from: a focus on changing oneself, and a focus on engagement and change within a community; a concern with the individual, and a concern with the group; the demands of self-activity and self-education, and the location of that self within the social surround. An emphasis on the needs and interests of each individual must become co-primary with faith in a kind of robust public that can and must be created. To be exclusively child-centered, to the extent that the needs of the community are ignored or erased, is to develop a kind of fatalistic narcissism, or, too often, a performance of whiteness; to honor the group while ignoring the needs of the individual is to destroy any authentic possibility of freedom. The challenge is to somehow hold on to the spirit of the old saying, "I am because we are, and we are because I am."

Education is an arena of struggle as well as hope: struggle because it stirs in us the need to look at the world anew, to question what we have created, to wonder what is worthwhile for human beings to know and experience; and hope because we gesture toward the future, toward the impending, toward the coming of the new. Education is where we ask how we might engage, enlarge, and change our lives, and it is, then, where we confront our dreams and fight our notions of the good life, where we try to comprehend, apprehend, or possibly even transform the world. Education is contested space, a natural site of conflict—sometimes restrained, other times in full eruption—over questions of justice.

William C. Ayers
Therese Quinn

Acknowledgments

This book has been produced out of a movement, and movements are made of people. There are too many people who have learned these lessons with us to thank them all, but they are present in the pages of this book.

We first and foremost want to acknowledge the organizations and their leaders whose work and knowledge are represented here, including the National Union of the Homeless, the Kensington Welfare Rights Union (KWRU), the Coalition of Immokalee Workers (CIW), the United Workers Association, the Media Mobilizing Project (MMP), the Michigan Welfare Rights Organization (MWRO), and National Welfare Rights Union (NWRU). We thank all 75 of the organizations from across the United States, led by the poor themselves, who make up the Poverty Initiative's Poverty Scholars Program.

We are grateful to William "Billy" Watkins, who recognized the importance of putting Willie's knowledge and experiences in written form and put us in contact with Teachers College Press. We would like to thank the staff at Teachers College Press, always gracious as they guided us through this process, including Emily Renwick, Beverly Rivero, Carole Saltz, and Aureliano Vazquez.

We would like to take this opportunity to celebrate those who were instrumental in the formation of the Poverty Initiative, including Amy Gopp, Jessica Chadwick, William Sloane Coffin, Paul Chapman, Janet Walton, Joe Hough, Cathlin Baker, Dick Butler, and Liz Theoharis.

We would also like to thank the faculty, board of directors, alumni, and students of Union Theological Seminary, whose constant encouragement and assistance have made the work of the Poverty Initiative possible, including Jan and Willie's uniquely Union teaching partnership, out of which this book was created. In particular we would like to acknowledge the support of President Serene Jones, Trustees Mitchell Watson, Art Trotman, Douglas Ades, Barbara Fiorito, David Callard, Mary White, Steve Hudspeth, Aiyoung Choi, Michaela Walsh, committee members Ted Pardoe, Susie Hermanson, Ela Dec, and faculty and staff Brigitte Kahl, Hal Taussig, Janet Walton, Su Pak, Daisy Machado, Barbara Lundblad, Paul Knitter, David Carr, and Maggie Richter.

Much of the content of this book was developed from the courses we taught together at Union between Spring 2007 and Spring 2010. We thank all those students who joined us in those experiences and particularly those students who agreed to let us publish their comments in the sections of our class discussion: Onleilove Alston, Ray Altmann, Adam Barnes, Miriam Boyer, Vanessa Cardinale, Jennifer Leath, Drew Paton, Aaron Scott, Jason Seymour, Charlene Sinclair, Jessica Van Denend, Alix Webb, and Colleen Wessel-McCoy.

The form and content of the book developed out of work with a great team of Poverty Initiative staff: Chris Caruso, Liz Theoharis, Alix Webb, Colleen Wessel-McCoy, and John Wessel-McCoy. A number of other staff assisted us at various points in the project, including Onleilove Alston, Adam Barnes, Crystal Hall, Charon Hribar, Dawn Plummer, and George Schmidt. We would like to thank Colleen Wessel-McCoy for coordinating the project and editing process. Without her this book would still be just an idea.

Lastly we thank our families, who have been a motivation for our continued work to connect knowledge and action to build a just society, especially our wives, Joanie and Brigitte, and our children, Alexis, Will, Frank, Jakob, and Paul.

This book is dedicated to all those who have played and will play a leading role in resolving the defining issue of our time: poverty.

Pedagogy of the Poor

Plight, Fight, and Insight of the Poor: The Need for a Pedagogy to End Poverty

Willie Baptist and Jan Rehmann

Education without social action is a one-sided value because it has no true power potential. Social action without education is a weak expression of pure energy. Deeds uninformed by educated thought can take false directions. When we go into action and confront our adversaries, we must be as armed with knowledge as they. Our policies should have the strength of deep analysis beneath them to be able to challenge the clever sophistries of our opponents.
—Martin Luther King, Jr., *Where Do We Go from Here?*, 1967

Our *Pedagogy of the Poor* is based on the assessment that an unprecedented polarity between wealth and poverty is the defining issue of our times. This argument is being strengthened by the current crisis, which has hastened the impoverishment of the working and so-called middle class. We are witnessing worldwide the worst human indignity and injustice of poverty in the midst of plenty, abandonment alongside an unheard-of abundance. The devastating economic and cultural consequences and all the continuing social ills of racial, gender, and other group inequities, which have been aggravated by this crisis, are far from over. Bankruptcies, unemployment rates, and foreclosures are rising at enormous rates. More and more families default on mortgages, student loans, auto loans, and credit card debt. The consequences have been a mounting toll of preventable deaths and unnecessary pains and miseries. These are among the many manifestations of a society whose economy is torn by deepening economic inequality. A major contributing factor to increasing inequal-

1

ity today is computerized, high-tech globalization, which has created a collision between an unprecedented production capacity and a declining world purchasing capacity.

For millions of people the real crisis of stagnating wages, contingent labor, and unemployment began long before the current financial meltdown started and will last long after the crisis is "officially" declared over. From the mid-1970s onward, we have been facing a devastating and rapidly increasing polarization of wealth and poverty. Whereas the richest 10% of the U.S. population owned about 30% of the national income in the time span between 1953 and 1973, their share soared to 44% in 2000 and to 49.7% in 2007, higher than in any year since 1917. At the same time the traditional correlation between the increase of productivity and the increase of wages, which was the economic bedrock of the "American Dream," was broken: While the productivity level rose continuously from the 1980s onward, real wages fell or stagnated. People started to borrow what they could no longer earn and plunged into debt. With the dismantling of the welfare state, the transition from unemployment or underemployment to dire poverty can happen even more quickly. Foreclosure and homelessness are often just one illness away.

The structures and power relations of high-tech capitalism that accelerated the spread of the precarious conditions and engendered the economic crisis have been successfully banned from the official discourse. Even relatively modest demands for federal work programs to alleviate unemployment or wage and unemployment benefit increases to strengthen the domestic demand are kept off the table. Although poverty is spreading throughout the country, rarely are the realities of poverty analyzed in a way that speaks to systemic causes. The stories and struggles of the poor are reduced to statistics and stereotypes. They are seldom portrayed as agents of change capable of fighting for themselves, thinking for themselves, speaking for themselves, and providing overall direction to a broader social movement. While poor communities are presently growing and becoming more disenfranchised, enlisting more members from the downsizing middle-income strata, their struggles for survival are too fragmented and weak to exert broader influence. They are still lacking critical analyses, coherent strategies, and a competent core of leaders developed particularly from the ranks of the poor to organize the latter into a united social force, a powerful voice that has to be heard.

In the midst of a reality of increased polarization, poverty, and disenfranchisement it is difficult to find opportunities for the intellectual study, dialogue, and reflection that provide the fodder for creative strategizing. Every attempt to open up such a space is severely hampered by, among other things, a deep disconnect between the struggles of the poor and research and debates in academia. Although the community organizing field has provided sophisticated methods for putting poor people into motion (e.g., the Alinsky model), the institutions that drive those methodologies usually do little to develop knowledge of structural inequities and are often confined to ad hoc mobilizing for "realistic" goals—this is in part caused by the tremendous influence of American pragmatism, which tends to separate practice from theory and thereby leads to eclecticism and narrow categorical thinking. While progressive scholars have provided multiple opportunities for the study of critical theories and society in academia, this work is usually cut off from social justice movements and therefore lacks grounding and relevance. The emerging practical struggles in communities and the theoretical work on the campuses represent two indispensable sources of knowledge and scholarship. However, their lack of combination and coordination weakens all parts. The poor are limited to simply managing their poverty, while the academics are limited to simply rationalizing poverty. Both the organized poor, working without access to critical analysis, and intellectual communities, functioning without grounding in the realities of poverty, are stalled in their ability to develop a vision for how things could be different.

The complexity, scale, and scope of the problems of poverty today demand a comprehensive pedagogical approach. This is especially true for the poor and powerless, as they have nothing but their numbers and are only reckoned with when organized and led by knowledge. *Pedagogy of the Poor* derives many of its approaches from the recent experiences and history of community struggles and academic debates. It draws on different kinds of knowledge and seeks to combine them in an interdisciplinary approach to education.

Our book cannot be traced back to a single origin. There were different events, encounters, and experiences that seemed coincidental at first and then, at a certain stage, coalesced into the idea that we needed a condensed publication to convey the experiences of our co-teaching.

There was, however, an early encounter that in hindsight proves to be formative. In October 1999, the Kensington Welfare Rights Union (KWRU) led many other organizations of the Poor People's Economic Human Rights Campaign (PPEHRC) in a monthlong March of the Americas from Washington, D.C., to the United Nations in New York City, where it delivered its protest against poverty as a human rights violation. When the march arrived in New York, hundreds of participants came to Union Theological Seminary and held a series of seminars on the campus about the spreading of poverty in the Americas and about how to organize a mass movement against poverty led by the poor. This was a crucial pedagogical experience for many students and faculty at the seminary: To their astonishment, they did not see poor victims to be pitied, but self-confident people with agency and creativity, and instead of being lectured to on the plight of poverty, they were listening and learning from what this organized grouping of poor people had to say, not only about the immediate experiences of survival, but also about the structural causes of poverty and the strategies to build up antipoverty movements. Academics got a sophisticated lesson in social theory and praxis.

Among the March of the Americas leaders who organized the seminars on campus was Willie Baptist, who at that time was the education director of the KWRU and co-coordinator of the University of the Poor, the educational arm of PPEHRC. Among the listeners was Jan Rehmann, who had just moved from Germany to the United States to teach philosophy and social theories at the seminary. A few years later, the student-based Poverty Initiative was founded, "dedicated to raising up generations of religious and community leaders committed to building a social movement to end poverty, led by the poor," as it declared in its mission statement. With the support of the then seminary president Joseph Hough, Willie became a scholar-in-residence at Union Theological Seminary, and the group grew into an educational center focused on poverty and social justice movements against poverty. It staged National Poverty Truth Commissions and organized regular poverty immersion trips for students to impoverished areas (e.g., the Gulf Coast, Appalachia, the Mississippi Delta, New York). It established a Poverty Scholars Program that brings together community organizers from New York City and nationwide who are organizing in their communities around such issues as water privatization, ecological devastation, eviction and foreclosures, housing, health care, food, education, living wages, and workers' rights. And it reached out to faculty members who were interested in including poverty and the experiences of poor people into their curriculums.

It was in the midst of these multiple activities that the pedagogical collaboration between Willie and Jan took off. At the time, Jan had just offered a class on the philosophical foundations of social justice struggles so that students had the opportunity to integrate their interest in antipoverty movements in their academic program. Encouraged by this experience, Willie and Jan developed an interdisciplinary approach that brings lessons from antipoverty grassroots activism, particularly from the experiences of the poor organizing the poor, together with social theory and ethical reflection.

It turned out that the classes they offered met a substantial need that was not yet covered in the seminary's curriculum. As a condensed result of this co-teaching, this book is meant to be useful for both grassroots organizers who feel the need to combine their practical work with a thorough analysis of society and for educators who are looking for resources on struggles for economic and social justice to incorporate in their curriculums.

Today's poverty is not an "underclass" phenomenon in which the pain and suffering of the poor are self-inflicted. It is a product of high-tech capitalism and its organization of labor. Technological innovations are not implemented in a way that they alleviate the work and shorten the labor time of all, but in a way that renders more and more people "superfluous" while extending the labor time of those who are still employed. The working class is split into those who are overwhelmed and exhausted by increasing work hours and those who are pushed out of sustainable jobs. Since poverty is produced by this systemic irrationality, it is not another "identity issue" but rather defines where our society is headed. It is the issue where the manifold injustices and oppressions in society in regard to class, gender, and race culminate and condense. This position gives the poor the least stake in the status quo. If consciousness of their social position could be created, a united and organized poor could have mass influence and impact. When Martin Luther King, Jr. transformed the traditional civil rights movement into the Poor People's Campaign, working across color lines, he stated in his December 1967 Massey Lectures before the Canadian Broadcast Corporation:

> The dispossessed of this nation—the poor, both white and Negro—live in a cruelly unjust society. They must organize a revolution against the injustice, not against the lives of the persons who are their fellow citizens, but must organize a revolution against the structures through which the society is refusing to take means which have been called for, and which are at hand, to lift the load of poverty. . . . There are millions of poor people in this country who have very little, or even nothing, to lose. If they can be helped to take action together, they will do so with a freedom and a power that will be a new and unsettling force in our complacent national life. (*The Trumpet of Conscience*, 1967, pp. 650–651)

In many ways, Martin Luther King, Jr. anticipated what we are trying to accomplish today when we propose a new approach to education, teaching, and learning. Our book tries to develop analytical tools forged from the perspectives of the poor and in the perspective of building a "new and unsettling force." Since the poor have little or no stake in the status quo, they have every incentive to understand the complex causes and mechanisms of misery and impoverishment without blinders, prejudices, and apologies. Since the movement of the poor is not just another "identity movement," it cannot be reduced to simply poor people leading poor people. Such a simplistic notion can easily be incorporated into a neoliberal system of governance that grants social groups and movements their "autonomy" while dismantling the welfare state, denying their economic human rights, and destroying their means of life. The aim is instead to build up a social movement that includes broad segments of society (including from the threatened "middle classes") and develops effective strategies to change the power structures that engender poverty. But the segment of the population most affected by the social problem that has the least or nothing to lose in its social solution must be brought with its basic needs and demands into the forefront of the struggle. Studies of social movements in the United States and in other parts of the world show the importance and indispensability of developing and uniting individual leaders to educate and organize such movements.

In the course of history, while small forces have overtaken larger ones, a dumb force has never overtaken a smart force. That is why the American slaveholders made teaching a slave to read an act subject to corporal punishment and even execution. Still today, there are many efforts to keep the majority of the people ignorant of the workings of the poverty-producing system and of what to do to change it. According to a widespread understanding of pedagogy, the oppressed and marginalized get a dumbed-down version of "popular education," while the intellectuals connected to those in power get rigorous academic study. Our *Pedagogy of the Poor* intends to question and to overcome this social division of education and knowledge. It is not just a book *for* the poor or about educating poor people. It is a pedagogy for all who are concerned about finding the appropriate solution to the defining issue of our times. It speaks to a broad range of people committed to the elimination of poverty, including practical organizers, university, college and seminary educators and students, high school teachers, religious leaders, denominational, ecumenical networks, and inter-faith social workers, and policymakers. This pedagogy questions the long-standing notion that the poor and poverty are to be viewed as categories unto themselves or separated entities. It poses the argument that the socioeconomic position of the poor is not one to be pitied or guilt-tripped about. Instead it argues that the predicament of the poor is indicative of a breakdown of the whole of society today.

To overcome the separation of grassroots movements and critical social theories is certainly no easy task. It requires a careful balance that avoids both theoretical hyperabstraction and simplistic explanations. A pedagogy of the poor has to deal with the contradiction famously expressed by Antonio Gramsci that *all* people are intellectuals, but not all "have in society the function of intellectuals." All people use their intelligence and wisdom to make sense of their lives and life conditions, individual and social, but most do not have the time and means to study systematically. This does not mean that we have on the one pole the "theory" waiting to be "applied" and on the other pole the immediate grassroots "experience" waiting to be "enlightened" by theoretical truth. Such a separation is as misleading as its pedagogical consequence is patronizing and ineffective. In reality, there is much theoretical reflection to be found in experiences of struggle and movement building, and every sound theory that relates to social realities needs to contain a lot of condensed life experience as well. The false dichotomy between "theory" and "praxis" is to be replaced by the concrete pedagogical task to combine different kinds and layers of knowledge and reflection that are currently separated and polarized in our prevailing education system.

Pedagogy of the Poor tackles this task by what might be described as a "hybrid text," that is, a combination of different idioms and discourses that permits one to look at the same subject matter from multiple perspectives. The book is framed and held together by an interview with Willie Baptist about his life in poverty and the lessons he draws from his participation in social justice movements against poverty. The interview is divided into six parts and interrupted by other chapters so that it can be read as a serial. Readers will notice from the outset that this not just an expression of "immediate" experience (which is a myth in itself rather than lived reality), but rather a narrative interwoven with social analysis and theoretical reflection. For example, readers will learn about the economic causes of the Great Migration from the South to the North and West and about the dynamics and ambivalent consequences of the Watts uprisings; they will get to know a differentiated account of the appeal and the shortcomings of black nationalism and the Black Panther movement; they will participate in an evaluation of the paradigm and strategy shift from the civil rights movement to Martin Luther King, Jr.'s Poor People's Campaign; they will become acquainted with Willie's analysis of the rise and demise of the National Union of the Homeless, and get an introduction into the debates on how to build up a broad movement to end poverty led by the poor as a social force united and organized across color lines. Willie argues that while the strategic task of uniting the poor across color lines could not be accomplished in history, this is becoming more of a possibility as well as an absolute necessity in today's conditions. The critical lesson underscored by both the defeat of Dr. King's

1967–1968 Poor People's Campaign and the demise of the National Union of the Homeless organizing drive during the late 1980s and early 1990s is that, especially in the initial stages, in the development of a social movement all energies and resources must be concentrated on the systematic education and training of an expanding core of committed and competent leaders in close connection with the practical struggles of the poor.

Complementing Willie's interview, Jan contributes four essays that were developed out of some of his in-class lectures. These lectures were buttressed by multiple readings, which the students prepared at home. They were designed to introduce the social analysis of poverty and the conditions of movement-building and often served as a starting point for a textual analysis in class. Chapter 2 gives an overview of four different perspectives on poverty, namely, traditional conservatism, liberal "modernization" concepts, neoliberal and neoconservative approaches, and liberationist perspectives that connect the struggle against poverty with an alternative project of society. Since religion plays a crucial role in the perception and interpretation of poverty, these different perspectives are described in such a way that they cut across politics and Christian denominations. Jan's introduction is further connected to contemporary debates about poverty by an in-class presentation by doctoral student Colleen Wessel-McCoy on Jeffrey Sachs's book *The End of Poverty: Economic Possibilities of Our Time* (London: Allen Lane, 2005). It shows an approach that tries to move from a neoliberal position to a neo-Keynesian one while remaining within the framework of global capital. Chapter 4, "Root Causes of Poverty," breaks down the complex mechanisms by which today's poverty is produced. After describing the ideology of a neoliberal "market totalitarianism" that became predominant in the late 1970s, the essay shows the devastating consequences of neoliberalism's social and economic policies. It also unveils the underlying development of a high-tech capitalism that transformed large sections of the traditional working class into contingent laborers (precariat) and the structurally unemployed. The current global crisis that is drawing more and more people into poverty, misery, and exclusion raises questions about the legitimacy of a system that reveals itself less and less capable of securing the "pursuit of happiness" for the world's citizens.

Chapter 8 provides an introduction to the theory of the Italian social theorist Antonio Gramsci (1891–1937), which we think is of crucial importance for building a social movement to end poverty. By focusing on the hegemonic (or ethico-political) aspects of struggles, he outlined the conditions necessary for a new class to actually become a "class for itself." His analysis of the production of consensus in "civil society" helps to avoid the two typical pitfalls of social movements, namely, to be either co-opted into the existing framework or marginalized. His theory of "organic intellectuals" is directed against any academic elitism and highlights the task of anti-poverty movements to educate its own competent intellectuals and leaders. Given the relevance of Gramsci's approach for social justice movements, we decided to complement Jan's contribution with a conversation between Willie and John Wessel-McCoy (who wrote a master's thesis on the relationship between Gramsci and Saint Paul) that brings Gramsci's theory in dialogue with Martin Luther King, Jr.'s Poor People Campaign and connects it with the uprisings and struggles in which Willie was involved.

Chapter 10 discusses the relationship between ideology theory and antipoverty movements, two areas that at first sight seem far apart from each other. But the topic of ideology theories—the study of how and why masses of people subject themselves actively and voluntarily to systems that exploit and oppress them—is certainly of importance for any social justice movement that organizes to change society. The chapter takes up a specific theory developed by the French philosopher Louis Althusser (1918–1990), whose key concepts "ideological interpellation" and "subject construction" became influential in the humanities (including in postmodernism and gender studies), and confronts his theory with a concrete example of poor people's resistance in community struggles. The pedagogic goal is to learn how to critically investigate the merits and shortcomings of a sophisticated social theory from the perspectives and the experiences of struggle of the poor.

Numerous subjects analyzed and discussed in our classes could not be presented in this book. On several occasions, for example, we invited scholars and community organizers as guest speakers and experts, to describe the basic manifestations of the current economic crisis, to learn from the struggles of the United Workers in Baltimore or the strategies of the Media Mobilizing Project in Philadelphia, to study the campaign Let Justice Roll or to share the experiences of the Zapatistas in southern Mexico and of the Movimento dos Trabalhadores Rurais Sem Terra (MST) in Brazil. One of our regular guest speakers, Chris Caruso, a doctoral student at the Graduate Center of the City University of New York (CUNY), presented a case study on the community struggles in postindustrial Detroit that revolved in particular around water privatization and its devastating consequences. We are glad to publish an enlarged version of this presentation in Chapter 6.

Our pedagogy implies a strong component of student participation. Each week, class is prepared by a working group consisting of two to three students who share with us the responsibility for the next meeting and kick-start the discussions on the readings. We have selected two class discussions that we believe are indicative of the culture of debate that developed in the course of our teaching and co-operative learning, one on resistance and un-intended consequences (in Chapter 3), the other on the question of whether Althusser's ideology theory is useful for understanding poor people's agency (Chapter 10).

Our *Pedagogy of the Poor* is determined not just by what is happening in the classroom or by whether we apply this or that sophisticated didactics. It is also important that our classes are embedded in and interact with the larger pedagogical framework of the Poverty Initiative at Union Theological Seminary. Many of our students participate in the immersion trips or in oth-er activities of the Poverty Initiative, which contributes to the consistency, motivation, and knowledge of the group. We therefore conclude our book with a chapter by Willie Baptist and Liz Theoharis that summarizes the pedagogical principles and lessons of the Poverty Initiative model. By laying out different teaching methods, forms, and activities, we hope to contribute to the emergence of many more educational projects that connect theoreti-cal reflection, social analysis, and building a movement to end poverty.

CHAPTER 1

Interview with Willie Baptist (I):
From the Cotton Fields to the Watts Uprisings

Jan Rehmann (JR): Willie, I will not enumerate all your activities here, nor your manifold writings and responsibilities. That would take up too much time. Let me confine myself to just a few selections.

As a youngster, you were a black student organizer in Los Angeles and worked closely with the local branch of the Black Panther Party; you then became a national organizer of the Union of the Homeless (1986–1991); then the director of education of the Kensington Welfare Rights Union (1991–2005); a lead organizer of the March of the Americas (1999); co-founder and lead organizer of the Poor People's Economic Human Rights Campaign; co-coordinator of the University of the Poor, since 1999; and, from 2004 onward, scholar in residence at Union Theological Seminary, with the mission to inform students and faculty about the realities of poverty and the experiences of the poor, not only about their plight, but also about their fight and insight.

Now, this interview is about your own biography, your life as someone who has experienced poverty, as someone who has been and still is an activist in the struggle to end poverty, and as an intellectual who critically reflects on his actions and strategies. That's how I got to know you during the March of the Americas in October 1999, when hundreds of participants in this march came to Union Theological Seminary and held a series of seminars here on campus about how to organize antipoverty movements led by the poor. I was struck struck when I heard you talking about the effort to organize a self-conscious and sustainable social movement. I was fascinated when I learned about the success and the difficulties to build up a reliable and democratically controlled leadership among the poor. I think the reason why I was so deeply moved while sitting there in your seminar was that it was the first time that I experienced poor people not as mere victims but as self-confident people with agency and creativity. Not just a populace to be pitied, which I always suspected to be an attitude from above, but a movement with which I wanted to be connected.

Let's transition to the interview. Willie, you were born in Corsicana, Texas, in 1948, and when you were five, in 1953, you immigrated with your family to Los Angeles. From then on, you grew up in Watts, one of the poorest neighborhoods not only of Los Angeles but of California. In 1965, when you were 17, you got involved in the famous Watts uprising, and this involvement awakened and politicized you. We will talk about these formative first 17 years of your life and about your reflections of these experiences. Would you like to tell us something about your family, and how you lived in Corsicana, Texas?

Willie Baptist (WB): I left Corsicana at the age of five—that was more than half a century ago—that's a long time to remember what happened to me at that early stage of my life. But there were certain things that struck me that I still remember—the main one being the prevalence of child labor in the planting, chopping, and picking of cotton. My parents, like other parents, would fashion cotton bags for children, and we'd be out there in the cotton field picking along with our parents. That was a very excruciating effort, especially for children. If you've ever experienced the cotton plant, the cotton fibers grow within a hard prickly shell, called a boll, that constantly pierces your skin as you attempt to separate the fibers from it. This excruciating activity has left an indelible impression on my brain. There's nothing romantic about it. Plus the dire heat in that area was upwards of 110 degrees, even in the shade. Those are the things I remember very vividly at that age in Corsicana, Texas.

JR: Were there still some connections to the sharecropper system that was installed after the Civil War? I remember reading that Martin Luther King, Jr. on a visit to an Alabama plantation in 1965, was shocked to meet sharecroppers who had never seen U.S. currency in their lives—they still traded at a plantation-owned commissary in scrip rather than money. Willie, as I understand, the casual labor your parents had to do was not directly part of the sharecropper system; in other words, they were not tenants and they were not paid with "plantation money," right? But it was different with your grandma. Will you specify this some?

WB: After the Civil War, Reconstruction was defeated and the sharecropper system was established, so dependencies were restored in modified form. From the outside it looked like a mutual agreement, but in fact, the former slaves sank more and more into debt, paid with "plantation money." You also had a lot of prison labor that picked the cotton. Both my father and my mother were in the peripheral element of the cotton production process. They were in the casual labor force, especially during bumper crops.

So while they were not formally in the sharecropper system, they would from time to time pick cotton. Anyone could sign up, pick cotton, weigh it, and get paid, like temporary labor today. For a year, we did live in one of the shacks on the plantation, but some people do it their entire lives. My great-grandmother, who we called Big Mama, my mother's grandmother, was a sharecropper along with her relatives in her generation and older, her parents. Big Mama was a very tough person and a disciplinarian. She would not spare the rod. She was a very strong force within our family, and she had to be because in the South you still had this climate of fear and you still were very aware of Klan activities. She kept the family disciplined to protect us. That whole climate was tied to the sharecropping period of cotton production.

JR: The exploitation of African Americans in the cotton belt played a crucial role for the entire U.S. economy, not only in the South, and not only during slavery, but basically until the mechanical cotton picker in the 1950s. Could you inform us of the role of the cotton economy and its impact on poverty?

WB: I wanted to have people look at the map here (Fig. 1.1). This map shows the area of the South, the so-called Black Belt, in which cotton was planted, chopped, and picked. When people refer to the Black Belt today they usually think in terms of black people, where they reside. While it's true that this is where you had the enslavement of the bulk of African Americans, what "Black Belt" originally referred to was the soil. A major geological feature of this region is the deposit of black alluvial soil left by the Ice Age thousands of years ago. It's a soil rich with mineral nutrients, which makes it conducive for cultivating the rigorous cotton plant. The high grade of cotton and the conditions that it required in terms of mineral nutrients could only be produced in this swamp-laden, mosquito-infested area called the Black Belt. Again, it comes from this black alluvial soil formation that developed out of millions of years of geological formation. I think this is very important to understand if you're going to understand the requirements of production.

For years, especially after the early merchant period of United States development, the cotton crop contributed the most value to the economic system. It delivered more than even the merchant and commercial activity that dominated the northern part of the United States. It was what made the South such a base of wealth, power, and influence. On into the 1860s, on the verge of the Civil War, you have tremendous profits being garnered from this crop, alongside other Southern crops—rice, sugar, tobacco—but "cotton was king." The North participated in the process in terms of procuring

Figure 1.1. Black Belt and Border Territory

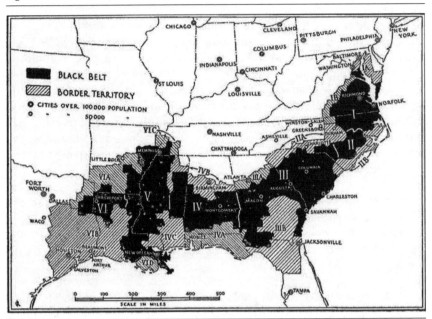

Source: J. Allen, "Black Belt and Border Territory," in *The Negro Question in the United States*, retrieved from http://www.mltranslations.org/Us/Rpo/aan/aan4.htm on December 31, 2010.

the cotton and helping to distribute it worldwide. The cotton industry became the base of the first major industrialization of the worldwide economy. Cotton was very powerful, especially this grade of cotton. India had a similar grade but it was more concentrated here. The end of the Civil War and the end of one human being owning another human being—slavery—did not end the fact that 55% of the world's highest grade of cotton, the most lucrative cotton, was produced on less than 5% of the earth's surface. That's the surface highlighted on the map of the Black Belt.

The question remained after the war: How you still procure this valuable crop without slavery? The answer took the form of sharecropping, a semi-slave form that lasted into the 1930s. As W. E. B. Du Bois has shown in his excellent study *Black Reconstruction in America*, the temporary attempts to create a true "abolition democracy" in the South were soon undermined and defeated by an alliance between the industrialists of the North and the Southern planters—"the appeal of property in the South got the ear of property in the North." The economic elites of the North needed to get that cotton. They had used black people as a battering ram in terms of

Reconstruction in order to beat back the political influence of the planters, to set the stage for Wall Street and railroad capital to penetrate that area and take advantage of that lucrative crop. Black labor was again reduced to unlimited exploitation, and the old plantation politics of dividing the poor along color lines and having the poor blacks policed by poor whites was reinstalled (Fig. 1.2).

If you want to find the derivation of Northern banking and railroad capital, a large part of that came as the result of tremendous industrialization of the South, especially in the form of railroads. The railroad system that existed before was one mainly for planters. It was different from the system in the North. Because of the preoccupation with the North and the war, and also because the Southern slaveholders dominated Congress, it was not possible to get the kind of policies that would help unleash railroad development. With the defeat of the planters they unleashed this tremendous railroad development.

In the map of poverty in the United States (Fig. 1.3), you can see that the former areas of the cotton crop along with the former areas of the slaves coincide with the highest rates of poverty. There is a concentration of poverty in the South as a whole, but the Black Belt area of the South has the highest, longest, deepest area of poverty still to this day. You can see in the wage system that the white worker in the South makes less money than the black worker in the North. The white worker in the South makes more money than the black worker in the South, but he makes less than the black worker in the North. There is a tremendous wage differential that reflects the continuity of poverty coming from slavery.

Figure 1.2. W. E. B. Du Bois on "Plantation Politics"

The system of slavery demanded a special police force and such a force was made possible and unusually effective by the presence of the poor whites. . . . It would have seemed natural that the poor white would have refused to police the slaves. But two considerations led him in the opposite direction. First of all, it gave him work and some authority as overseer, slave driver, and member of the patrol system. But above and beyond this, it fed his vanity because it associated him with the masters. Slavery bred in the poor white a dislike of Negro toil of all sorts. He never regarded himself as a laborer, or as part of any labor movement. If he had any ambition at all it was to become a planter and to own "niggers." . . . The result was that the system was held stable and intact by the poor white.

Source: W. E. B. Du Bois, *Black Reconstruction in America: 1860–1880* (New York: The Free Press, 1998) (Originally published 1935).

Figure 1.3. Percentage of Individuals in Poverty in the United States by County

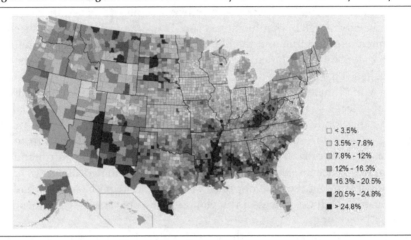

Source: Retrieved from http://www.statjump.com/lists/individuals-poverty-dp3c167ts.html/

These are factors that are at play when you consider the fact that they identified blacks from the west coast of Africa to come work this area as slaves to produce this tremendous crop and then after slavery re-enslaved that mass and segregated them to continue to produce that crop through the sharecropping system. That was the prevailing factor. It wasn't just that they didn't like black folks. That came as a rationalization for this tremendous profit. It should be noted that what is rarely given historical mention is the fact that the continued lucrativeness of the cotton crop also reduced millions of poor whites to this same form of semi-slavery.

JR: Now, what happened, when the mechanical cotton picker was put to work on a mass scale? Did this affect your family?

WB: In the early 1940s International Harvester successfully tested the commercial mechanical cotton picker, which was soon produced on a mass scale. It could outpick fifty sharecroppers, rendering our labor superfluous, both black and white. As a result millions of black and white sharecroppers were turned off the land. Some of the poor whites had the option to get into the textile industry, but most of the blacks did not. This gave rise to what has been called the Great Migration out of the South (Fig. 1.4). Some estimates have it that in the second wave of the Great Migration between 1950 and 1970, 11 million migrated, including about 4 1/2 million blacks. This map shows the earlier period, between 1916 and 1930, but the patterns are the same. You can see how the streams of movement developed. The people from the Carolinas and Georgia basically went to Philadelphia, New York, Newark. Out of Mississippi, they went straight up to Chicago. They call Chicago "Up South Down South." The reason you have Blues coming out of Chicago is that a lot of it comes out of that plantation area in Mississippi. Because of the racist housing covenants and other similar measures the Great Migration of blacks found themselves concentrated into the inner-city ghettoes. Whereas Southern poor whites were more dispersed.

I came out of the Black Belt—Navarre County, Corsicana; we migrated to California. Because of the fact that my father had been involved with casual labor in cotton production and other jobs that surround that economic activity, there was this whole effort to try to find a better and more secure living standard for the family. In 1953, the whole family spent that last year picking cotton. After it was all said and done we had $100 and we were able to purchase a jalopy. We made our way to the West Coast by way of this jalopy through Dallas, then on Highway 20 to Los Angeles. My uncle and my auntie had moved there earlier and encouraged us to come, saying there was much more stable employment.

At that time California had become a major center of munitions and military production. The workers' paychecks gave rise to a lot of secondary industries. That was the basis on which my uncle and my auntie were calling us to "come on over here, baby, get a better job out here. Do whatever you

Figure 1.4. The Great Migration, 1916-1930

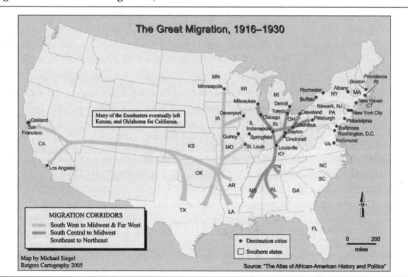

can to get on out here." But the main reason was the introduction of the mechanical cotton picker that put millions of agricultural laborers out of work. Later, you had a burgeoning chemical industry that produced much more effective fertilizer for a higher grade of cotton and also chemicals that could serve as pesticides that would eliminate the need for chopping cotton. Chopping cotton means getting rid of the weeds, through manual labor, so that the cotton grows straight up, and is not hampered by the weeds. But with the development of the chemical industry they were able to use chemicals as opposed to people, manual labor. That cut down on the need for labor and so it forced a larger sector, African Americans but also poor white workers, to migrate to find jobs.

JR: The Great Migration caused by the mechanical cotton picker is generally considered as one of the largest and most rapid internal mass movements of people in U.S. history. It also caused a fundamental sociological change, from a predominantly rural to a largely urban population, concentrated in the inner cities. How did you and your family experience this fundamental transition?

WB: One of the things that I noticed as I was coming up in Corsicana, which was primarily rural, is that our family and other black folks were very scattered. Our churches were very small. We had a very isolated community. When we were picking cotton we lived in a shack that belonged to the plantation owners. We knew the other black folks that were around, and we saw white folks, too. But for the most part, I didn't see the kind of concentration of black folks until I moved into Watts, a community in South Central L.A.

Urban churches in L.A. were much larger than churches in the plantation areas of the South. I went to Paradise Baptist Church, a huge church to me. Seeing all these people—the concentration of black people—that's the thing that I remember from that age. Looking back on it, you can see how the Klan's influence was effaced, because the Klan is not built for that kind of concentration of black people. What I noticed was that the fear of the Klansmen ceased to be a factor. The Klan's position in terms of control and intimidation was taken over by the police. That kind of concentration could only be managed by a standing police force. A lot of the Klansmen became policemen. Because of the economic conditions in the Watts ghetto, the relationship between the police and the black youth was very tense all the time. I remember that any time we had an encounter with the police, it seemed like every policeman was a southerner. He had the southern accent, and I don't care how many times you gave him your name, your name was "nigger." Those were the kind of encounters we had and which eventually ignited the uprising.

My father worked as a dishwasher for a while, went to different kinds of casual labor, finally got into the construction trade, and worked himself up. Both my mother and my father only went to the 8th grade, so for him to pursue that and get that kind of promotion was a significant accomplishment. But it was only over time, after I was grown up and out of the house. My mother worked as a domestic laborer for some rich white folks in Beverly Hills. When we first arrived we went from one relative to another until we could finally settle into a home. We kept moving from one home to another. I remember we were living around the train tracks.

JR: How would you describe the social conditions in Watts that finally exploded in the uprising in 1965? Was it a revolt out of poverty and unemployment or primarily against the unremitting racism, especially at the hands of the police? Or both together?

WB: At that time I thought it was only the issue of race. But on further reflection, you could see that at the same time as blacks were coming into the area a process of automation developed in the various industries and services, not only in the L.A. area but also throughout the U.S. economy. When the economy was restructured, blacks were among the first fired. That's when the slogan "last hired, first fired" evolved. Because we were among the latest immigrants to arrive in the region, we were "last hired" into these plants, and when they restructured, especially when they developed new technologies, we were the "first fired," since we represented the unskilled and semiskilled laborers. That's where African Americans predominated, so we were laid off temporarily and often permanently, leaving concentrations of unemployment, especially affecting the youth, with unemployment rates reaching 70% among the black youth. Of course, drugs were not as much of an issue then. Gang activity wasn't as high because the drug activity was not as high. But on each corner, you had huge congregations of black youth not having anything to do.

That environment was ripe for this kind of police relationship that was constantly antagonistic and would frequently erupt in some form. There were a lot of rumors, many of them true, about what police had done. There were cases of girls as young as 15 that were taken into the back of police cars and raped. There were a number of stories where African Americans were asked to get their identification and when they reached into their pocket to get it they were shot in cold blood, dead, under the pretext of having been reaching for a gun. There were bad relationships, but underneath that were the economic factors of unemployment. How do you contain and control people, especially the youth element, under those conditions? With an aggressive and racist police force. This could not help but to give rise to these kinds of tense situations.

One night I was hanging outside and fell asleep next to a tree. I was woken up by this helicopter from the LAPD 77th precinct. The whole street lit up like daytime and I was surrounded by all these policemen who were yelling, "Nigger, get up," and "Nigger, wake up."

And I said, "What's up, man?"

They said, "Get the hell up," and "What are you doing here?"

I asked, "What did I do officer, I live just across the street. What did I do? Why are you calling me all of these names?"

And they said, "Shut the fuck up," et cetera. "They called into our office saying you had robbed something."

I said, "I didn't rob anything, I've been right here. I live right across the street."

These are the kinds of incidents that created rage within the community. These incidents ignited the movement.

In terms of what happened in August of '65, the rumor we heard was that the uprising was incited at Nickerson Gardens housing projects, where there was a concentration of unemployed youth and people on welfare. It was a rough place because of the economic conditions. Even other blacks wouldn't want to go into Nickerson Gardens. What we heard was that Marquette Frye was pulled over by some Irish and Southern police officers and accused of drunk driving. What would happen, especially during the summer, is every time the police would arrest somebody people would come out to watch, because they were concerned that something was going to happen in terms of police brutality. People would congregate to monitor the situation, and then the rumors would flow from there.

So the night the riots started, this younger man Frye was pulled over and told to walk the line. He said he didn't need to walk the line. They had a little scuffle. His mother came out of the project saying they shouldn't mess with her son. The police ordered her to stay out of the way, but she refused. Nobody knew what these police would do because the police squad could do anything, especially if they take you away, so she was there trying to keep them at bay. She insisted on them leaving her son alone. One of the cops took his baton and hit her in the stomach with it, and the rumor that went around was that she was pregnant.

Stories of that went throughout the community and you had something like 60,000–100,000 people hitting the streets after hearing about the incident. Within a couple of days, the police force was paralyzed. The police basically operated on the principle that became famously discussed in relationship to the Rodney King incident: You concentrate a whole force against a small force. That's basic military strategy. When there was some kind of bust the police would assemble in a vacant lot in the area and then descend on one spot at the same time. When you have 60,000–100,000 people on the street at one time, that nullifies the police strategy. Police were basically rendered null and void. So they brought in the National Guard.

JR: How did you yourself relate to the uprisings? Were you personally involved? What did it mean for your personal development?

WB: As a way of protecting me and my brother, my father had started a Little League baseball team, and that saved my life. People I grew up with went through and sustained a lot of death over time as a result of going to Vietnam and also because of street activities. I was involved in a baseball Little League and I went on through intermediate, into senior and semi-pro. That's where I got my name, Willie. At that time Willie Mays was the man, so if you played baseball and your name was William, Wilbur, or anything that suggests Willie, they'd call you Willie.

When the Watts uprising took place my father was concerned not only about me but also about the other players in the team and their parents. He made an effort to keep his sons from getting out there and getting into the fray and getting killed or something like that, as well as calling to make sure other people on the team were cool. He tried to keep me under wraps, but he had to go to work during the day and I snuck out on two days. At the first occasion, I went out to an area just watching stuff. You could see the situation just turning upside down in the midst of all this danger, the looting, sniping, the police play and stuff like that. You had this kind of festival atmosphere. At the corner this wino was drinking some Ripple or something like that—a bottle of very cheap wine—with a bag on top of it, and he directed traffic. I'll never forget that. Everything was turned on its head. People identified places where they had bills they couldn't pay and they would take the furniture and clothes from those stores.

Another day while my dad was working my friends came by and said, "Hey, man, come on out here. We're having fun." I didn't want to be a poop-butt sitting home protected by momma, so I found my way out there. When I got out there I acted timid—I wasn't trying to die out there. I saw tanks going up and down the community. I saw the sheriff's department riding in long car caravans with their shotguns sticking out the windows to intimidate people. When we got to the area where some of the looting was taking place, we were trying to size up what we were going to do and before we knew it, here come the helicopters, like from Vietnam or something— that was all we could think about. The helicopter started chasing people with the microphones out saying, "Stop what you're doing," and "Freeze," so we got the hell out of there. As we ran, my group split up and went all different ways, and I unluckily got caught with some other brothers that the police were able to round up by way of the helicopters. They pointed machine guns at us and had us get down with our face in the ground. I will never forget that experience. If that don't wake you up to the social realities that this thing involved more than just your own individual situation, I don't know what will. That this is a situation of the society and its military forces having to come down on a community left an indelible impression on my mind and helped shape my understanding today about the social character of these struggles we are currently involved in.

CHAPTER 2

Different Perspectives on Poverty: An Introduction

Jan Rehmann

I would like to kick off the discussion about poverty by giving you an introduction into different perspectives on poverty. For the purpose of simplicity, I've decided to reduce the many different approaches to the four main paradigms that you see in Figure 2.1. Since religion plays an important role in the perception and interpretation of poverty, I have arranged the sections in a way that they cut across politics and Christian denominations.

Before we enter into a discussion of these paradigms, I have to specify what they do and do not describe. First, they do not claim to depict an "objective" reality, but a set of worldviews, and by doing so they rely on how these tendencies define their own worldviews. I use them in order to grasp the inner logic of these views. Second, the sections represent what social analysts usually call "ideal types." The term goes back to the sociologist Max Weber (1864–1920) and means a typological concept that does not grasp *all* the characteristics of a phenomenon but highlights only those that help to determine its specifics. And third, since the history of ideas and worldviews is always in motion, such a diagram can only grasp some tendencies as if in a frozen picture. In reality, the four columns are not strictly separated from one another but rather intersect and overlap at times.

THE CONSERVATIVE PARADIGM

Let's start out with the left column of the chart. In the traditional conservative paradigm, poverty is "just *there*," regrettable, but unavoidable. There have always been rich and poor; that's the natural order. You cannot, and therefore should not, try to change this fundamentally. The relationship of rich and poor is a not a question of social power relations; it's not a struc-

FIGURE 2.1. Different Perspectives on Poverty—Political and Religious

	POLITICAL	RELIGOUS	EVALUATION
Conservatism	Poverty is unavoidable. Compassion of the rich.	**Conservative Christianity** Original sin. "The poor will be always with you."	Religion as ideology of submission. Justice as obedience to the "law" (Aristotle).
Modernization	Poverty is backwardness.	**"Liberal" Christianity** Faith in social and moral progress.	Linear concept of "progress." "Technological determinism." Neglect of social power relations. Criticized by "dependency theories."
Neoliberalism/ Neoconservatism	Blaming the poor (and welfare programs). "Culture of poverty."	**"Religious Right"** "Moral Majority." "Prosperity Gospel."	Racializing images of (black) "underclass." Moralizing of poverty victimizes the victims. Unable to explain the causes of poverty.
Liberational Paradigm	Poverty founded in unjust system. Related to the accumulation of wealth.	**Religious Socialism and Liberation Theology** Preferential option for the poor. Justice as economic redistribution. "Structural sin." Theology as "orthopraxis."	Poverty linked to power relations. Takes the agency of the poor seriously.

tural one caused by exploitation and social injustice; rather, it is a personal one. The ethical response to poverty is not to be understood in terms of an economic redistribution, but can only be individual: The rich should show compassion and forbearance toward the most destitute; they should engage in acts of charity. In this fixed order, those at the margins—the widows, the orphans—should be cared for to a certain degree, but the poor have to accept their place in life humbly.

This traditional conservatism has been buttressed by conservative strands of Christian theology, across different denominations. One of the basic reference points is a specific interpretation of the doctrine of "original sin": Humans are fallen creatures. They are not allowed to get out of their state of sinfulness; they are never capable of building up an egalitarian society free of hierarchies and privilege; each attempt to try to do so is contrary to human nature; the only consolation in this vale of tears and sorrow is an afterlife in heaven.

Another reference point is the famous New Testament passage in which Jesus countered the disciples' objection to the expensive ointment that Mary poured over him: "For you always have the poor with you, and you can show kindness to them whenever you wish; but you will not always have me" (John 12:1–11). There is a long exegetical and theological debate about whether this passage literally means that there will always be the poor and poverty in the world, and I won't go into any details. I'd like to mention just one plausible alternative interpretation: "You, my disciples, always have the poor with you, because you are *my* disciples. We've always been with the poor in our journey so far, and you will certainly continue to do so once I'm gone, because that's just our mission. But now, take care of the one that's soon departing." Furthermore, biblical scholarship points out that this quotation is linked to the description of Sabbath and Jubilee codes in the Hebrew Bible that proclaim a slave and debt release every seven years and a comprehensive redistribution of land designed to end poverty: "There will be no poor among you . . . if only you will obey the voice of the Lord your God" (Deuteronomy 15:4–5). In referring to these codes, Jesus reminds his followers to continue this social justice commitment.

The conservative perspective on poverty has been the predominant trend for most of the history of Christianity. One could say that it became predominant in the fourth century C.E. when the Roman emperor Constantine converted to Christianity and transformed it into the official religion of the empire, its religious state ideology. But you can find this trend in all major denominations: in the medieval Catholic doctrines of "natural law" that legitimized the existing feudal order, in Luther's call to humbly accept the rank God has put you in, and in Calvinist views (not of Calvin himself, though) that distress and poverty on earth are to be seen as visible signs of being reprobated by God. The hegemony of this paradigm lasted at least until the Second Vatican Council in the 1960s when the doctrines of the Catholic Church shifted toward a modernization paradigm and even opened up a space for an emerging liberationist paradigm. Similar changes can be observed in other Christian denominations at that time as well.

Within this religious conservatism, the theological arguments vary between the different denominations, but the basic message is quite similar: You must humbly submit to the established hierarchical order that has been ordained by God and must be upheld. In this framework, "justice" means to follow the laws of the authorities that have been installed by God. Throughout the history of religion there have always been movements in each denomination that challenged the predominance of conservative doctrines. One can even argue that this top-down concept of "justice" does not belong to the Judeo-Christian tradition at all, because it has its roots neither in the Hebrew Bible nor in the New Testament, but rather in Aristotle's philosophy that identifies justice (in general) with lawfulness. Book V of his *Nicomachean Ethics* is on "justice," and here, he explains, "What is prescribed by legislation is lawful, and we hold that every such ordinance is just" (Book V, 1129b). From this perspective, Rosa Parks's refusal to give up her seat on the segregated bus would not only be "unlawful," but also "unjust," and therefore "un-Christian." But it was predominantly through the combination of Church doctrines with Hellenistic philosophies that this conservative paradigm became part of the Christian tradition. As far as religion functions as an ideology of obedience and submission, it contradicts the biblical concepts of justice, which are linked to the exodus from Egyptian slavery, to the social redistribution proclaimed by the Sabbath and Jubilee codes, and to the prophets' sharp criticism of wealth accumulation.

THE MODERNIZATION PARADIGM

Let's move on to the next column. Similar to the conservative paradigm, the modernization paradigm does not challenge the unequal distribution of wealth as such, but it tends to be more optimistic with regard to social change. It believes in the "progress" of humankind, most notably in the benefits of technological development, which is supposed to bring about progress in civilization, morality, and social justice. Since this approach is historically linked to Enlightenment philosophy and influenced by modern science, it shows in general more faith in human capacities and in the potentials of education.

This optimism is represented by more "liberal" strands of Christianity that tend to interpret the kingdom of God in ethical terms of the social and moral progress of humanity. The church is compelled to contribute to that progress. In this paradigm, poverty is seen mainly as "backwardness." It shows that a country or a part of the population is not yet modernized, not yet fully integrated in the world market. The main answer to poverty is the enhancement of economic growth, which is usually explained as the result of an enhancement of unrestricted markets.

In terms of social theory, modernization concepts have often been criticized for their superficial concept of progress as a linear, evolutionist process. In fact, this theory is structured by a simple dichotomy: On the one hand you see progress and modernity, on the other hand "traditionalism," and both poles are being linked by the concept of "development," which is understood as a matter of traditional societies, regions, or sectors moving toward modernity, toward industrialization and developed capitalistic markets. This framework does not consider *to what ends* and *in what social relations* the technologies are being used. Modernization theories usually do not address the destructive potentials technologies can have, both ecologically and economically, when they are introduced for the sake of profits: Instead of being used for a general reduction of labor time, they have the effect of throwing large parts of the population out of work.

On an international level, modernization theories came under fire from "dependency theories" that claimed that United States–led modernization programs benefited rich countries rather than poor ones, and within poor countries only the elites. In most of the cases, foreign transnational companies took the lion's share of the profits out of developing countries. Similar developments are to be observed within the United States as well. Rampant poverty in Appalachia was usually explained by the "backwardness" of a region that was "left behind" by the Industrial Revolution. But it is more accurate to say that Appalachia was an "internal colony" that made the Industrial Revolution possible by providing the industry with the raw materials it needed. Whereas modernization concepts explain poverty by the circumstance that countries or regions are *not yet* fully integrated into the capitalistic world market, dependency theorists hold that poverty is the very result of *how* and in what position these areas are integrated in the world market.

NEOLIBERALISM AND NEOCONSERVATISM

Let's move on to the next column, which shows two different but also largely intersecting tendencies. The term "neoliberalism" is not to be confused with the common use of "liberal" in the United States, which usually describes moderately "progressive" folks, concerned with social justice and tolerance. Rather it designates a radical market ideology that became predominant in the late 1970s, in the United Kingdom in 1979 with the victory of Margaret Thatcher, and in the United States in 1980 with the presidency of Ronald Reagan. It stands for an economic politics that aims at dismantling the welfare state, the privatization of public services from railroad systems to water, and the weakening of trade unions (see Chapter 4 and the case study on Detroit in Chapter 6). Its hegemony is closely linked to a computer-driven transnational high-tech capitalism. Proclaiming "individual freedom," neoliberalism proposes to bring all human actions and desires into the domain of the market.

Especially in the context of U.S. politics, this neoliberal market radicalism has, to a large degree, taken on the ideological form of "neoconservatism." Republican administrations from Ronald Reagan onward, and recently that of George W. Bush, connected a neoliberal economic politics with conservative notions of national pride, military virtues (including the right to go to war when American interests are at stake), family values, crusades against gay and lesbian rights, and so on. Neoliberalism and neoconservatism are certainly not the same. They have different intellectual origins and sometimes come into conflict with each other. Furthermore, neoliberal economic politics have been adopted by the Democratic Party as well, and they are still predominant under the Obama administration, which has decided to leave the creation of jobs almost exclusively to the private sector.. In the United States in particular, neoliberalism and neoconservatism were able to build a stable alliance for many years.

It was especially the neoconservative part of this alliance that has been widely approved and buttressed by different strands of the Religious Right, which successfully organized a populist grassroots movement around the questions of abortion and the nuclear family. With regard to poverty, the neoliberal and neoconservative approaches tend to lay the blame on the poor themselves and on the welfare programs that pretended to protect them against poverty. The reasons for poverty lie with individuals, and specifically in the choices they make. Welfare programs only encourage them to make the wrong choices: not to take a poorly paid job, not to stay in school, not to get married. Through this, the welfare programs support a culture of self-perpetuating unemployment and foster an "underclass" in inner cities. One of the specifics of the right-wing approach is the tendency to turn poverty into a racial issue and, at the same time, to criminalize it. The basic assumption is that the poor could work themselves out of poverty if they just tried hard enough. Poverty is a matter of individual morality, and the answer to poverty lies in individuals assuming the moral responsibility to provide for their own and their families' needs.

It is also important to recognize that interpreting poverty as a result of laziness, immorality, drug abuse, female-headed families, and so on is widespread not only in the media, but also in common sense notions of poverty. Many seem or pretend to know someone who became poor because of bad individual decisions. But such individual examples can never explain poverty as a *mass* phenomenon. Drug trafficking and inner-family violence might be one of the effects of poverty, but they cannot explain the causes of the mass impoverishment, for example, in the deindustrialized "Rust Belt." Statistics also show that most poor people in the United States are *not* unemployed. The majority are in fact working poor who work their hearts out, while overexploitation and the lack of sustainable jobs prevent them from getting out of poverty. The concepts that start out from a particular culture, psychology, or behavior have no explanatory value when it comes to the structural causes of poverty. And when poverty is moralized, a tremendous moral pressure is placed on the poor making them feel like failures and thus destroying their self-esteem.

THE LIBERATIONIST PARADIGM

Now we get to the column on the right. For the liberationist paradigm, poverty is not a part of the natural order, a hangover from the past, or the result of individuals' failures, but is mainly caused by a system founded in injustice. One cannot come to terms with the phenomenon of poverty without putting it in relation to the accumulation of wealth. Since poverty is not the result of a lack of integration into the world market, but of a certain position *within* the capitalistic world order, you cannot overcome poverty without changing and transforming this order itself.

In the religious history of the United States, this approach has been developed mainly by religious socialists who were partly connected to the old Socialist Party of America of Eugene V. Debs. On the international level, it was most famously presented by liberation theology, which emerged in the 1960s and 1970s in Latin America. It began as part of a movement of modernization of the Catholic Church that culminated in Vatican II in the early 1960s. But it also turned against the economic modernization programs in South America that did not alleviate poverty as promised. Its key concept is the "preferential option for the poor," which basically means that throughout the Hebrew Bible and the New Testament, God's chosen people are primarily the dispossessed, the humiliated, the downtrodden and marginalized. It is predominantly this option that defines the biblical concept of divine justice: not as virtue of submission to the earthly rulers, but as a call for liberation from slavery, exploitation, and oppression and for economic redistribution. The promised "kingdom of God" is not about investing your hopes and longings in an afterlife, but is a pledge for liberationist praxis in the here and now. In this context, the concept of *sin* shifts its meaning toward an understanding of "structural sin"; that is, sin is not primarily conceived as a moral flaw lying in the inner core of the individual (as a necessary expression of the original sin), but sits in the social structures of injustice that create the greed for private profits, widespread misery, and moral degradation. And finally, liberation theology defines itself as a liberating "praxis" rather than as a new dogma, as something to be *done*, namely by poor people themselves, who organize in base ecclesial communities (*comunidades eclesiales de base*) to read the Scripture in the context of their economic and political conditions. Rather than elaborating a new orthodoxy, a "right doctrine," it wants to create a new "orthopraxis," a "right practice."

Liberation theology has been harshly criticized by the Vatican, especially by the former cardinal Ratzinger, as a Marxist ideology clothed in pseudoreligious language. Liberation theologians defended themselves with the argument that they use Marxism not as an overall materialistic philosophy (including an atheistic worldview), but as an analytical tool for understanding economics and politics—a tool that helps them sharpen their Christian faith and practice. This didn't protect them from being silenced by the Church. In addition, they lost parts of their popular influence through the rising influence of conservative evangelical Protestantism. But I would caution against the fashionable interpretation that liberation theology is "outdated" or even "dead." It has survived in other forms and enriched its approach with new developments of empire-critical, gender-critical, and postcolonial studies. I would even argue that the current left turn in several Latin American countries can in part be traced back to the ongoing subterranean influence of liberation theology.

It is important to recognize that each of these paradigms, whether we like them or not, have their strongholds in common sense, including among the poor themselves. (1) "We're poor, because that's what God preordained us to be: Some are big, some are small, some are smart, some are stupid, some are rich, some are poor. That's how it is. Period!" (2) "We're poor because we lack modern technology and a health clinic, and we're not well educated either—once the corporations arrive and invest, the profits will trickle down and we'll be better off"; (3) "We, or mostly *they*, the undeserving poor, are poor, because they drop out of school after having out-of-wedlock children"; (4) or finally, "We are poor because the rich are rich, all too rich: They increase their profits by lowering our wages below the poverty line; they decide how the wealth is produced, how new technologies are introduced, and even if they are not always mean and greedy persons, they fire us as soon as we are not profitable to them anymore." If you try to mobilize and organize in social justice movements, you have to be aware that these contradictory perspectives can be found side by side within the same individuals. People's common sense is not homogeneous but full of contradictions and inconsistencies, and this is true not only for "others" but also for each of us. It is neither sufficient nor helpful to denounce the paradigms we might oppose as if they were mere fantasies or errors or illusions. Instead we have to learn to listen intensely to these contradictions and to work with them. That's one of the reasons why we will take some time to deal with Gramsci's theory of common sense and hegemony (see Chapter 8).

I don't pretend to give you a value-free presentation as though I were hovering above the fray. I actually think that the liberationist paradigm has the strongest analytical and explanatory potentials, not in the sense that one finds here handy solutions for getting rid of the scourge of poverty—far from that. The struggle to end poverty is a long-term one that does not promise an illusory quick fix. It is mainly for two reasons that I advocate the liberationist approach: 1.) In terms of social analysis, you cannot understand poverty without relating it to the distribution of wealth and without taking into account the economic, political, and cultural power relations that heap up the riches on the one side and accumulate misery on the other; and 2.) only the liberationist paradigm allows for a social movements approach that takes the agency of the poor seriously. Poverty cannot be overcome without developing a social movement to end poverty, led by the poor themselves, capable of forging broad alliances that can put governments under pressure.

CHAPTER 2 SUPPLEMENT

A Critique of Jeffery Sachs's *The End of Poverty*

Colleen Wessel-McCoy

Economist Jeffery Sachs was involved in the "shock therapy" policy guidance that characterized the neoliberal takeover of the International Monetary Fund and World Bank in the 1980s and 1990s, reining in extreme hyperinflation in Bolivia through severe austerity measures and helping transform communist Poland into a market economy.[1] In both cases, these measures contributed to enormous increases in unemployment and poverty. But Sachs has had a conversion, to apply religious language to what he describes as lessons learned from experience in the field. In his 2005 bestseller, *The End of Poverty*, Sachs offers his alternative to the extreme "economic freedom" arguments and the structural adjustment development practices, saying that liberalized and privatized free markets will not in themselves end poverty. He distinguishes between three degrees of poverty: extreme, moderate, and relative. One billion people—one-sixth of humanity—are "too ill, hungry, or destitute even to get a foot on the first rung of the development ladder." These people living in "extreme poverty"—calculated by the World Bank as a purchasing power parity of less than $1 per day—are found only in developing countries concentrated in East Asia, South Asia, and sub-Saharan Africa. "Extreme poverty no longer exists" in the "rich" countries, whose 1 billion people are one-sixth of the world population (Sachs, 2005, p. 3). Although there are cases of relative poverty, defined as "a household income level below a given proportion of average national income," all people in developed countries "are enjoying twenty-first-century affluence" that accompanies economic progress (p. 20).

In poor nations where extreme poverty exists, mostly in sub-Saharan Africa and parts of Asia, Sachs says, capitalist markets fail to sufficiently address situations where disease, harsh climates, and geographical isolation prevent people from participating economically in the global market. By intervening in the market system just long enough to fix those particular barriers, global capitalism can expand to include those who are not yet consumers or laborers. Because these preconditions have not been met, capitalism's economic progress has bypassed those Sachs calls "extremely poor." The resulting gulf between rich and poor is "a new phenomenon" that resulted from economic progress occurring in some geographic areas at faster rates than in others (p. 29). In other words, it isn't capitalism that makes people poor; being bypassed by capitalist markets makes people poor. For Sachs, ending poverty in practice means bringing all people into the modern capitalist economy. When poor people are helped onto the "ladder of development, at least a foothold on the bottom rung," they can climb out of the downward spiral from there. For Sachs, we end poverty when we put people to work in sweatshops, because "sweatshops are the first rung on the ladder out of extreme poverty" and are "opportunities for personal freedom" (p. 11). People can climb their way up from there to the "riches" of the developed world.

Despite proclaiming distance from free-market fundamentalism, *The End of Poverty* still shares many assumptions with neoliberal economic theory and practice. Prominent is the belief that capitalist markets don't cause poverty. Where markets haven't worked, we need to create conditions in which they will work. It's the inadequacy of the conditions that prevents market systems from working successfully. Similarly shared is the argument that wages set by competition in the labor market are accurate, even if they seem unjust or violate economic human rights. This is where Sachs's endorsement of sweatshops finds its theoretical justification. Making those opportunities possible is another neoliberal premise found in *The End of Poverty*: States are responsible for creating good business climates for investors. An element of neoliberal practice (even if not explicitly part of neoliberal economic theory) shared by Sachs is that nongovernmental organizations and foreign aid are good ways to both infuse our values globally and keep us safe from riotous mobs of poor people—those who do not benefit from the current global system. Beneath all of this is the unquestioned assumption that the capitalist market system is the best way to organize society, locally and globally.

Sachs has thrown his weight and thinking behind the United Nations Millennium Development Goals (UNMDG), which aim to reduce by half worldwide the number of poor people living on less than $1 a day by 2015, along with other benchmarks. If "rich" nations can provide the preconditions of basic infrastructure and human capital, including basic health services, capitalist market forces will do the rest of the work. This would cost "donor nations" only 0.7% ($0.15 of every $100.00) of their gross national product (GNP) per year until 2025. In *The End of Poverty*, the threshold of the "end" of "poverty" is people having at least $2 per day, which would precipitate and enable poor people to climb out of poverty. But it is not a plan for ending or even ameliorating "relative" poverty found in countries where GNP indicates that (as a mathematical average) no one is poor. The "end" of poverty in *The End of Poverty* is the elimination of *extreme* poverty, not all poverty. The goal is, according to Sachs, "still less to equalize world incomes or to close the gap between the rich and the poor" (p. 289).

Far from being the consequence or cause of extreme poverty, for Sachs the consolidation of wealth in the hands of the few is the solution to extreme poverty: It is "taxpayers with incomes at the very top of the charts" that will solve much of the problem through either modest increases in taxation or large-scale philanthropy (p. 289). He suggests that if "the top four hundred richest taxpayers (in the United States) . . . could give 10% of their 2000 income, or $6.9 billion . . . this would be enough to save millions of lives per year, for example, through the comprehensive control of malaria in Africa" (p. 307). The real questions are the ones Sachs never asks: Why do we tolerate a system where four hundred people have an income of $69 billion per year when others cannot afford to buy their own mosquito nets? Why tolerate a system that allows the top twenty Wall Street hedge fund managers to earn an average of $658 million in one year while middle-income auto workers are being permanently laid off and their pension funds and health care benefits are decimated (Ozanian & Schwartz, 2007)? Since Sachs does not consider the way transnational high-tech capitalism squeezes out and degrades human labor, he cannot formulate a realistic and sustainable strategy against what he calls "absolute" poverty.

Sachs has recently sharpened his criticisms of Friedrich von Hayek, the intellectual father of neoliberal theory and policies, and has given increasing attention to Nordic social democratic state interventions, where he argues that higher taxes and strong social welfare programs are not "antagonistic to a prosperous market economy" (Sachs, 2006). However, the central argument about Sachs and similar anti-extreme-poverty policy proposals remains: Even while expressing concern for those in poverty, economic and political thought loyal to global capital will always seek stabilizing solutions to potential challenges (like poverty and inequality) to capitalist market systems, whether in neoliberal form or more Keynesian and social-democratic forms. Our critique should not be limited to focusing on "bad" economic policies or "bad" people, but should primarily target the fundamental structure that generates and needs them both. Otherwise our analysis is limited to pulling leaves off the branches of the problem and not pulling up its roots.

Terms like "relative poverty" are not simply a prioritizing of higher-risk cases of poverty, but change the analysis. How we define poverty affects the strategies we choose to pursue in ending poverty. Instead of artificial benchmarks that put poor people in competition with one another for being the most poor, the solutions to poverty lie in poor people themselves realizing how much they have in common across the borders of "rich" and "poor" nations.

NOTE

1. This presentation was given in Willie Baptist and Jan Rehmann's spring 2007 course. It was drawn from my MDiv thesis from the same year, focusing specifically on *The End of Poverty*, and does not incorporate Sachs's subsequent work.

REFERENCES

Ozanian, M. K., & P. J. Schwartz (2007, May 21). Wall Street's highest earners. *Forbes Magazine*. Retrieved, December 31, 2010, from http://www.forbes.com.

Sachs, J. (2005). *The end of poverty: Economic possibilities for our time*. London: Allen Lane.

Sachs, J. (2006, November). The social welfare state: Beyond ideology. *Scientific American*. Retrieved, December 31, 2010, from www.scientificamerican.com.

CHAPTER 3

Interview with Willie Baptist (II): The Contributions of Malcolm X and Martin Luther King, Jr.

Jan Rehmann (JR): As I understand it at the time of the Watts uprising you were much more fascinated by Malcolm X than by Martin Luther King, Jr. Why was that?

Willie Baptist (WB): During that period the scale of Watts inaugurated a whole period of uprisings in urban areas; some 300 cities or more were involved. This left a tremendous impression on me and others. And in this situation, Malcolm's speeches, in particular his famous "Message to the Grassroots" of 1963, hit the mark. We got a hold of his albums and I just played them over and over again. He said there were "field Negroes" and there were "house Negroes," and he was a "field Negro." We read that, looked at our situation, and said we're definitely field Negroes, we ain't got nothing (Fig. 3.1).

It was clearly not the upper-class professional blacks in Baldwin Hills that were involved in the uprising, but largely the lower-income ghetto folks. This notion of class differentiation even among the blacks became punctuated during the uprising. What we associated with the upper class was that they were bourgeois "Uncle Toms." Their philosophy was that of Martin Luther King, Jr. or A. Phillip Randolph, people who were pushing for integration. We didn't want to identify with that, because at that time we saw all white people as our enemy.

It was during that time that black nationalism became our philosophy. I developed such a strong black nationalism I couldn't deal with white folks or anything white. At that stage of my life I wouldn't even wear white underwear. I wore black underwear. I just didn't like white folks. It was a time when we were awakening to our own sense of pride and Malcolm X was the primary mover in my life in terms of those feelings, studying Africa and the eruption of the national liberation struggles throughout Africa and Asia, and the constant reference between what was happening in the United States—the civil rights movement and later the uprisings—and the developments in Africa. Malcolm spoke to those issues.

Figure 3.1. Malcolm X on "House Negros" and "Field Negros"

The house Negroes . . . loved the master more than the master loved himself.
. . . If the master said, "We got a good house here," the house Negro would
say, "Yeah, we got a good house here." Whenever the master said "we,"
he said "we." . . . If the master's house caught fire, the house Negro would
fight harder to put the blaze out than the master would. . . . On the same
plantation, there was the field Negro. The field Negro—those were the
masses. . . . The Negro in the field caught hell. He ate leftovers . . . guts.
That's what you were—gut-eaters. . . . When the house caught on fire, he
didn't try to put it out; that field Negro prayed for a wind, for a breeze.

Source: Malcolm X, *Malcolm X Speaks: Selected Speeches and Statements*, edited by G.
Breitman (New York: Merit, 1994), pp. 10–11.

It was different with King. Even though there was a certain respect because this cat was going to jail, because he was talking about integration, at
that stage of my life I couldn't deal with it. You had the situation where the
upper classes of blacks were supporting integration, especially among the
black preachers in the bigger churches. Those of us in the lower classes, in
the ghettos, we were more inclined toward black nationalism. I took on an
African name, Busara Akili, it meant "knowledge and wisdom" in Swahili.
My brother and I got into that because it was a pride thing, awakening to
the soulful singing of James Brown, "Say it loud; I'm black and I'm proud."
This refrain could be heard throughout the streets of the ghettoes. That
was where I was at in that stage of my development. You had in Malcolm
X not only this recognition of the role of race, but also a budding class understanding. When I look back on it I can see that what you were dealing
with was race, class, gender; all of these things were inseparable from what
was impacting my life and the lives of others like me during that uprising
and later on the uprisings that engulfed Detroit, Newark—all the places that
erupted in 1967 and 1968.

JR: Let me throw in a provocative statement, for the sake of a lively
debate. I am always a bit puzzled when I read or hear the widespread understanding that Martin Luther King, Jr. was a lukewarm and all-too-moderate
black leader, compromising with the white liberals that supported the civil
rights movement, whereas Malcolm X was the really radical leader, the real
revolutionary. I am not sure whether this is true for his economic perspectives. Looking at one of his speeches at Harvard on March 18, 1964, he de-
clares that "black nationalism" in the economy was just to teach the people

to spend their money in the black neighborhood and to "create employment for ourselves." In this definition, at least, there is no fundamental challenge to the economic structures. In contrast, Martin Luther King, Jr. during his last years not only focused on preparing the Poor People's Campaign, but also clearly challenged the very system of capitalist injustice and impoverishment. Isn't he the one that formulated a more substantial and sustainable critique of social injustice and poverty?

WB: What you were dealing with is much more complex than that. What King was proposing in terms of integration at the time, before he started to prepare the Poor People's Campaign, never challenged the capitalist market system. His main drive was for the black masses to be integrated into a system that locked them out through Jim Crow. The black upper classes stood to gain a lot from that integration in terms of them being able to participate in the market as capitalists. Even with the militant expression that Malcolm represented, even in that separatism, there was still a resonance between that position and markets, setting up your own businesses, and becoming part of the market system. The idea was that instead of white folks coming into the community and setting up businesses, that should be done by black folks. So in both of the approaches at that stage—integrationism and nationalism—there were no challenges to the market system or capitalism, even though Malcolm's statements were very radical, provocative, and militant.

Studying their words and work in the last periods of their lives you can see that they both begin to develop an anticapitalist orientation. Coincidentally, or not so coincidentally, these well-known leaders were killed as they were becoming more anticapitalist in their thinking and actions. You can read Malcolm's last year and you can see some of his statements that talk against class oppression and exploitation. He says there will be a war but doesn't think it will be a race war. Instead it will be a war between the haves and have-nots. This is one of his last statements. In London he made similar statements about exploitation. Not long after he had been talking to some of the more leftist wings of the National Liberation Fronts in Egypt and Algeria, as well as in sub-Saharan Africa, Ghana, and Tanzania. The people he developed a strong relationship with as he pursued the human rights question with the United Nations were all killed around the same period. Karl Evanzz's book *The Judas Factor: The Plot to Kill Malcolm X* exposed the fact that the national organizer of the Nation of Islam was an FBI agent and explains how that contributed to the death of Malcolm X. And then you had King in the latter period of his life taking up these questions that challenge the market system.

JR: It is well known that Martin Luther King, Jr. was very critical of the urban uprisings. But he also gave a very thoughtful analysis of them. For example, he observed that there were only very few cases of black violence against persons. And it is true that almost all the deaths were inflicted on the rioters by the military. The violence of the rioters was almost exclusively against property. Martin Luther King, Jr. concluded they were so violent with property "because property represents the white power structure, which they were attacking and trying to destroy." Can you confirm this observation, and what do you think about his explanation?

WB: It's often described as a riot, but it was not a riot. It was an uprising against the inhumane conditions. Many participants like me are proud of that moment in history when the downtrodden people of Watts stood up. The hurting but determined voice of the voiceless was heard around the world. If you really sum up the participation of most of the people in the uprisings, their activities were mainly that of mass looting— going to a furniture place and getting furniture, going to a clothing place and getting clothing, going to supermarkets and getting food. These are basically the activities of most of the people in all the so-called riots. Even though just about every "riot" was ignited by police relationships, the response of the people was to target the areas where they had accumulated bills. Most of these areas were owned by white businessmen and so the notion of white and black was there, but underneath were these prime economic questions, which dictated the participation of most of the people in the "riot" situation.

You had a lot of black veterans who had learned to use weapons in the Vietnam War. We had this one place in our neighborhood that was looted, the Whitefront Department Store, which was almost like Walmart. They sold guns, but also food, clothing, everything in the store. There was an orchestrated move on the part of a number of black veterans where they climbed to the roof, first in order to get into the building and open the doors for the people, and then to use the vantage point of the roof to keep off the police through gunfire. There are pictures of them climbing ladders. You saw this onrush of regular people going into Whitefront to get food, clothing, and that kind of stuff, and you had this orchestration between the black veteran snipers and the people mostly taking items to meet their needs.

Now of course the most deaths were sustained by the residents of the black ghettoes. In the Watts uprising, there were something like 34 deaths of blacks, while deaths among the white police were in the single digits. A lot of the activities, even though they were very violent and disruptive, were mostly directed toward this violation of property rights—taking furniture, taking a company's clothes or food. I think that King's statement was very instructive, not only in regard to Watts, but also to the other cities that erupted in the late 1960s. It shows both the class issues in the sense of property—who owns and who doesn't—and also the simultaneous influence of the race question (Fig. 3.2).

JR: I'd like to turn to the complicated problem of the uprising's outcome. From what I know and understand, and please correct me if I'm mistaken, the result is ambivalent. On the one hand, it showed the agency of the impoverished blacks in the cities, their will and capacity to resistance, and I think the antipoverty activist and scholar Francis Fox Piven is right when she points out that without the urban riots, the Johnson administration wouldn't have expanded their government programs against poverty. On the other hand, it can hardly be denied that the riots provided the ideological fodder for a white, right-wing backlash. In Detroit, for example, working- and lower-middle-class whites were rallying around explicitly racist candidates like George Wallace. So without revolt there would have been no concessions; but one could say that the riots finally opened the way for Ronald Reagan's victory in 1980 and the victory of neoliberalism. Is there a way to sort this out?

WB: The only way to approach it is again realizing its complexity and going beneath the surface of events to try to look at all the different sides to this thing, to look at the contradictions. On one level, especially a tactical level, this onrush and outbreak of outrage, spearheaded by lower-class black youth, forced the hands of the government and certain concessions were made. Programs were brought into Watts; certain makeshift jobs were

Figure 3.2 Martin Luther King, Jr.'s Analysis of the Urban Uprisings of the Late 1960s

---

The blood-lust interpretation ignores one of the most striking features of the city riots. Violent they certainly were. But the violence, to a startling degree, was focused against property rather than against people. . . . The much publicized "death toll" . . . and the many injuries were overwhelmingly inflicted on the rioters by the military. . . . A handful of Negroes used gunfire substantially to intimidate, not to kill; and all the other participants had a different target—property. . . . The focus on property . . . is not accidental. It has a message; it is saying something. . . . Property represents the white power structure, which they were attacking and trying to destroy.

Source: M. King, *A Testament of Hope: The Essential Writings of Martin Luther King*, edited by J. Washington (San Francisco: HarperCollins, 1986), pp. 648–649.

created. The Ford Foundation and others came in and set up different programs to get people working raking up trash and clearing up the wreckage. More blacks were brought onto the welfare rolls as a result of upheavals of the 60s. This outbreak of violence in over 300 cities in the latter half of the 60s was the largest violent social upheaval since the Civil War. This was not some small thing. Through our engagement in that process during the Watts uprising we were able to force the hands of the police. In the first four days, the police receded. I can't tell you what that meant for the ghetto black youth. We were constantly hearing about incidents and many in our ranks had had encounters with police harassment and negative epithets. To know that they had to retreat was elating for us. We kicked ass, if only for a minute! And this is not only some good feeling. It is strategically important, because the uprising showed that the poor themselves can have not only agency but also a leading agency, that we can stir the nation.

On the other hand it is certainly true that the powers-that-be were able to utilize the uprisings for their own purposes. They were successful in depicting the poor blacks as lawless criminals and to organize an all-class-white "law-and-order" backlash that gave rise to demagogues like Ronald Reagan and successive right-wing neoliberal and neoconservative presidencies from 1980 onward. It can also be observed that the predominant media representations of poverty changed from the mid-1960s onward. At first, they were dominated by the white rural poor of Appalachia, and these pictures of the "deserving poor" helped support President Johnson's "War on Poverty." But then, the media representations shifted to the "undeserving poor" of the inner-city blacks and helped create the image of a black "underclass" detached from the moral values of America and held captive by a "culture of poverty."

JR: Would you then say in hindsight that Martin Luther King, Jr.'s concept of "massive civil obedience," specifically the strategy of a nonviolent *and* aggressive *and* dramatic disruption, would have been a better way?

WB: This is for me an abstract question. You cannot rewrite specific historical moments. When you're in the middle of the action you have to deal with the concrete situation as it is. King himself said the "riots" were "the voice of the unheard." He understood where we were coming from after going in and talking to people like me. If there had been mechanisms for people on the bottom to speak, to have their stories and demands heard, they wouldn't have needed that violent outlet. I was 17 years old then, and I'm still learning from Watts. I go back and visit the much-respected Watts

Tower—this incredible structure put together by a poor Italian immigrant, made out of broken bottles and cans. My father took me to this structure when I was much younger, way before the uprising. My sister and I revisited it recently, after my mother's funeral. It is still amazing that while everything else was leveled during the uprising, the Watts Tower was left unharmed. It became a symbol of respect for those who stood up, especially for those who lost their lives. Even to this day a lot of people who participated in the uprising go back to the Watts Tower and look at it and proudly say, "We were involved in this!" This is especially true now that the Watts uprising is celebrated as a rebellion and not simply as a "riot." But at the same time it is romanticized now and used as a tourist attraction.

What remains is the valuable experience that we as lower-class blacks did something extraordinary, at least for a moment. I'll give you an example: In the middle of the uprising, when the National Guard had come in after the police were paralyzed and the uprising was expanding, the armed forces issued a command to turn back the ships that were taking troops to Vietnam and instead to stay on alert nearby in case they were needed to control the uprising. For two weeks they didn't send those troops to Vietnam. So an open letter was sent from Vietnam to the "People of Watts" thanking us for saving the lives of the Vietnamese and of the American soldiers. Things like that don't leave you. Here you have the bottommost of society—those who are the most exploited, vilified, criminalized, and talked about as being nothing—asserting themselves.

Such hindsight questions are only productive if you use them to learn for present and future struggles. For instance, this unprecedented moment of history taught first of all that the success of a social struggle requires a connected, clear, competent, and committed collective of leaders that is able to anticipate some of the unintended consequences of certain actions and to preemptively counter the attempts to divide and control, the strategies to manipulate the outcome or to co-opt the leaders or parts of the movement. Secondly, in 1965, we did not have the experience of King's preparations of a Poor People's Campaign across color lines in 1967 and 1968. It is certainly not a coincidence that he was killed at the time when he tried to transform the civil rights movement into an encompassing human rights movement that focused on the economic needs and demands of the poor. His launching of a project to organize an interracial movement of the poor marked a new quality that we have to build on. Any study of the strategic significance of the move Dr. King made to unite the poor across color lines against the backdrop of U.S. history would show that his last campaign was an answer to the racial manipulation of "plantation politics," the pitting of poor whites against poor blacks.

CHAPTER 3 SUPPLEMENT

Class Debate on Resistance and Unintended Consequences

The following excerpted conversation took place after Willie Baptist and Jan Rehmann discussed the contributions of Malcolm X and Martin Luther King Jr. during the course they taught in the spring of 2007, "Poverty – Social Theories – Alternative Models?", at Union Theological Seminary.

Jason: As I understand the predominant gist of the last sections of the interview, you are saying that it is dangerous to start out with actions of resistance without knowing the possible unintended effects. But every action, every communication has unintended effects. When I say something to you, it has unintended effects; everything has unintended effects. Doesn't your warning then lead to the conclusion that we shouldn't do anything for fear of unintended effects? That path just leads to inaction and cynicism. Whatever story you try to tell in the media, it's going to come out according to the interests and people that have control of the media anyway.

Tim: I'd like to challenge Jan's criteria for "radicalism" by which he tries to demonstrate Malcolm X's lack thereof. I don't think that the critique of the capitalist system is an appropriate measurement. There are so many examples where such a critique is done in an abstract way, in the absence of a visceral movement.

Jennifer: First of all, especially when we're talking about African American embodiment, we don't have to do anything. We don't have to be bad or good, or violent or nonviolent, for negative images to be portrayed of us. It's not going to matter if we riot, if we jump off bridges, or if we excel. The images are already there and the mold is already there. The stereotypes are already in effect, and they are used to perpetuate certain things. Maybe this is an ignorant perspective, but it is just one that feels consistent with my experience, with that which I learn from my family, my friends, and people around, and with what I've read in terms of African American history as well.

So, in terms of unintended perspectives that others might have of African American communities, I would not agree that the violence of Watts hurt black people's image, or the image of the poor. It was certainly used like that, but it didn't do that any more than if they'd been using other means. One of the undercurrents of the conversation I was hearing in the conversation was a rejection of Watts as a valuable uprising—and the question has been raised of what was intended by it. And I think in part I have the sense that it was more organic than intentional.

Once you get 60,000 people organically rallied around the fact that some violence has occurred, people are not necessarily thinking about it systematically. This dynamic is not the same as in the organizing work that MLK did, sit-ins and boycotts that were occurring, because these activists were well prepared, instigated, and motivated in this sense. There is also the question on the table about the value of violence. Part of the reason why there has been a disparaging tone about Watts was because of the violence that was exercised in it. I think the experience of the people in Watts as it was evidenced in what Willie was saying was one of constant and continuous violence, all the time. So, to talk about the response to violence as violence is slightly unsettling for me, because real violence was what promoted this response.

Charlene: The first thing I want to say is that I do agree with Jennifer around the questions of black embodiment and the images of black folks, but I also think that doesn't mean that we don't have to remanipulate and reformulate these images in some ways. To say, it does not matter, because we're going to be portrayed badly anyway, is very detrimental. We have to think beyond that to create contradictions in people's common sense as a result of some of those reformulations. The second piece: Even with the organic nature of the Watts riot, the question then becomes, what do you do with 60,000 to 100,000 people that are confronting the social order? And in that respect, I don't think there is much difference to what happened with Rosa Parks. Smaller in Alabama, but still, a moment in time, that people who were ready took advantage of something that grew and escalated into something bigger. The organic nature of Watts—that's what I'm hearing as Jan's challenge—is how do we take the moment to move it into a movement, because people are in motion; they are expressing their anger against social systems and structures in a multitude of different ways.

In regard to the question of violence, I agree totally, that what happens all over the country, now and then, are violent acts. I have to challenge though whether we let violence off the hook. I don't think that violence begetting violence makes that latter violence okay. I am conscious of what can be a slippery slope. Young people being confronted by a whole host of different things, but the image I always have is what to tell the mother whose son got shot and killed? There has to be a sense of responsibility around violence. How do we define radicalism; how do we define revolutionary stances? What means are appropriate or legitimate to restructure what society looks like?

Jennifer: Okay, Charlene, I agree that it is somewhat defeatist to say that just because the image of black people is construed outside of the reality or actions of black people it should not be a concern for black people. In other words, I agree that we ought to think about the image we project. Furthermore, I agree with the point that you made to distinguish yourself from the defeatism I may have conveyed. However, I think there are two important possibilities within my observation that the images of blacks are not determined by black reality or action that I would want to articulate: First, when we blacks know that people will think whatever they want regardless of what we do, there is something liberating in this knowledge insofar as it frees us to *be* something that is outside of the norm and, in fact, counterhegemonic. There is a different opportunity to reject the problematic societal norm. Second, to the extent that non-blacks selectively create the images of blacks, *they*, not blacks, should be held responsible for those images. Whatever is within the power of blacks to control about our own image is our responsibility. However, history has proved that this is mostly out of our hands.

Furthermore, what black historian Evelyn Higginbotham identifies as the "politics of respectability" has been exposed for its shortcomings: blacks spent a whole lot of time trying to be more Victorian than the most Victorian English folks to no avail in terms of social advancement. So, I guess this would make me a little bit sensitive about the notion of blacks being overly concerned about projecting a certain image. Non-blacks must be held accountable and blacks ought to be liberated to develop a unique identity that is not dictated by the dominant culture.

Rob: When you are black and come out of a history where you were owned by whites, the black nationalist rhetoric of "black is beautiful," "black pride," and so on helps you a lot to own yourself—this is a radical move.

Alix: This discussion of violence is deeply moving to me and speaks to so many lives, but I find that the conversation has revolved largely around the race dynamics of black and white. I have been struggling to determine whether and how to insert my story as an Asian woman in this country. I find it difficult to figure out how to not have my story become a comparison in the identity politics that frame this history, because that isn't what my story is about. If nothing else, my history is simply another installment of the cruel manipulations of capitalism's ability to divide and conquer. When I do try to fit the concepts of violence versus nonviolence into my own history, I feel confused. My mother was born in the Merced Relocation Camp during the World War II internment of Japanese Americans in concentration camps on U.S. soil (a birth into another violently oppressive situation). Most of the history I know of this experience is that my people went into these camps quietly and lived there with minimal outward struggle for years. I feel that Japanese Americans have been in some ways judged as harshly for their nonviolence as others are judged for situations of "violent uprisings." Primarily in that this history is barely remembered (and that stories of resistance that did exist—like more militant struggles at some of the camps—have been silenced). And then some would say that my people were passive along with the ton of other stereotypes that surround this history. Others would say they honorably chose nonviolence. I sometimes think perhaps they should have struggled more, more violently, and I can't tell that I think that nonviolence is always the right thing. Other Japanese Americans may argue about this with me, but I really feel that this time in history was the death of my people in this country—today the communities no longer exist or are shattered and the families are broken. If they had struggled would we somehow have been able to fight harder to hold on to one another and our communities after our families were released? On the other hand I think that this country looks at a struggle like the Watts uprising, and is willing to call that resistance. The media's history of Japanese Americans tells a story of nonresistance. I think that there are other forms of resistance, though. For example, all of my cousins and I are mixed heritage with white. Is this "assimilation" violent or nonviolent? Is this a defeat? Or is it in fact a form of resistance?

Brian: I'm white, and I'm oppressed because of my sexual orientation. I think the religious dimension is missing in our discussions. I'd like to talk more about religion and ethics. And I'd like to question the assumption that violence can ever be justified. Jesus turned against Peter when he drew his sword. Something achieved by violence has no lasting effects. Think about the golden rule.

Paul: The question of violence seems to me more complex than this. When you look, for example, at the Stonewall Riots of 1969 in New York, you can see that these violent clashes between the police and groups of gay and transgender people were an achievement. It became a watershed for a global gay rights movement, because it was the first time that gay and transgender people have resisted police harassment on such a large scale.

Drew: I've been living in Nicaragua for some years, and when I talked with people about the Sandinista revolution, I got a paradoxical response: For one, the revolution "had to happen," in spite of the bloodshed and civil war that followed; for two, it should never happen again. Such a contradiction shows us the complex character of historical changes, in particular if they are as condensed as revolutions.

Willie: Discussions about violence and nonviolence can become very abstract if they are not connected to a concrete assessment of the respective situation. The term *violence* is being used in many different ways and can mean many different things. There is a huge difference if you talk about violence against persons or "violence" against objects, property. Some would call a sit-in or a blockade of streets and railways "violence," because car drivers or train passengers are stranded, or a strike, because the factory comes to a standstill. But to employ the same word for phenomena that are so different is misleading. The "violence" to break the locks and occupy a house so that homeless people find a home for their families and kids can be literally a life-saving operation, whereas the structural violence whereby the economic power relations condemn a growing part of the population to unemployment or underemployment, to foreclosures, to a lack of health care, to hunger and cold, is a crime against basic human rights. A discussion on violence has therefore to look carefully at the entire historical context, the specifics of the situation and the concrete options people have at hand.

These discussions and considerations of concrete tactical options were by and large missing from the forethought of the fighters of Watts and the other uprisings of the 1960s. Even though I participated in the 1965 Watts uprising I'm still learning the lessons of that mass black ghetto resistance to very exploitative and oppressive conditions. I remain a student as well as a product of Watts. Three of the primary lessons I continue to draw from that life-shaping experience are 1.) it was the impoverished, what Malcolm X called the "field Negroes," that revolted, not the black upper classes; it was Watts, not Baldwin Hills, that erupted; 2.) the impoverished stood up as a social force with such powerful initiative and agency that it shook world opinion and still claims historic importance; and 3.) the impoverished as a social force had no organic core of theoretically and politically trained leaders. There were no sufficiently conscious elements among the ghetto combatants to strategically anticipate what has been referred to as "unintended consequences," to anticipate the manipulations of race and racism by mainstream media and the other instruments of the "powers-that-be." There was no intellectual force prepared and positioned to consider and coordinate the political and ethical implications of the use of nonviolent or violent tactics.

Jan: I agree with Willie's analysis. I always find it one-sided to get morally outraged by the violence of looting and scuffling with the police without mentioning police brutality and without talking about the structural violence of racism and classism that drives people into misery and desperation. But even if we take all this into account, we cannot get rid of some serious political and ethical problems posed by a violence that endangers or harms people's lives—so I am not talking specifically about Watts. In terms of politics: As soon as a social movement is portrayed as "violent," such an image drives away the possible allies that one would need to get out of isolation. If urban riots have the effect that possible allies like the white working class or the middle classes turn against you, this effect is to be carefully analyzed and taken into account. Antonio Gramsci, who experienced the rapid and devastating turn from revolutionary workers' uprisings in northern Italy in 1918–1919 to the fascist victory of Mussolini's March to Rome in 1922, once said that there was no worse strategy than to scare away people by a militant rhetoric that is in no way backed up by real power. In terms of ethics, I think Charlene and Brian are right, when they point out that it is dangerous to separate ends and means. If the means do not represent or at least foreshadow the ideals you are striving for, you are creating a fundamental inconsistency that risks damaging the credibility of the movement. In this sense, ethics and politics are closely linked.

Let me conclude with a methodological remark. When Willie and I set up our interview, we were not interested in conveying a negative judgment on the Watts uprising, but we wanted to enhance a dialectical analysis of its complexity. Let me give a tentative definition of *dialectics*, without getting too much into a philosophical expertise: *dialectics* comes from the Greek words *dia*, "through," and *lego*, "to talk," which gives us the literal meaning "to talk something through." Starting from this literal meaning, *dialectics* means something like talking through the different aspects of a complex phenomenon, unveiling the inner contradictions of a complex phenomenon. Dialectics is mainly directed against a moralistic dualism, against a simplistic either-or way of thinking that claims to determine that something is either good or bad, positive or negative, productive or self-defeating. Against such dichotomies, dialectical thinkers point out that life is more complicated and that its phenomena contain different and contradictory elements at the same time. Dialectical analysis is then a method of sorting out the inner contradictions of a phenomenon and, on the practical level, an art to move skillfully in these contradictions, so that one has "the wind of history in one's sails," as Walter Benjamin put it.

A social event, and especially an explosion like an uprising, can be at the same time very productive in one respect and detrimental in another respect, for example, very productive for the agency and self-esteem of a movement, and at the same time easy to be manipulated by the mainstream media in order to encapsulate the movement, to scare away possible allies like the white poor. Both can be true at the same time, and if we are ready to analyze both aspects, we might be able to overcome the rifts within and between different social movements. It could turn out that each of the opposite approaches has some relative "truth" in it that risks being turned into a fallacy as soon as it is made an absolute value. The political skill could then be to find a new perspective that overcomes the blockades between polarizing tendencies and combines the respective strengths without carrying on the weaknesses.

CHAPTER 4

Root Causes of Poverty: Neoliberalism, High-Tech Capitalism, and Economic Crisis

Jan Rehmann

"In my neighborhood, I saw a welfare recipient driving a BMW—there is so much fraud going on," a young woman recently said in a heated discussion I helped organize, and it was evident that this story considerably framed how she perceived welfare recipients. I later learned that she grew up in poverty herself and, as a single mother, struggled to make ends meet. This was, for her, the dignified poverty, the acceptable one that has nothing to do with welfare, the virtuous one where you work hard and pull yourself up by your bootstraps. Those on welfare rolls represented for her the lazy ones, the slackers, the cheats. It was not that she was insensitive about the problem of social injustice; there is no need to tell her how poverty felt. But it remained a purely individual issue, to be resolved in private. Her worldview was structured by the dichotomy of "deserving" and "undeserving" poor.

COMMON SENSE AND SOCIAL ANALYSIS

I am telling you this story because it reveals the weight of common sense on our perception and understanding of the world around us, revealing the importance of a critical social analysis. According to Antonio Gramsci's famous definition from the early 1930s, common sense is an incoherent set of generally held assumptions and beliefs, which "contains Stone Age elements and principles of a more advanced science, prejudices from all past phases of history . . . and intuitions of a future philosophy." The task of a "philosophy of praxis" is then to critically work on the coherence of common sense (1971, pp. 324, 330–331). Each ideology that tries to build up political consent has to anchor itself in common sense by connecting with certain elements of it, splitting them from or pitting them against others. When we are confronted with poverty, we usually have certain images and explanations that we think are authentic, coming out of what we've seen and experienced directly. In fact, these images and interpretations are often determined by the prevailing media images and the predominant ideologies about poverty.

A widespread commonsense understanding is that poverty is caused by individual fate or bad choices people make in their lives: dropping out of college, getting pregnant, getting divorced, ending up in one of the famous female-headed families that haunt the "moral" debates on poverty, having a "culture of poverty," sliding into the "black underclass" of the inner-city ghettos, lacking an education, failing to adapt to the demands of the economy, and so on. And some of us might know examples where certain fateful events, choices, or cultural characteristics actually *do* play a role. We might even know welfare recipients (or have heard about them) who are "lazy," are drug addicted, or cheat the system—examples that seem to validate the impression that these characteristics are the causes of poverty.

Social analysis can help us to mistrust such widespread images. This might start on the basic level of statistics that contradict the widespread myth of the "lazy" poor: In 1997, 48% of poor families with children had at least one family member who worked full-time, 29% had at least one family member who worked part-time, only 24% were excluded from the labor market (Iceland, 2006, pp. 78–79). If you add up the full-time and part-time percentages, you can see that over three-quarters were indeed "connected" to the labor market, and less than a quarter were not. Since the share of contingent labor has considerably increased since 1997 (in particular, in the service industry), the numbers of "working poor" are certainly much higher today. Poverty is therefore not sufficiently understood as people being "excluded" from the labor market and its beneficial "work ethics" for "psychological" or "cultural" reasons. It is more accurate to describe poverty as the destiny of working poor who cannot get out of poverty because of the lack of sustainable jobs or because of overexploitation.

One of the differences between commonsense notions and social analysis is the latter's insistence on carefully distinguishing between structural causes of poverty as a mass phenomenon and the psychological and cultural consequences, that is, the ways poverty is being lived and experienced. For example, no one would deny that alcohol and drug abuse play a devastating role in poor communities—nobody knows this better than poor people's movements, whose organizing efforts are constantly undermined by drug trafficking and addiction. But it does not make sense if one tries to explain the mass impoverishment in the devastated coal-mining areas of Appalachia by blaming the drug trade or specific cultural patterns. Studies on poor people's habits and cultures can be fruitful if they are embedded in an analysis of the specific structural conditions and power relations in which poor people have to develop their strategies of survival.[1] But without such a connection, these studies are doing little more than supporting the predominant pattern that blames the poor for their poverty.

And finally, social analysis can help to reconstruct how the images of poverty that we've got in our heads have been carefully prepared by think tanks, produced by the media and other ideological apparatuses. It can contribute to critically challenging what presents itself as spontaneous evidence. One example is the racialization of the image of poverty that started in the mid-1960s: Before 1964, the predominant media representation of poverty was the white rural poor of the Appalachian coalfields. These pictures of the "good poor," the "deserving poor," stirred up public sympathy and helped support President Lyndon B. Johnson's "War on Poverty." By 1967, 72% of media representations of the poor were African Americans (Gilens, 2003, pp. 101–130). Unfortunately, this has nothing to do with a heightened racial sensitivity of the press. Rather, it became part of a strategy of "othering": Poor black folks became the "undeserving poor." This occurred at the same time that stories about the War on Poverty turned negative. Even in states with very few African American poor, people were convinced that poverty was mainly "black." The black "underclass" was portrayed by two faces, namely the male gangbanger and the teenage single mother—a very effective combination of racist and sexist stereotypes as it turned out. These images enforced racist reactions from the white middle classes and white blue-collar workers who saw their tax money being "wasted" on inner-city hustlers and drug addicts. The ideological connection of poverty and black crime prepared the ground for turning the "war against poverty" into a neoconservative "war against the poor."

The widespread explanations of poverty by psychological or cultural factors suffer from the fundamental weakness that they dissimulate the social structures by which poverty is being produced, the relations of power in our economy, and the way the wealth in this rich country is being distributed. I'd like to focus on the connection between poverty and the system of social inequality, and for this purpose I'll go back a bit in history to the late 1970s and early 1980s, because it is at that time that the market radicalism that we experience today came to power.

INCREASING SOCIAL INJUSTICE

Data from *The State of Working America, 2006/2007* (Mishel, Bernstein, & Allegretto, 2007) helps illuminate this shift. Figure 4.1 shows the income share of the top 10% of the population from 1913 to 2003, comparing the United States and France. Generally speaking, it shows that the

Figure 4.1. Top Decile Income Share in France and in the United States from 1913 to 2003

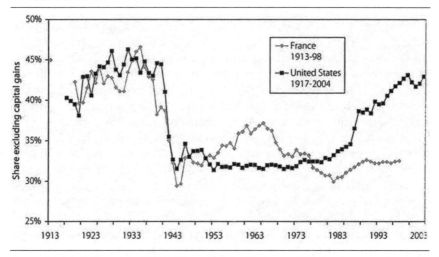

Source: L. Mishel, J. Bernstein, and S. Allegretto, eds., *The State of Working America, 2006/2007* (Ithaca, NY: Cornell University Press, 2007), p. 348.

richest 10% proportionately accumulated a much larger portion of the pie. If we look at the time span between 1953 and 1973, we can see that this top bracket of the U.S. population owned little more than 30%, whereas the French upper classes were relatively better off, owning up to over 35% in the 1960s. But the dynamics changed at the end of the 1970s and the beginning of the 1980s: The top-decile share of income in the United States reached 44% in 2000, while the share of the French elites remained relatively low. In 2007, the top decile share in the United States was equal to 49.7%, a level higher that any other year since 1917 (Saez, 2010, p. 2).

A similar tendency can be seen in Figure 4.2, which compares the family income of the top 0.1% of the population of three countries (France, the United States, and the United Kingdom). We can see again that between the 1950s and the mid-1970s their share remains quite stable (between 2% and 3% of the national income). And then, the U.S. share rocketed upward in the late 1970s and early 1980s (reaching about 7.4% in 1998), leaving the elites of the other two countries far behind. These two charts illustrate how the income inequality has increased in the past 30 years, especially in the United States. The ratio of the median compensation of a worker to the median salaries of a CEO was still 1:30 in 1970, but by 2000 the ratio had soared to 1:500 (Harvey, 2005, p. 16).

Figure 4.2. Top 0.1% Family Income Share in France, the United States, and the United Kingdom

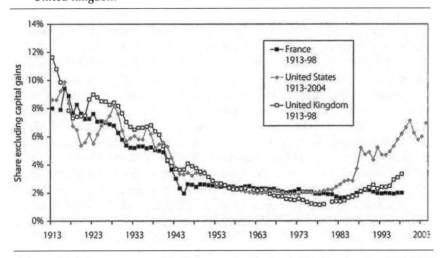

Source: L. Mishel, J. Bernstein, and S. Allegretto, eds., *The State of Working America, 2006/2007* (Ithaca, NY: Cornell University Press, 2007), p. 348.

What happened in between? Why did the income inequality increase so sharply from the late 1970s onward? One of the answers points to the predominance of "neoliberalism," which began in the late 1970s.

A NEOLIBERAL THEOLOGY OF THE MARKET

What is neoliberalism? The term is not to be confused with the commonsense understanding of "liberal" in the United States, which usually designates a moderate left-wing attitude, concerned with the welfare state, social justice, and tolerance. Rather, neoliberalism is the opposite. It has become the general designation for an economic politics that claims to realize a market order that is "free" from government interference, especially from any attempts toward wealth redistribution in favor of lower classes or marginalized groups. Its proponents advocate for the dismantling of the welfare state, the deregulation of labor relations, and the weakening of trade unions' bargaining power, all in the name of a "free market society" and its entrepreneurial spirit, both of which are in danger of being stifled by a patronizing state bureaucracy. Proclaiming "individual freedom," neoliberalism proposes to bring all human actions and desires into the domain of the market, since it regards market exchange as an "ethic in itself," capable of substituting for all previously held ethical beliefs (Harvey, 2005, p. 3).

Contrary to its polemics against government interference, neoliberalism in power never reduced the state as such but solely those institutions in which substantial social compromises had been hammered out during the preceding period of Fordism. Whenever neoliberal parties conquered the "commanding heights" of the state, they strengthened the military and repressive apparatuses and reorganized the state's internal structure by its marketization ("public-private partnerships" and the like).[2] In this context, it is important to know that neoliberalism's economic politics were first implemented around 1975 by Augusto Pinochet's cruel dictatorship in Chile—with the active support of the "Chicago School" around Milton Friedman. But neoliberalism's hegemony cannot be reduced to force or forgery. It has become an ideology with a strong impact on common sense, an ideology that could win an active or at least passive consensus, not only among elites, but also among wider milieus of middle and popular classes. In the United States it has taken on a kind of religious aura that permeates everyday culture to a degree to which we are often not aware. Its victory became clear with the election of Margaret Thatcher in 1979 in the United Kingdom and of Ronald Reagan in 1980 in the United States.

Looking to the origins of neoliberal theory, I confine this discussion to one of its leading figures, Friedrich A. Hayek, an Austrian economist and philosopher, who emigrated from Austria to London in 1931 and then, in 1950, to Chicago. In 1947, he organized the first international association, the Mont Pèlerin Society, that helped many neoliberal think tanks all over the world. His *Road to Serfdom* (1944/1994) became a bible for the British neoliberals around Margaret Thatcher. In 1976, he published *The Mirage of Social Justice*, where he argues that the concept of social justice, in any form, is empty and misleading. According to Hayek, employing the term is either thoughtless or fraudulent, a dishonest insinuation that is intellectually disreputable and destructive of moral feeling (Hayek, 1976, pp. xii, 97). Why? Justice can only exist among individuals, he assumes, and therefore cannot be applied to the "Great Society of free men," which he defines as (and actually reduces to) the anonymous and spontaneous mechanisms of the market. He frankly admits that this market "gives to those who already have. But this is its merit rather than its defect" (p. 123). One cannot apply a standard of "social justice" if there is no one in charge who can be blamed and to whom one could appeal if the standard is not met. The market is like a "game" with its own rules, and when you lose you have to accept the outcome as fate.

If we step back and look at Hayek's arrangement, we can see that he establishes the market as a kind of deity whose decrees are to be followed without questioning and whose realm is not to be touched by human planning or reasoning. Its invisible hand has some interesting functional similarities to the deeds of a hidden God, *deus absconditus*, in Calvinist theology: *It cannot be known.* For Hayek, the claim to understand the spontaneous workings of the market constitutes a fundamental fallacy of the Age of Reason, which he associates most notably with the traditions of Karl Marx and Sigmund Freud. *It cannot and must not be influenced.* Any attempt to interfere in the market game in the sense of redistributive justice leads straight to full-fledged socialism and is totalitarian by definition (pp. 64, 75–56, 136). But while Hayek's portrayal of the market is reminiscent of the ideological form of traditional theology, it is also the exact opposite of its Judeo-Christian substance. Hayek's hidden God is definitely not the biblical God of the Exodus and the Jubilee Year, of liberation and social justice, but the reified rule of money, capital, and shareholder values, namely, the very fetishism the Bible so forcefully condemns as idolatry, epitomized in the "golden calf."

As Fredric Jameson remarks, the neoliberals' free market is Leviathan in sheep's clothing (1991, p. 273). Market totalitarianism is indeed incompatible with a Christian ethics that starts from the sacredness of the human person, "realized in community with others," because from this ethical perspective the economic institutions have to "serve" human needs, and not the other way round. In the words of the famous Catholic pastoral letter *Economic Justice for All*, "Wherever our economic arrangements fail to conform to the demands of human dignity lived in community, they must be questioned and transformed" (National Conference of Catholic Bishops, 1986, p. 15). From Hayek's starting point of an unquestionable market game, it is consistent that he turns against any notion of economic human rights. In his view, President Franklin Delano Roosevelt's Four Freedoms (of speech, of worship, from want, from fear) and the United Nations Declaration of Human Rights, which proclaims the social right to decent jobs, housing, health care and education (Fig. 4.3), are fundamentally flawed because they combine individual freedoms with social and economic rights, which he says are not compatible with a market society and lead to socialism (Hayek, 1976, pp. 103–104). But the totalitarian state socialism he invokes is more part of a scarecrow scenario than the real target, which is the "social-liberal" attempt to connect individual and social rights. Neoliberalism first and foremost targets the economic doctrine of Keynesianism and the social compromise it represented.

Figure 4.3. Economic Rights in the Universal Declaration of Human Rights (excerpts)

Article 22: Everyone, as a member of society, has the right to social security and is entitled to realization, through national effort and international co-operation and in accordance with the organization and resources of each State, of the economic, social and cultural rights indispensable for his dignity and the free development of his personality.

Article 23: (1) Everyone has the right to work, to free choice of employment, to just and favorable conditions of work and to protection against unemployment. (2) Everyone, without any discrimination, has the right to equal pay for equal work. (3) Everyone who works has the right to just and favorable remuneration ensuring for himself and his family an existence worthy of human dignity, and supplemented, if necessary, by other means of social protection. (4) Everyone has the right to form and to join trade unions for the protection of his interests.

Article 24: Everyone has the right to rest and leisure, including reasonable limitation of working hours and periodic holidays with pay.

Article 25: (1) Everyone has the right to a standard of living adequate for the health and well-being of himself and of his family, including food, clothing, housing and medical care and necessary social services, and the right to security in the event of unemployment, sickness, disability, widowhood, old age or other lack of livelihood in circumstances beyond his control. (2) Motherhood and childhood are entitled to special care and assistance. All children, whether born in or out of wedlock, shall enjoy the same social protection.

Article 26: (1) Everyone has the right to education. Education shall be free, at least in the elementary and fundamental stages. Elementary education shall be compulsory. Technical and professional education shall be made generally available and higher education shall be equally accessible to all on the basis of merit. (2) Education shall be directed to the full development of the human personality and to the strengthening of respect for human rights and fundamental freedoms. It shall promote understanding, tolerance and friendship among all nations, racial or religious groups, and shall further the activities of the United Nations for the maintenance of peace (United Nations, 1948).

THE DISMANTLING OF THE KEYNESIAN WELFARE STATE

Keynesianism was the mainstream economic doctrine in the United States and Western Europe between World War II and the late 1970s. The term is derived from the economist John Maynard Keynes (1883–1946), a counselor of the British government, who advocated for the very economic policies that Hayek, Milton Friedman, and other neoliberals later strictly rejected: Keynesianism promoted a mixed economy, in which both the state and the private sector played an important role and an active fiscal policy oriented toward the macroeconomic goals of economic growth, full employment, and citizens' welfare—goals excluded in Hayek's concept of a purposeless society. Most notably, Keynes advocated for the state's responsibility to strengthen demand, for example, through, real wages, so that people would have enough money to buy the commodities that businesses produced. Keynes, whose doctrine had a strong impact on Roosevelt's New Deal politics, was certainly not a "socialist." When he stepped into the debates about how to overcome the Great Depression, he promised not to institute revolution but to save capitalism. According to his economic doctrine, the government has the responsibility to pursue macroeconomic policies that ensure people have long-lasting jobs, decent wages, and social protection systems. In other words, it has the duty to provide some social justice by redistributing wealth toward the lower-income segments.

For a long time, neoliberalism was a minority movement of intellectuals that could not match the predominance of Keynesianism in public opinion. This began to change in the 1970s, when the economy stagnated, and the economic and political elites came to the conviction that Keynesian strategies did not work anymore. The changing tide could be seen in 1974 and 1976, when Hayek and then Friedman received the Nobel Prize in economics. Four years later, Margaret Thatcher and Ronald Reagan were in power.

Looking back at the increase of social inequality from the early 1980s onward, illustrated by Figures 4.1 and 4.2, we can see what was really going on behind the smokescreen of antigovernment and market "freedom" slogans. Neoliberalism in practice can be described as the successful strategy of the elites to restore their economic power as well as political and ideological hegemony. The neoliberals achieved this goal by different means, out of which I only select a few.

First, in terms of financial markets, the beginning of neoliberalism can be described as the transition from the "Bretton Woods system" to "a new dollar–Wall Street regime" in the early 1970s. Through the abolition of gold as the material anchor of money flows ("Nixon shock") and the abandonment of fixed currency prices among nation states, most international financial relations were taken out of the control of state central banks and turned over to private financial operators (Gowan, 1999, pp. 17–30). The economic balance of power shifted to private banks and created the predominance of a financial sector seemingly detached from the "real economy"—a specific "disembedded" variety of capitalism, frequently dubbed "turbo-capitalism" (Edward Luttwak) or "casino capitalism" (Susan Strange).

Second, the Reagan administration and its successors issued dramatic tax cuts for the rich, in both corporate taxes and top personal tax rates. As you can see in Figure 4.4, between 1979 and 1990 the tax rate for the highest bracket dropped from 70% to 28%.

Third, Reagan's victory over the air traffic controllers' union (PATCO) marked the beginning of a massive assault on labor unions. Figure 4.5 shows that the proportion of unionized workers declined from 29% in 1975 to 12.5% in 2005.[3] At the same time, capital investments moved away from the unionized Northeast and Midwest into the nonunion South and West. This decline had an immediate effect on poverty, regardless of what one thinks about the quality and political integrity of labor unions. Often, the mere existence of a union makes the difference between working in poverty and working your way out of it.

Figure 4.4. United States Tax Rates for Higher and Lower Brackets, 1913–2003

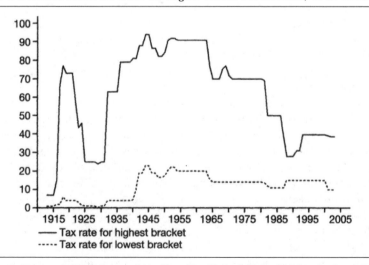

Source: D. Harvey, *A Brief History of Neoliberalism* (Oxford: Oxford University Press, 2005), p. 26.

Figure 4.5. Union Coverage in the United States, 1977–2005

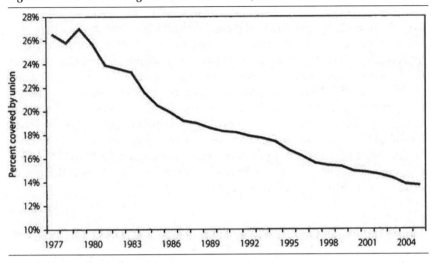

*Covered by a collective bargaining agreement.

Source: L. Mishel, J. Bernstein, and S. Allegretto, eds., *The State of Working America, 2006/2007* (Ithaca, NY: Cornell University Press, 2007), p. 182.

Fourth, the economy was deregulated: Public services like transportation, education, care of the environment, and energy and water supply were increasingly privatized, commodified, handed over to the stock markets. In terms of labor relations, "deregulation" means basically that employers could hire and fire their workforce as they liked. It is one of neoliberalism's main characteristics that it engendered a considerable increase in unsecured, contingent labor, especially for women.

Finally, many of these tendencies can be summarized by the catchphrase "Walmartization of the economy." Walmart is not only is the world's largest corporation, but it is also a model for a new type of low-salary, low-benefit employment practice that systematically bulldozes local small businesses by setting prices so low that no one can afford to match them. Walmart's salaries usually do not equal a sustaining family wage; its health care packages are so expensive that over half of its employees cannot afford them and are therefore forced to rely on Medicaid and other government programs financed by taxes. All of a sudden, the much-vilified role of the state in the economy becomes vital again, but only as a source of corporate subsidies: Taxpayers have to absorb the health care costs for the employees of a corporation with huge annual profits.

This is a very incomplete list of how neoliberalism has worked in practice. One of its outcomes can be observed in Figure 4.6, which shows wage decline starting again at the end of the 1970s, interrupted by a rise from 1995 to 2000 in the famous "New Economy" period, but ending by the recession of 2001. The most remarkable finding in this chart lies in the relationship between wage levels and the productivity curve. From the 1960s to the mid-1970s, you can see a correlation between the increase of productivity and the increase of wages—which corresponds to a basic commonsense notion of "fairness": When the pie gets bigger, salaries should go up. But from the late 1970s onward, this correlation is broken up. Although productivity rates accelerated again from 2000 to 2005, real wages fell and the number of families in poverty grew (Mishel, Bernstein, & Allegretto, 2007, pp. 17–21).

FROM THE "WAR ON POVERTY" TO THE "WAR AGAINST THE POOR"

The hegemony of neoliberalism produced immediate consequences in the general perception of welfare politics and poverty. This manifested in the prevailing opinion (famously laid out in Charles Murray's *Losing Ground*, 1984) that poverty was caused mainly by welfare programs themselves.

Figure 4.6. Real Wages and Productivity in the United States, 1960–2000

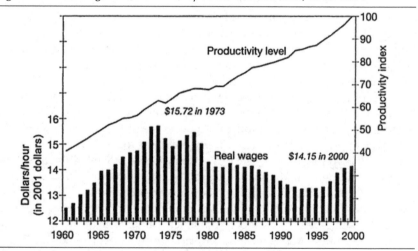

Source: D. Harvey, *A Brief History of Neoliberalism* (Oxford: Oxford University Press, 2005), p. 25.

The argument is simple: It's not the social structure or class position that determines your economic success but rather the individual choices you make. The social welfare programs established by Roosevelt's New Deal and augmented by Johnson's War on Poverty created negative incentives that keep people in poverty—not taking a poorly paid job, not staying in school, not getting married because this would reduce the welfare benefits. In this explanation, we see "welfare queens" collecting their money from various agencies. The moral decline constitutes an irresponsible and criminal "culture of poverty," the culture of a "ghetto underclass" that perpetuates poverty. The argument is based on the (counterfactual) assumption that the poor can work themselves out of poverty if they just tried hard enough.

This pattern has been taken up efficiently by the propaganda machine of the Republican Party. A passage from the inaugural address of President George Bush Sr. in 1989 reveals how the blaming of the poor can be coated in a seemingly caring and compassionate language: "There are homeless, lost and roaming. . . . There are those who cannot free themselves of enslavement to whatever addiction—drugs, welfare, the demoralization that rules the slums. There is crime to be conquered, the rough crime of the streets" (January 20, 1989; quoted in DiFazio, 2006, p. 2). One might have to read this passage several times over before one recognizes the scandal: Welfare is being depicted as an "addiction" and thereby is directly associated to drugs, immorality, and street crime! We can see here how neoliberal ideology is intensely trying to shape a commonsense image of poverty, which is, if not critically deciphered, accepted as self-evident. In Newt Gingrich's "Contract with America" (1994) we read: "Government programs have bred illegitimacy, crime, . . . and more poverty. Our Contract with America will change this destructive social behavior." We will eliminate the "culture of poverty" and replace it with a "culture of productivity" (DiFazio, 2006, pp. 2, 72). Poverty, engendered on a mass scale by deregulation, deindustrialization, and a race to the bottom of the labor market, has been transformed into a "behavior" to be cured by labor discipline.

It is one of the bitter experiences of liberals and progressives in the United States that it was the of Clinton administration that took the decisive step to implement this program. The Welfare Reform Bill of 1996 pushed welfare recipients toward low-wage jobs by curtailing their benefits. The Welfare to Workfare programs certainly caused a reduction of the number of welfare recipients, but they did not reduce poverty. Most workfare jobs paid so poorly that they didn't help poeple climb out of misery. Even if official poverty rates declined slightly in the late 1990s (through the New Economy boom), extreme poverty as measured by the "poverty gap" (Fig. 4.7) and rates

Figure 4.7. Family Poverty Gap and Family Poverty Rates, 1959–2005

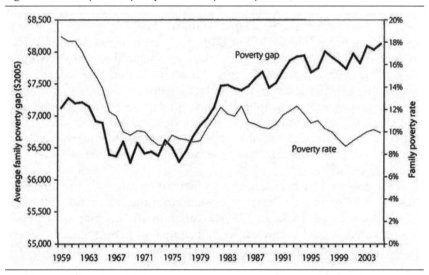

Note: Poverty gap is the dollar gap between a poor family's actual income and the poverty threshold.

Source: L. Mishel, J. Bernstein, and S. Allegretto, eds., *The State of Working America, 2006/2007* (Ithaca, NY: Cornell University Press, 2007), p. 289.

of "poverty below half the poverty line" have constantly deepened. Emergency food and shelter providers report a significant increase in the numbers of people they must help, most of them working poor: In New York City, for example, most of those who depend on soup kitchens and food pantries are people with one or more jobs.

HIGH-TECH CAPITALISM AND CONTINGENT LABOR

Thus far, I have portrayed neoliberalism in two ways, on the level of an ideology that can be described as an idolatry of the market, and on the level of an economic and social policy that dismantled the Keynesian welfare state, weakened trade unions, and created an unprecedented polarization of wealth and poverty. But I think neoliberalism cannot be adequately grasped without looking at the underlying emergence of a new type of transnational high-tech capitalism. Some scholars argue that the hegemony of neoliberalism emerged from the management of a transition to a new level of high-tech production (Haug, 2003, p. 42). Indeed, at the same time as the Bretton

Woods system was abolished and replaced by the dollar–Wall Street regimen dominated by private financial institutions, the first commercial microprocessor was introduced. High-tech capitalism can be defined as a mode of production based on electronics and computer systems, combined with an explosion of the Internet during the 1990s. The term "transnational" describes a new stage of globalization: It is not only that national economies are linked to one another through trade and finances, but the production process itself is dispersed all over the globe, so that, for instance, the individual parts of a car are manufactured in different "developing countries," the assembly may occur in Brazil or Japan, and the management may be coordinated from a central computer in Detroit. Production takes place in a kind of transnational spider's web that stretches over the globe.

Now, to produce useful things with the help of the most developed technologies could in principle be a very beneficial innovation. These technologies could alleviate painstaking labor and shorten the labor time of all of us so that we had more leisure time—time for taking care of our partners, children, or parents, time for culture, community commitment, and for our friendships. If well designed, they could even reduce the ecologically harmful waste of natural resources. But this is not the way technological innovations are usually introduced in a capitalist society, which is driven by the accumulation of private profits. Under these conditions, technologies tend to devalue human work and to squeeze human beings out of the labor process. Marx criticized this tendency as a systemic alienation that is most irrational and destructive: Since the values produced by the working class end up in the pockets of the factory owners, they can be used to replace their producers; "the working population therefore produces both the accumulation of capital and the means by which it is itself made superfluous," so that the employed part of the working class is overworked, whereas the unemployed or underemployed sections are condemned to "enforced idleness" (Marx, 1867/1990, pp. 783, 789).

A closer look shows therefore that poverty is not only caused by a particular economic and social policies, but is also engendered by new strategies of how high-tech capitalism organizes the labor process. The attributes of these economic transformations— deregulation, lean production, subcontracting, outsourcing, the just-in-time principle, and so on—are well known. The French sociologist Pierre Bourdieu has coined the term "flexploitation," which became a widespread means of describing the new combination of flexibilization and exploitation. Many social analysts use the term "precariat" instead of "contingent labor," and the term "precarization," in order to grasp the economic and social processes that render labor and labor relations contingent. The concepts are formed in analogy to the classical concepts of the "proletariat" and "proletarianization." Similarly, liberation theologians in South America have coined the term "pooritariat" (*pobretari-ado*). These different terms point to the deep structures that generate instability and impoverishment. They designate a process that happens not outside or at the margins of capitalist production but at the core of its class relations.

Precarization is a general and encompassing process that concerns large segments of the working class and also parts of the middle classes. It is not always linked to unskilled jobs, but can also be found among white-collar professionals, "independent contractors," all kind of freelancers, different varieties of "franchising," and qualified IT jobs performed by a highly individualized "cybertariat" (Huws, 2003). Microsoft is organized as a two-tier system, in which some engineers and programmers received stock options that make them wealthy—at least until the economic crisis hit—while the majority is composed of contingent workers ("white-collar sweatshops"). Even in better-paid positions, the lack of long-term contracts causes conditions in which poverty might be just a few steps away. As the economy has headed into a downturn, the anxiety of loosing one's job has reached the middle of society. In "developing countries," the "informal economy" makes up between 50% and 80% of social labor, which means that it is not "substandard work," but has become the real standard. On a global level, the "informal proletariat" is the fastest-growing group of the world's population.[4] What we see is not only a decomposition of the traditional industrial working class—with all its undeniable phenomena of fragmentation, desolidarization, competitive individualization, and so on—but also at the same time a recomposition of class, in the course of which contingent labor is the most dynamic part of the labor force. Mario Candeias describes the precariat as a new class faction that has the potential to become a "universal social figure" of the working class, because it epitomizes the new flexible mode of production of high-tech capitalism, in which insecurity and overexploitation are moving toward the center (Candeias, 2007, p. 9).

NEOLIBERAL CAPITALISM AND ECONOMIC CRISIS

It is evident that the precarization of labor and the stagnation of real wages have played a decisive role in kicking off the crisis with which we are confronted. "Since employers succeeded in keeping wages from rising, the only way to sell the ever-expanding output was to *lend* workers the money to buy more. . . . By 2006, the most stressed borrowers—'sub-prime'—could no longer pay what they owed. This house of debt cards then began its spiraling descent" (Wolff, 2010, p. 76). When the International Monetary Fund (IMF) talks about "the largest financial crisis in the United States since the Great Depression," this description, as dramatic as it sounds, is still an understatement, first, because the crisis is not restricted to the United States, but has gone global, and second, because it is not only a financial crisis, but also a full-fledged economic crisis that is sweeping through the "real economy," affecting all sections from construction to the auto and consumer goods industries. Not only are several of Wall Street's big investment banks gone, we have also experienced more than half a million (533,000) job losses in one month alone (in November 2008).

It is obvious that the ideology of neoliberalism that has been predominant for about 30 years is in crisis right now. The big corporations, financial or nonfinancial, that had vilified state intervention as a socialist infringement on their property rights have lined up to apply to be bailed out with huge sums of taxpayers' money. The mainstream press that had celebrated market radicalism as a sacrosanct religion has now shifted to blaming Wall Street and corporate "greed" and sometimes to denouncing the same deregulation of financial markets it had fallen for before. Even Alan Greenspan, who headed the Federal Reserve Bank of the United States for 18 years, declared that he is in "a state of shocked disbelief" about how a system based on "the self-interest of lending institutions" could have found itself in such a mess (McNally, 2008, p. 3). The economic and political outcome of this crisis is difficult to determine and will depend on the relations of force. Must we expect a right-wing backlash and authoritarian neoliberalism? Or is it realistic to bet on a Keynesian economic policy with a re-regulation of the financial markets and some elements of a "green capitalism"? Or is there the chance for a new wave of social movements to emerge that target transnational capitalism as a system that reveals itself as being less and less capable of securing the "pursuit of happiness" for the majority of people?

Unfortunately, it is not primarily the beneficiaries or ideologues of neoliberalism who pay for the crisis. Behind the average of 10% unemployment lie still more revealing numbers as soon as you relate the unemployment rate to the different levels of annual household income: Toward the end of 2009, the unemployment rate in the lowest income group (out of 10) was 30.8% and in the next lowest income group 19.1% (Herbert, 2010, p. A27). The dismantling of the welfare state has created a situation in which the transition from unemployment to dire poverty has become extremely short. As soon as employees are fired, they lose the health benefits that had been covered through the workplace. According to public health experts, "On average, for each jobless worker who has lost insurance, at least one child or spouse covered under the same policy has also lost protection" (Pear, 2008). In their need, the uninsured turn to the emergency rooms as their only option (obliged to see all patients, regardless of their ability to pay), which leads to overcrowding, overburdening of doctors and staff, and endless waiting lines (Abelson, 2008). The health care crisis goes hand in hand with a deepening of the mortgage crisis, which kicked off the financial meltdown in the first place. At the end of September 2008, a record 1 out of 10 American homeowners with a mortgage was either at least a month behind on his or her payments or in foreclosure at the end of September ("One in 10," 2008). It is to be expected that foreclosures will multiply and homelessness will swell further, to enormous proportions.

It is fair to say that neoliberal high-tech capitalism has not only, from the early 1980s onward, been increasing social injustice, squeezing real wages, and creating mass impoverishment, but also has engendered the crisis that is drawing more and more people into poverty, misery, and exclusion. Over the next weeks of this course, we will take on the task of carefully analyzing the economic crisis, how it is related to social injustice and poverty, how it is connected to the fundamental structures and power relations of our capitalistic economy, and how it concretely affects people's lives. We will also deal with the question of how this worsening situation might lead to new forms of resistance, and how we can help to strengthen social movements to end poverty that are able to resist and to counteract in these difficult times.

NOTES

An earlier version of this chapter was published as "Poverty—What's Neoliberalism Got to Do with It?" in Poverty Initiative (ed.), *Appalachia: Listening with Our Hearts* (New York: Poverty Initiative, 2007), pp. 23–35.

1. A famous example is the study *The Weight of the World*, edited by the French sociologist Pierre Bourdieu and others (1999).

2. An important case in point for the neoliberal strengthening of the repressive state apparatus is the enormous buildup of the prison system in the United States from the mid-1970s onward so that in 2000 the U.S. incarceration rate (per 100,000 inhabitants) was about 7 to 8 times the respective numbers in France and Germany and more than 10 times the numbers in Sweden and Denmark (Wacquant, 2009, pp. 59–62).

3. Union membership further declined to 12.3% in 2009, and this was the first time that more union members worked in the public sector than in the private sector: Whereas union membership grew to 37.4 % in the public sector, the share of unionized workers fell to 7.2% in the private sector (Greenhouse, 2010, p. B1).

4. According to UN calculations, the "informal proletariat" will reach approximately 2 billion to 3 billion in 2030, more than the 1.5 billion to 2 billion working-class participants in formal labor relations (Davis, 2004, p. 13; 2006, pp. 176ff, 199ff).

REFERENCES

Abelson, R. (2008, December 9). Uninsured put a strain on hospitals. *New York Times*. Retrieved December 31, 2010, from http://www.nytimes.com

Bourdieu, P., et al. (Eds.) (1999). *The weight of the world: Social suffering in contemporary society*. Stanford, CA: Stanford University Press.

Candeias, M. (2007). Unmaking and remaking of class: The "impossible" precariat between fragmentation and movement. *Rosa-Luxemburg-Stiftung*, Policy Paper 3.

Davis, M. (2004). The urbanization of empire: Megacities and the laws of chaos. *Social Text*, 22(4), 9–15. Retrieved December 31, 2010, from http://muse.jhu.edu/journals/social_text/v022/22.4davis.html

Davis, M. (2006). *The planet of slums*. London & New York: Verso.

DiFazio, W. (2006). *Ordinary poverty: A little food and cold storage*. Philadelphia: Temple University Press.

Gilens, M. (2003). How the poor became black: The racialization of American poverty in the mass media. In S. Schram, J. Soss, and R. Fording (Eds.), *Race and the Politics of Welfare Reform* (pp. 101–130). Ann Arbor: University of Michigan Press.

Gowan, P. (1999). *The global gamble: Washington's Faustian bid for world dominance*. London & New York: Verso.

Gramsci, A. (1971). *Selections from the prison notebooks of Antonio Gramsci* (Quintin Hoare and Geoffrey Nowell Smith, Eds.). New York: International.

Greenhouse, S. (2010, January 23). Most U.S. union members are working for the government, new data shows. *New York Times*, p. B1. Retrieved December 31, 2010, from http://www.nytimes.com

Harvey, D. (2005). *A brief history of neoliberalism*. Oxford: Oxford University Press.

Haug, W. F. (2003). *High-Tech-Kapitalismus: Analysen zur Produktionsweise, Arbeit, Sexualität, Krieg und Hegemonie*. Hamburg, Germany: Argument-Verlag.

Hayek, F. A. (1976). *Law, legislation, and liberty, vol. 2: The mirage of social justice*. Chicago & London: University of Chicago Press.

Hayek, F. A. (1994). *The road to serfdom*. Chicago: University of Chicago Press. (Original work published 1944)

Herbert, B. (2010, February 8). The worst of the pain. *New York Times*, p. A27. Retrieved December 31, 2010, from http://www.nytimes.com

Huws, U. (2003). *The making of a cybertariat: Virtual work in a real world*. London: Merlin Press.

Iceland, J. (2006). *Poverty in America: A handbook* (2nd ed.). Berkeley, Los Angeles, & London: University of California Press.

Jameson, F. (1991). *Postmodernism, or, the cultural logic of late capitalism*. Durham, NC: Duke University Press.

Marx, K. (1990). *Capital: A critique of political economy, volume 1 (1867)* (B. Fowkes, Trans.). London: Penguin Books. (Original work published 1867)

McNally, D. (2008). *From financial crisis to world slump: Accumulation, financialization, and the global slowdown.* Retrieved March 1, 2010, from http://marxandthefinancialcrisisof2008.blogspot.com/2008/12/david-mcnally-from-financial-crisis-to.html

Mishel, L., Bernstein, J., & Allegretto, S. (Eds.) (2007). *The state of working America, 2006/2007.* Ithaca, NY: Cornell University Press.

Murray, C. (1984). *Losing ground: American social policy, 1950–1980.* New York: Basic Books.

National Conference of Catholic Bishops. (1986). *Economic justice for all: Pastoral letter on Catholic social teaching and the U.S. economy.* Washington, DC: U.S. Catholic Conference.

One in 10 Americans behind on mortgage or in foreclosure. (2008, December 5). *San Francisco Sentinel.* Retrieved December 31, 2010, from http://sanfranciscosentinel.com

Pear, R. (2008, December 7). When a job disappears, so does the health care. *New York Times.* Retrieved December 31, 2010, from http://www.nytimes.com

Saez, E. (2010). *Striking it richer: The evolution of top incomes in the United States (Updated with 2008 estimates).* Retrieved December 26, 2010, from http://www.econ.berkeley.edu/~saez/saez-UStopincomes-2008.pdf

United Nations. (1948). *Universal Declaration of Human Rights.* Retrieved December 31, 2010, from http://www.un.org/en/documents/udhr

Wacquant, L. (2009). *Prisons of poverty.* Minneapolis & London: University of Minnesota Press.

Wolff, R. D. (2010). *Capitalism hits the fan: The global economic meltdown and what to do about it.* Northampton, MA: Olive Branch Press.

CHAPTER 5

Interview with Willie Baptist (III): King's Poor People's Campaign, "Operation Cereal Bowl," and Labor Struggles at the Steel Plant

Jan Rehmann (JR): Willie, if you look back at the whole period from the civil rights movement to the ghetto riots of the '60s, what would you say are the main lessons for you?

Willie Baptist (WB): Looking back at this history, I have to say I am less interested in the leading personalities as such—the question of at what points Malcolm X was right or Martin Luther King, Jr. was right. I'm looking primarily at the dynamics of how social movements develop, and it is from this vantage point that I am discussing questions of leadership, rather than reducing it to a few figures.

What interests me is what happened to the civil rights movement after the Montgomery bus boycott in 1955. Prior to the boycott the civil rights movement was more or less a movement led by lawyers. The main organization that was at the forefront was the NAACP (National Association for the Advancement of Colored People), and their main strategic approach was in the area of litigation. They would find cases in an elementary school or college that they would take before the courts, where they would try to get some kind of redress to the problems faced by black folks generally. The Montgomery bus boycott represents a point of departure and a challenge to that approach. And for the first time you have a real crystallization of a strategy that combined litigation with direct nonviolent mass action. White ministers and many others came to see that legal Jim Crow was wrong and got involved in this massive protest that was backed up by a legal strategy. The Montgomery bus boycott utilized a new kind of commitment and a new way of fighting, which required new types of leaders. And this new core of leaders formed into the SCLC (Southern Christian Leadership Conference) in 1957.

JR: Why are you insisting on the importance of the leadership? The way the story of the Montgomery bus boycott is usually told is that it was triggered by the courageous decision of Rosa Parks not to obey the bus driver's order that she give up her seat to make room for a white passenger.

WB: Well the whole matter of Rosa Parks is not fully appreciated in terms of the economic, social, political, and even religious factors that were involved in her decision to not get up from her seat. People even mistakenly assume that what she did singularly ignited a whole movement, and that is not what happened in history. Parks was a leader in the black community. She was a longtime secretary in the National Association for the Advancement of Colored People and had received training at the Highlander Folk School in Tennessee. Highlander was and still is a leadership training school and cultural center for workers' rights and racial equality. It was founded in 1932 by Myles Horton, who had studied at Union Theological Seminary. This training plus her long experience as a leader in the black community prepared Ms. Parks in terms of consciousness and skills for the leadership role she played in the boycott. That put her in a position to take advantage of social and economic developments, like the implementation of the mechanical cotton picker, which shifted the black population into cities, creating the possibility and necessity for mass activity in the black communities to deal with racially discriminatory relationships. Behind the single act of remaining seated there is a longer history of organization and intense training that is usually not noticed and reported. It wasn't just that she got tired; she and leaders like her were trained and prepared to take advantage of the historical moment that made effective mass action possible.

The relationship between consciousness-raising and organizing on the one hand, and changes in conditions and spontaneous revolt on the other, is complex. The most effective protest actions of the civil rights movement were due to a careful preparation that required a well-trained leadership. Another example is the Student Nonviolent Coordinating Committee's (SNCC) massive sit-in movement that was the result of trainings and workshops about the situation, timing, and the need to take action in a coordinated manner. You have to be trained; leadership has to be developed. And that leadership has to understand the moment in history—the forces and factors favorable for certain kinds of actions. SNCC's training prepared them to be effective. The black community at that point was in a position that the status quo of Jim Crow segregation conflicted with their basic needs—social and economic. So they were compelled to fight it, they were in a position with a certain level of concentrations in urban areas to fight it, and they fought it with a new strategy that combined legal maneuvering in the court system with mass action.

JR: Now, the last campaign Martin Luther King, Jr. was preparing was the Poor People's Campaign. Could you tell us how this campaign was designed, how it started, how it unfolded, and what came out of it?

WB: The purpose of the Poor People's Campaign in 1968 from the point of view of King and other key leaders such as Robert Kennedy was to unsettle the thinking of the masses of the American people. King realized that the ending of poverty could not take place unless you moved the thinking of the majority of the American people, and the best way to do that was to organize and unite the poor across color lines and across religious and gender lines. What that meant strategically was the unity of the poor around their common basic economic human needs and rights. This was his answer to this kind of "plantation politics" that W. E. B. Dubois discussed earlier, in terms of how the politics of the United States were formed historically on the basis of keeping the bottom of this country disunited and turned against one another. Race derives from this country's long history of the slaughter of American Indians and enslavement of blacks and has been constantly used to divide and conquer the most exploited and oppressed of this country.

The Poor People's Campaign challenged the major economic and social contradictions of those times. In King's assessment the period had moved from the era of civil rights—dealing with merely racial relationships—to human rights—dealing with the inseparability of racial relationships, economic exploitation, and foreign policy, especially as expressed in the Vietnam War at that time. He spoke in these last years of his life about the need to have a "revolution of values," to change the sense of priorities of this country. He insisted that the country's whole house has to be put in order. He was not simply talking about changing Jim Crow laws—which he said were obtained at no cost to America—but about reconstructing the whole political and economic power relationship. Uniting the poor across racial lines as a "new and unsettling force," the Poor People's Campaign would generate the power to shake and move the thinking and behavior of broader sections of the American people. Those who were the most victimized by poverty, who had the least to lose by the change in the economic status quo and the ending of poverty, that is, the poor whites, and poor blacks and other non-whites, had no choice but to unite. That is what he set out to do. This was not about poor people just getting some kind of temporary relief in the forms of minimum-paying jobs or food stamps. This was about ending poverty all together. Dr. King's analysis told him that at that time the economy had already developed the means and productivity that made it possible to eliminate poverty.

The initial phases of the Poor People's Campaign would take the form of a mobilization and marches from different locations throughout the country—from Appalachia, the South, northern states, as well as the West Coast, and from Native American reservations. Led by a "Mule Train" from Marks, Mississippi, the different routes of the marches would converge on Washington, DC. Encamping in a tent city on the Washington Mall, like the Bonus Marchers did the 1930s, they would proceed to mount a series of massive civil-disobedient operations focusing national public attention on the issues of poverty and pressuring government officials to deliver on the demands of the Poor People's Campaign. As you know, Dr. King was assassinated before the march took place. However, it went on as planned and a major tent city was set up, named Resurrection City, a clear reference to the Bible. The campaign fell short of its objectives, which were to keep attracting more numbers and even risk long-term jailings toward pressuring the federal government to enact a Poor People's Bill of Rights. This set of demands included the right to a job or adequate guaranteed annual income. If you didn't have a job, you had a guaranteed adequate sustenance—not just for poor folks—but for everybody to have a descent standard of living that was necessary for the existence of human beings with dignity.

JR: How would you see the relationship between the civil rights movement and the Poor People's Campaign? Was it a continuation of the former or did it have a completely new quality?

WB: Certainly there were some continuities, but the entire social alignment was different. Often the distinctions are obscured, making the poor people's movement a part of the civil rights movement and therefore de-emphasizing the real importance of the Poor People's Campaign's strategic departure. In the civil rights movement, every section of the African American community was involved and had a stake in that movement. In terms of ending legalized Jim Crow segregation and racial discrimination, it affected every class strata of the black population, bringing together poor blacks and middle-class blacks, in part with support from the ruling elites—represented by the Kennedy administration and the Johnson administration, based on the problems of de jure racial oppression.

With the Poor People's Campaign, King shifted to another problem, to another era, dealing with some of the fundamental questions of economics and the politics in this country that created poverty and kept poverty intact. Unlike the civil rights movement, the focus of the Poor People's Campaign was not only on black folks. It widened its focus to all who were in poverty and in pain, including poor whites, poor Latinos, poor Asians, poor women, and you-name-it poor. He recognized that the section of blacks who most benefited from the civil rights legislation and the voter rights legislation were the upper-class blacks. The mass of the poor blacks in the ghettoes didn't get very much out of the civil rights legislation. He pointed out that there is little effect on the black masses if you are now able to go into a restaurant without the sign "White Only," but you can't afford a hamburger.

So even though he and others had been influenced by the civil rights movement—including the poor blacks—and therefore were able to take the movement's sense of social responsibility and experience of struggle into this next period, the next period was different and posed a new alignment of social forces than the previous one. This relationship between these two historical periods is very important for those of us today who are taking up the issue of poverty. It means that there are lessons we can draw from the Poor People's Campaign that we can't draw from the civil rights movement.

JR: Was this new focus on economic human rights the reason King lost the support of his allies in the white upper and middle classes, the mainstream press, and the Johnson administration?

WB: To answer this question it is important to appreciate that the culmination of the civil rights movement as a mass movement coincided with the interests of the upper classes in that historical moment. Specifically the ruling class needed to expand industry into the southern United States, which practically required breaking legal segregation. Taking advantage of the mass destruction of Europe in World War II, those in power in the United States were moving to secure hegemony over world economics and politics. Plus there were huge industrial and financial profits to be gained by expanding industry and production to reconstruct Europe. Under Truman, a White House national planning committee found that for an industry to go into the South it would need to have two bathrooms, two cafeterias, and so on. That made no economic and political sense domestically or internationally, so legal Jim Crow social and labor policies and their political protectors, the Dixiecrats, had to go. And thus you had the Truman, Eisenhower, Kennedy, and Johnson administrations to a certain extent siding with the civil rights movement because the upper-class interests, which these administrations represented, coincided with the interests of the civil rights movement.

But then with the struggle against poverty, King began to raise the problem of poverty as being in conflict with the fundamentals of the economic and social systems of this country—capitalism. Those ideas posed a major threat. He was calling into the question the entire system. It was particularly threatening because he was calling the system into question at a time when he enjoyed tremendous credibility. He had just obtained the Noble Peace Prize and was now an internationally recognized and legitimized leader. When he took up the peace movement, linking it to the struggle against poverty and racial relationships, he became the embodiment of what the poor embodied, that is, the combined interests of the antiwar movement, antiracism movement, and a movement against economic exploitation and poverty. He embodied all the different processes. At that time you had a tremendous antiwar movement, and a tremendous motion of the poor, especially in the black ghetto as a result of the black uprisings, and he had inherited a tremendous unquestioned influenced over the civil rights movement. In his person, he threatened to bring all these currents together. The prospect of bringing them all together in terms of the Poor People's Campaign (PPC) became a major threat and point of antagonism to the upper classes and to the Johnson administration, and therefore to mainstream media. The corporate media had given tremendous coverage of the civil rights movement and was key when King gave his talk in 1963, the March on Washington. The whole world was listening to his speech. But again when the civil rights movement began to make this transition to the PPC then that alignment with corporate media became an antagonism, an opposition. Thus there was an attack on King and the PPC and a blackout by the major press and TV news networks.

This is an important historical lesson because it suggests that in order to guarantee a voice we need to create our own media. We can't expect strategically the kind of alignments that would provide us with a voice, because we are talking about a realignment of certain class and social relationships, similar alignment of the class and social relationships that took place with regard to the PPC.

JR: King's critics in the SCLC argued that the Poor People's Campaign was unrealistic—not enough staff, no real infrastructure. Weren't they right in hindsight?

WB: The question about the Poor People's Campaign being unrealistic raises issues that are at the heart of leadership, that is, the art of leadership and the art of politics generally being the art of the possible. In other words, the ability to figure out, at any given moment in history, what is possible and therefore, in social conflict, what is usually necessary. It means an assessment of the situation and what was happening. From our point of view, looking back at the PPC we have to look at the historical forces at play. What were the options people had at that particular time? I think the struggle of the poor was definitely at play and King attempted to give that struggle consciousness, unity, and organization (Fig. 5.1). It was definitely a possibility posing a definite threat, although the economics and politics of the times limited what it could accomplish. For instance, unlike today, when the so-called middle class is experiencing major social dislocations and impoverishment, the middle-income strata in the 1960s were enjoying their highest standards of living. This placed major historical constraints on the struggles of the poor at that time and made it more difficult, if not impossible, for the Poor People's Campaign to win public opinion and thereby mount sufficient political pressure. However, despite these limiting conditions, the campaign and King obviously posed a huge threat to powerful elements of the government.

You can't really understand the factors that go into making a movement possible, if you have an outlook that is influenced by this narrow, pragmatic, antitheory, anti-analysis approach, which dominates our culture. And what's more, you miss out on the total lessons of that period in history. For instance, the limits of those times tell you a lot about possibilities for struggles of the poor today, particularly regarding the tremendous opportunities for winning increasing sections of the so-called middle class of the American people over to the necessity of ending poverty.

I want to again emphasize how it is very difficult to appreciate what is possible in a certain time period unless you deeply understand the historical context. For example, the Jesus movement—the early Christian movement—was basically a minuscule movement against the Roman Empire, the most powerful political and economic structure that had ever existed up to that time. You could look at that early Christian movement in a very superficial way and say it was a failure, and therefore it was unrealistic. But the fact of the matter is that it gained such a credibility and such an influence that the Roman power structure through its representative, Pontius Pilate, the governor of Jerusalem at that time, had to execute Jesus Christ

Figure 5.1. The Lack of New Grassroots Organizers for the Poor People's Campaign

Under immense pressure to create a meaningful movement, King hoped black preachers could be the spark plugs for a new struggle to end poverty. Backed by a Ford Foundation grant of $230,000 for ministerial training, SCLC gathered about 150 ministers from fifteen cities at its Ministers Leadership Training Program in Miami. Its purpose was to "create a common force of grass roots people to affect positive changes in the ghetto." . . . On February 23 King addressed the ministers in a talk titled, "To Minister to the Valley," telling them that they . . . could change the nation. . . . But FBI reports said most black ministers in Miami remained noncommittal about the Poor People's Campaign. . . . King faced a contradiction of means and ends, trying to build a poor people's movement with essentially middle class ministers.

Source: M. K. Honey, *Going Down Jericho Road: The Memphis Strike, Martin Luther King's Last Campaign* (New York: W. W. Norton), pp. 188–189.

by nailing him to the Roman cross. You could interpret that as a failure and unrealistic, but the fact of the matter was that the values that Jesus represented—bringing good news to the poor, lifting up the "least of these," and organizing a movement that had a totally different program and morality than the Roman Empire—set the stage for the powerful growth of the Christian movement, even in Jesus Christ's execution. To this day, you wouldn't have the kind of widespread influence of Christianity if you didn't have the development of the early Christian movement, with the core leaders, the disciples, taking up the cause that Jesus represented. It was a notion of a revolution of values that they begin to use in their message that built the Christian movement.

So when you look at the tremendous credibility and legitimacy that King has come to represent, and look at the last years of his life—which tend to be covered up and obscured—where he took up the issue of poverty and moved the issue, there are tremendous lessons and legitimacy for those of us today. We would be at an extreme disadvantage in what we are doing today if those struggles hadn't taken place. And even though there was a whole period of quiet as a result of King's assassination and the disorganization of that effort, life asserts itself, and movements of the poor who are having to fight are looking at history for lessons and legitimacy, especially in this crisis, this chronic crisis, that is continuing to mature in this system making more and more people poor. If you study that movement further, you will see that King and other leaders of the Poor People's Campaign themselves used lessons from history as guides. They looked to the struggle of the Southern Tenant Farmers Union where white farmers and black farmers came together to organize for themselves. They looked to the Bonus Marchers, composed of black and white veterans, whose tent city became a model for the Poor People's Campaign's Resurrection City. All of these examples give us tremendous lessons for today and suggest that, given the historical and political situation in which we find ourselves, we have to reignite the Poor People's Campaign and this effort to unite the growing class of poor and disadvantaged across color and religious lines to impact majorly the thinking of the American people so as to move the economics and politics of this country. All of history suggests that this is what has to be done, and certainly King's experience, and the way that the powers-that-be moved against King, suggests that this is a real threat to power relationships because it threatens change.

JR: Why was King then killed? Out of mere racism, be it by the individual racist James Earl Ray or by the institutionalized racism of the FBI?

WB: The fact is that the problems of the Vietnam War and foreign policy involved the poor in a major way. They needed the black poor and the white poor as cannon fodder at the frontlines, where they sustained far and away the highest death and casualty rates. It was the major concern of the powers-that-be, particularly military intelligence, that the organization of a successful PPC would have demoralized the fighting spirit of these frontline forces and upset the overall war effort in Vietnam. Even though the struggle for civil rights involved the leadership by and large of upper-class blacks, the poor blacks played a mighty role in the civil rights movement. They were the main troops. This was true of the Montgomery campaign as well as the other major campaigns. The main mass of the whole civil rights network involved poor folks. Then you had in the black ghetto eruptions in the late '60s, the largest violent social upheaval since the Civil War by the so-called black "underclass." King in his person embodied and had influence over these tremendous energies. He emerged as a very influential factor in all those major processes, and his effort to pull together a PPC meant bringing together all those forces. This was a real threat and made gaining major concessions around the issue of poverty and interrupting the policies and efforts of the powers-that-be a definite possibility. That's why they killed him. The transcripts from the 1999 Martin Luther King, Jr. assassination trial in Memphis, Tennessee, proved this and that the PPC represented the possibilities of throwing a wrench in the machinery of the powers by obstructing both domestic and foreign policies. The transcripts showed that King was not killed by a lone racist. It showed that his death was an execution with every level of government participating. I invite everyone to go over these historic transcripts for yourself. They can be found at the website of the King Center at http://www.thekingcenter.org/.

JR: Willie, let's move on with your own experiences. From 1965 to 1969, directly after the Watts uprising, you were a student organizer, and then, from 1969 to 1971, you initiated a community organization in Watts called Operation Cereal Bowl that was connected to a local branch of the Black Panther Party and distributed free breakfast meals for kids. This is not the Black Panther Party as it was portrayed by the media, is it?

WB: Well, you know, the media's portrayals of the Panthers have been very superficial, biased, and even manipulative. They exploited the Panthers' principle of "self-defense" and depicted them as this violent group of black people that wanted to kill white people, but that wasn't what they were about. This erroneous generalization that has stuck reflects a one-sided depiction of the sensationalized shoot-outs that the Panthers were cornered into. The reality was much more complex than that. In regard to the Panthers' relationship to violence, I would like to refer you to Huey P. Newton's book *War Against the Panthers: A Study of Repression in America* that traces the FBI's systematic efforts to "expose, disrupt, misdirect, discredit or otherwise neutralize" the Panther Party—this is a quote from a FBI memorandum of 1967. The Panthers must be examined in their concreteness, in the different phases of their development. Of all the inner-city movements that reacted to police conditions and the conditions of unemployment, the Panthers were the most organized ones. This was the main reason why they became a tremendous inspiration for me and a lot of other people.

To give you an example, there is a lot we can learn from the experience of the Black Panther Party based in Oakland, California. Maybe you've heard of Amory Bradford's book *Oakland: Not for Burning*. What the title indicates is the following: Despite the fact that Oakland was one of the centers of black ghetto concentration, it did not have a riot, and one of the reasons was that the movement in the ghetto took an organized form in the Black Panther Party for self-defense. With their police patrol they went around and preempted and monitored activities of the police. They organized mainly around the poor youth. One of the most effective programs they had—and this came out of the FBI's findings—was their free breakfast program for children. According to the FBI evaluations, that was the most dangerous aspect of their activities. It was the infiltration and provocation around the violence that provided the police and politicians a pretext to counter with much greater violence, to kill or to jail its leaders and to destroy the Panthers. But even in their taking up the gun in self-defense—and at that time it was legal in California to openly carry a gun—the intent was to inspire blacks to resist the wanton beatings that the police subjected on the population.

You have to be part of a community that is constantly under siege by the police department to really understand this dynamics. The motto of the police department is very respectable: "protect and serve." And many join the force for good reasons. However, you have less respectable police policies, and a number of police officers use the power of the badge to do things other than protecting and serving the community. They take advantage of the fact that they have guns and they come in and beat the shit out of you. This is ghetto reality. So what are you going to do in that situation? The Panthers preempted the process of police harassment by organizing police patrols. There are a lot of lessons from the early period of that group. Toward the end they were highly infiltrated and became stereotyped and isolated, which set the stage for their eventual defeat and demise. These days everybody says they were a member of the Panthers. You can't talk to a black person from the ghettoes of those times who wouldn't say, "I was in the Panthers." Not everybody was in the Panthers. But at the height of the Panthers development it was said that "every minute a new person joined the Panthers." That's how popular they were, and it was because they stood their ground against police brutality.

We were mostly interested in the Panthers' breakfast program. We wanted to organize in the communities that were devastated in the aftermath of the Watts uprisings. So we developed Operation Cereal Bowl, where we gave free breakfasts to children in the community. Through that relationship, we were able to get into the community with the parents and raise the issues of police brutality, jobs, and economic justice. The life situation of the people in Watts was complex and had many interrelated sides to it. In my life experiences, this narrative is constantly one of the interplay of race and class, of race and poverty. Starting with Operation Cereal Bowl, we organized in a primarily black ghetto community, yet clearly the class issues and economic issues were so dire that kids were going to school having not eaten. They couldn't compete educationally because they were diverted by hunger pains. So we started this program to deal with black people, the people of my community, but we were also dealing with the class issues connected to the fact that parents couldn't afford adequate breakfast for their kids. There was definitely interplay between class and race.

JR: At the same time, you were still in college. How did you experience the interplay between class and race there?

WB: I didn't graduate from college, but for 3 years I attended Pepperdine College, now called Pepperdine University, now in Malibu, California. To understand the class dynamics, one has to consider that Pepperdine was a very expensive conservative college, second in cost only to the University of Southern California. I received a baseball scholarship, which paid for my tuition. That was the only way I could have gone to that college. This was the case for a lot of the black athletes, most of whom were from the lower classes. A number of my friends from Watts went to similar schools on similar scholarships. Pepperdine College was voted by the John Birch Society as the number-one school to send your kids. The black athletes there on scholarship felt embattled in the midst of this very expensive, very conservative college. At the same time we felt exploited by the way we were used as advertisements for the college. We really felt under siege.

During that period, I was among a group of students, mostly athletes, who helped form the Black Student Union (BSU). We black students fighting for black studies and for increasing the quotas of blacks on the campus. But then you had another upper-class section of blacks from places like Baldwin Hills, from high-income professional classes. So there was a tussle within the

BSU about our objectives. We were all blacks trying to defend our rights as blacks and to have a black studies program, but while the upper-class blacks were really enamored with cultural nationalism—wearing African garb and adopting African names—for those of us from the lower classes, especially the black athletes from ghetto neighborhoods like Watts, even though we dabbled in that kind of thing for reasons of black pride and appreciated the liberation struggles in Africa, that wasn't our main focus.

For us, the main issue was the killing by a white guard of a 15-year-old black youth who was trying to use the college's basketball court. Pepperdine was located in the middle of a black low-income community, but wouldn't allow the community to come in and use their athletic facilities. We black athletes thought that these facilities should be open to the community. Larry Stokes, a black kid from the community, came with his friends onto the campus with a basketball in his hand and the white guard put a 12-gauge shotgun at his chest and blew him away. The officer who shot him had been quoted as saying he was going to kill him a nigger, and to add insult to injury, he was later acquitted in court. This ignited a whole resistance out of which we formed the BSU. It was connected to athletics in the sense that Larry Stokes wanted to use the basketball court, and as athletes we felt he should have a right to do that.

In my life story, these two factors are constantly interplaying. In my experience—and I think the greater narrative corroborates this—I find it very difficult to detach the economic factors of class from the social factors of race, as well as gender and other social identities. There's an increasing interrelationship between these dynamics, at least in my analysis. Certainly my early experience corroborates their inseparability.

JR: And then, in the early 1970s, when you were 23 or so, you worked and organized in a steel plant in Torrance, near L.A., and became a shop steward for the United Steel Workers of America. This was a period when your struggle against racism directly interconnected with a commitment in the labor movement. Could you tell us something about this period of struggle?

WB: After leaving Pepperdine, I got a job at the steel plant, and it was there that I led two protests. One was a walkout and another was a protest against discrimination against the black workers. At Martin Marietta the plant was divided into a munitions part and a faucet fixtures part. I was in the latter section, mainly assembling these fixtures. The manager of that particular section objected to workers having beards. It so happened that the only people who had beards were the black workers. We thought it was a statement of disrespect and racism. We were adults and could handle ourselves in that environment with beards. It turns out he was arbitrarily pursuing his own kind of racial policy around the beards; other sections of the plant didn't have that policy. So a couple of black workers and I organized a protest. We took over the manager's office and were prepared to stay there until he gave us the dignity and respect we deserved. He had to back down because the general management stepped in saying we don't have a "no-beard" policy and we don't want to be embarrassed by negative press.

JR: Were you supported by the white workers?

WB: Yes, we got a lot of support out of that struggle. I was able to use the organization of black workers in that plant as a base for general organizing. In our department, we had mostly men who did the supply work and mostly women who did the assembly of the fixtures, and we had more whites than blacks. We did a walkout with almost everyone in that department around the ventilation question. The factory had the ventilation directed only at the fixtures while we were soaking up the smoke and grime. We said those fans need to be turned on human beings, not just the equipment. So we organized a general walkout—whites and blacks, women and men. Since it was a wildcat action, meaning it wasn't authorized by the United Steelworkers Union, we also had to confront the leadership of the union. Here again the class factors intersect with the race factors. You can picture me as the big mouth confronting the black leadership of the union saying, "You guys ain't doing shit to deal with the conditions of this plant, so we decided to do it on our own. We're going to do it whether you like it or not." So there was a confrontation between me, representing this multiracial struggle, and the predominately black leadership of the established local union.

There's a complexity there. Life is more like a dice than a dime; it has many sides, not just two. You have to really engage your intellectualism in order to understand the concreteness of it, to understand these questions in their specific contexts and divine the kind of tactics that allow you to make impact in that particular situation. We were able to get the company to back down on the ventilation. They began to turn the fans halfway toward us, and we felt like that was a victory. Out of that action I was elected shop steward and carried on the struggle from there. I had a relationship with both the white and black workers, but I was still black. I didn't give up who I was. But I knew that we had to figure out the common basis of unity for all the workers in order to impact that plant, to deal with the management or even to deal with the upper echelon of the trade union leadership, which in that instance was the United Steelworkers Union. As the shop steward I took everybody to the third and highest stage of the grievance procedure, even for minor complaints. I wanted the workers to see the whole process and see how it was inadequate and that the union hadn't negotiated a contract complete with dignity. By taking them all the way through the process, even though I knew they would lose at the end, they were able to see the bankruptcy of the union misleadership. In every step we did, we had to deal with those complexities.

JR: Why did you stop working there in 1975?

WB: A whole section of us were laid off. It wasn't for political reasons; it was the production cycle. Periodically you would hear of other plants in the area doing layoffs. It's what they do; they lay you off when they can't make a profit.

I should say that I met my second wife during this steelworkers' struggle. My first wife was involved in the Black Student Union organizing. She was African American and from Baldwin Hills. When we got into the midst of that struggle we closed the whole school down by buying big chains from the hardware store, locking up the administration buildings, and standing in front of the doors. She was at the forefront of it—she was a militant something. But then her parents got wind of it in Baldwin Hills and they moved her back to Louisiana. After a long saga, I helped get her back to L.A., and we married. But this again shows the class contradiction between the Baldwin Hills' "house Negroes" and the Watts' "field Negroes." There were points of unity, but there were also constant differences in terms of approach, even though she was particularly militant and prepared to fight it out. But the questions of relations are certainly much more complex than that.

In the steel plant I met my second wife, who was a poor white Italian. We separated for about 4 years recently, but then made amends and are still together today. This relationship with a poor white woman is different than the relationships I had with other whites because she was not a middle-income white liberal. I guess she couldn't afford liberalism. We would battle straight up. She wouldn't back down when I'd try to guilt-trip her by saying, "You've been exploiting us for 400 years." She'd cuss me out. Man, she's tough. And she's a committed fighter. She has what I imagine was the attitude of the poor white American hero, John Brown. It was a very interesting experience having a relationship with an upper-class black woman, going through the divorce process and then meeting this poor white lady at the steel plant. It's in these so-called private relations that I again was hit by the complexities of passionate class, race, and gender struggles.

JR: The period after you were laid off from the steel plant in 1975 was the time when you were on workfare. What was that experience?

WB: I worked on several other odd low-wage jobs in the L.A. area. Later, my family, my wife and two children, had moved to Chicago, in the Near Northside neighborhood. In Illinois they had the Aid for Families with Dependant Children Unemployed Parent Program, under which unemployed fathers who were heads of households could be on welfare, but they would have to get on workfare. In other words, you had to find a makeshift job and work for your welfare check. So I washed dishes at the Salvation Army and then repaired plumbing.

It was while working on the plumbing in the basement of an elementary school that I learned the dynamics of welfare reform, long before it was implemented in 1996 under the Clinton administration. I was working alongside some plumbers who taught me enough about plumbing that I could do most of the work. They could just drink coffee and joke around while I did their work. It turned out they were making upward of $18–19 per hour and I was making on average $2.50–3 per hour on my welfare check. It became very clear to me that if I were an employer concerned about the bottom line—maximum profits—I'd rather hire a guy I only have to pay $2.50 an hour than to hire someone I have to pay $18 an hour. That gave me insight into this welfare reform. It wasn't about these "welfare queens" and lazy people who want to live off welfare. It's about changing the wage structure to compel people to work for poverty wages so as to be more competitive and garner more profit. That set the stage for the welfare reform in 1996.

CHAPTER 6

A Case Study on Organizing:
The Struggle for Water in Postindustrial Detroit

Chris Caruso

Detroit and Highland Park, Michigan, have become the center of the struggle over access to water in the United States, with 40,000 to 45,000 families cut off water annually since 2001 and some of the highest water rates in the country. This chapter examines the drive to privatize water in the context of the shift from Fordism to flexible accumulation and "accumulation by dispossession" (Harvey, 1990, 2003) and the agency of those most impacted by water shut offs in challenging these privatization efforts. Postindustrial Detroit, with among the highest foreclosure and unemployment rates in the nation, anticipated the challenges of many areas of the country as the United States moved into the recession of 2008. As the fiscal crisis facing cities and towns across the United States is used as a pretext to impose austerity measures, analyzing the experience of Detroit is important in understanding the trajectory of privatization, the erosion of democracy, and efforts taken to challenge them. In this chapter, I will examine how local groups have responded by building organization among those most affected and making powerful appeals to democracy and human rights.

WATER AND WATER PRIVATIZATION

Water is a $400 billion global business—it is 40% of the size of the oil industry and one-third larger than the pharmaceutical industry, and it is growing rapidly. Water privatization began in the 1980s in Latin America and East Asia; it spread to South Asia and Africa in the late 1990s and to the Western world in the 2000s (Varghese, 2007). In the early 2000s, the three largest water companies in the world were the French Vivendi, the German RWE, and the French Suez respectively. Ranking in the top 100 among Fortune's Global 500 List, Suez operates in 130 countries and Vivendi in over 100; the combined annual revenues of the two French companies are over $70 billion. In 2003, RWE revenues were over $50 billion, the company having recently acquired British water giant Thames Water (Public Citizen, 2003). In 2006, however, RWE announced its divestment from the global water business (Varghese, 2007).

Despite strong support for water privatization from the World Bank, the International Monetary Fund, and others, water multinationals have faced a series of financial and political setbacks in their projects in the developing world. Led by Suez, with a self-declared mission to bring water to the world's poor, water multinationals began withdrawing their investments in the developing world. Suez announced in January 2003 that future investments will favor "the quickest free cash flow generating projects and contracts," avoid long-term investments, and concentrate on the soundest markets of Europe and North America (Hall, 2003b). Another element of these policies is a strategy of departure when an investment goes sour. When the currency collapse in the Philippines adversely affected their investments, Suez abandoned their concession in Manila and then sued the Philippines for $303 million to recoup their losses (Hall, 2003a).

As multinational water companies withdraw from the developing world, they are set to aggressively expand in the United States and Europe:

> Eighty-five percent of all water services in the U.S. are still in public hands. That's a tempting target for conglomerates like Suez, Vivendi, and RWE. Within the next 10 years, they aim to control 70 percent of water services across the United States. (Barlow & Clarke, 2003)

Vivendi, Suez, and RWE have each bought up the leading U.S. water companies, U.S. Filter, United Water, and American Water Works, respectively. Through the purchase of American Water Works, RWE gained control of the largest U.S. private water utility. This expanded its customer base from 43 million to 56 million people (Rothfeder, 2001). Water is a $150 billion industry in America and growing fast (Varghese, 2007).

THE CASE OF WATER IN DETROIT AND HIGHLAND PARK

The largest city in Michigan and the second largest city in the midwest, Detroit is the 18th largest city in the United States. Once the fourth largest city in the United States, Detroit's population has been declining since the 1960s. In the decade between 2000 and 2010, Detroit lost a staggering 20% of its population, the largest decline in any large U.S. city other than New Orleans. Its population in 2010 was 713,777 with over 80%

Black residents (Seelye, 2011). As industry deconcentrated and Detroit lost its base of manufacturing jobs, it has also lost its tax base. When Chrysler left Highland Park (an independent municipality within the Detroit city limits), the population therein dropped from 60,000 to 16,000 (Public Citizen, 2003). Detroit and Highland Park, which maintain independent water systems, inherited decrepit infrastructure with large deferred maintenance costs that their current tax base is unable to address. The solution on offer for distressed communities like Detroit and Highland Park is water privatization. Former water industry consultants were appointed as heads of water departments in Detroit and Highland Park. They have implemented aggressive austerity measures to soften up these communities to accept privatization and improve the revenue stream of the utilities prior to putting them on the auction block.

DETROIT

Between July 1, 2001, and June 30, 2002, the Detroit Water and Sewage Department cut off water to 40,752 households in the Detroit area (Lords, 2003). Since 2001, between 40,000 and 45,000 households have been cut off from water every year. The new chief administrator of the Detroit Water and Sewage Department (DWSD) arrived from a high-level position with the Thames Water Corporation (a subsidiary of RWE). Within one month of taking office, he hired a consulting firm which was involved in the privatization of Atlanta's water, instituted double-digit rate increases, and launched an aggressive policy of debt collection and cutoffs for nonpayment. Despite corporate customers accounting for over three-quarters of the money owed to Detroit for back water bills, he focused the collection efforts on individuals. This included DWSD workers' cementing areas around shutoff valves to prevent residents from turning their water back on (Michigan Welfare Rights Organization [MWRO], 2004).

HIGHLAND PARK

The state of Michigan took Highland Park into receivership in June 2001. Governor John Engler appointed an administrator to run the city. The elected mayor and City Council no longer had power over any decisions that affect the budget. Highland Park's emergency financial manager immediately imposed an extreme austerity program. She "shut down City Hall. She closed the library and the recreation center. She slashed the workforce to a skeleton crew, then cut further" (Angel, 2002). For months, she refused to authorize the expenses involved with turning on the lights at City Hall so that City Council could meet. She closed the city's district court. Public safety officers accuse her of creating a pay crisis to destroy their union

(Angel, 2002). Highland Park resident Marian Kramer adds that in Highland Park they "don't have people checking fire hydrants anymore. When there is a fire, everyone is afraid. Whole blocks burn because the fire hydrants are not working. Neighboring cities' fire departments refuse to help. Who will pay them? They just let the city burn" (interview, Chris Caruso, January 2007).

In addition to service cuts, a move towards privatization began with the hiring of a former vice president of a privatization consulting firm based in Atlanta to perform the daily administration of the city. He hired a fellow former vice president to run the water department in Highland Park. This new administrator raised the water rates steeply and subcontracted the water department's collection to a private firm, which sent employees carrying firearms to shut off people's water. The city administrator has instituted a policy of adding delinquent water bills to the property tax owed for a home. The city then began to foreclose on homes of people who could not pay their water bill. In some cases, children were seized from parents who could not pay their water bill and placed in foster care (Litowich, 2004). Highland Park's new water rates are among the highest rates in the country. It should be no surprise, then, that almost half of Highland Park households have been slated for water shutoff. At the same time, these two administrators were paid $300,000 a year for the part-time work they perform for the financially strapped city.

The city administrator spent 18 months negotiating in secret with the Rothschild Wright Group (RWG) to privatize the water in Highland Park. No other bids for managing the water department were considered, and RWG admitted that they have no prior experience running municipal water departments (Sweetwater Alliance, 2004). The proposal between Highland Park and RWG wrote in millions of dollars of guaranteed profit to RWG and stated that if the deal was canceled before its 10-year term, RWG would recoup all its costs and profits at Highland Park's expense (Sweetwater Alliance, 2004). Under this contract, RWG would also be allowed to use water from the public reservoir for bottled water sale. This withdrawal and privatization of public services is consistent with a capitalist logic that says that a population whose labor is no longer required for accumulation is a "surplus population" that is undeserving of basic services (Glimore, 2007).

A BRIEF HISTORY OF ORGANIZING IN DETROIT

Through the 19th and early 20th centuries, American industry roughly followed a pattern of centralization. As William Cronon documented in the case of Chicago, factors such as topography; access to transportation routes, including rivers and railroads; and proximity to raw materials were important in the centralization of industry in the United States (1991). The level of technical and organizational development of the production process reached in the 20th century—known as Fordism—also tended to centralize industry into large factories where large numbers of workers worked together on long assembly lines. Detroit was one such "central city"—situated on the powerful Detroit River with access to the Great Lakes. By the mid-20th century, Detroit had become a major center of world capitalism, and was perhaps the most concentrated and technically advanced site of industry in the world. Sixty percent of that industry was the automobile industry (Sugrue, 1996).

Karl Marx argued that the concentration of large numbers of workers in large factories (such as the River Rouge Plant in Detroit, which employed 85,000 workers at its peak) created favorable conditions for labor organizing. In *Capital, Volume 1*, Marx wrote, "Hand in hand with this centralization . . . there also grows the revolt of the working class, a class constantly increasing in numbers, and trained, united and organized by the very mechanism of the capitalist process of production" (1867/1990, p. 929). Perhaps not surprisingly, Detroit was home to some of the most militant labor organizing and most powerful trade unions in the United States. The roots of Detroit's militant labor movement are in the Unemployed Councils that developed during the Great Depression. These Unemployed Councils were strongest in 1932 and 1933 with marches, housing takeovers, and other efforts to fight hunger and homelessness. The Unemployed Councils took their fight against hunger to the auto manufacturers in 1932; "out of this mass drive came the seeds for organized labor to organize the shops in the city" (Baker, 2010). In the winter of 1937–1938, the United Automobile Workers (UAW) organized sit-down strikes in over 100 Detroit companies (Babson, 1986). The period between the Great Depression and World War II was one of substantial gains by the union movement. This organizing was at the point of production and was focused on leveraging strikes to win concessions around wages and working conditions.

DETROIT'S REVOLUTIONARY UNION MOVEMENTS

Although Ford Motor Company was hiring African Americans in the 1940s, African Americans were not hired into Detroit's factories in large numbers until the labor shortages of World War II. Many African American workers were alienated by labor's White conservative leadership, and by the 1960s

> a much more radical current of black working-class activism developed in Detroit. Only weeks following King's assassination, black workers at the Detroit

Dodge Main plant of Chrysler Corporation staged a wildcat strike, protesting oppressive working conditions. (Georgakas and Surkin, 1998)

This wildcat strike led to the formation of the Dodge Revolutionary Union Movement (DRUM) and inspired the development of many revolutionary union movements (RUMs) throughout the auto plants in Detroit. Workers at these factories formed the League of Revolutionary Black Workers (LRBW) in June 1969 (*Finally Got the News*, 1970). One of the leaders of the LRBW was General Baker who is directly linked to the current struggles around water privatization:

> We developed an organization, not a caucus, not tied down by union rules. I got fired leading a wildcat strike and we decided to use my discharge as a calling card to build an organization called DRUM... We used it to say that, you have declared war on us and that's the only decision that you will make. We will decide...the terms of the engagement...We are going to fight you everywhere we can. (Baker 2010)

This radical organizing had strong roots in the Black freedom struggles in Detroit dating back to the 1940s and 1950s through organizations including the Negro National Congress (NNC), the National Negro Labor Council (NNLC), Local 600, the March on Washington Movement (MOWM) and others (Theoharis and Woodard, 2003; Kelly, 1996; Dillard, 2007).

WELFARE RIGHTS MOVEMENT

In addition to these organizations of African American workers, welfare rights organizing was also very strong in Detroit. Reacting to a racist and discriminatory history of welfare and taking inspiration from the civil rights movement, the National Welfare Rights Organization (NWRO) struggled to register thousands of destitute women and men, especially people of color, for the welfare roles in the 1960s and 1970s. This movement was led by poor women of color and claimed a membership of hundreds of thousands at the height of its organizing (Nadasen, 2004; West, 1981). The Detroit Metropolitan Welfare Rights Organization was one of the five largest welfare rights organizations in the late 1960s and distinguished itself by increasing welfare rolls in large numbers (Piven and Cloward, 1979). Welfare rights organizing in Detroit was closely linked with union and other radical working class organizing that was happening concurrently. There is a valuable body of scholarship on this organizing in Detroit (e.g., Fine, 2000; Goldberg, 2010; Smith, 2001; Thompson, 2004; and Ward, 2006).

THE DEINDUSTRIALIZATION OF DETROIT

Thomas Sugrue (1996), in *The Origins of the Urban Crisis*, points out that deindustrialization actually happened earlier within the auto industry than in other industries. Between 1947 and 1963, Detroit lost 134,000 manufacturing jobs. Advances in communication and transportation technology; the transformation of industrial technology, including automation; the acceleration of regional and international competition; and the expansion of industry in low-wage regions, especially the South, are responsible for this job loss.

As opposed to the centralizing tendencies of Fordism of the previous period, in this new period of flexible accumulation, processes of industrial decentralization became dominant. (Harvey, 1990). Decentralization was an effort to seek cheaper labor costs and to escape the large unions that were concentrated in urban areas like Detroit. An additional aspect of this deindustrialization was automation, which in the late 1940s and 1950s was pursued aggressively by Detroit automakers as another way to reestablish control over the labor process.

For Detroit in the period of Fordism and industrial centralization, the main contradiction was between capital and labor, the struggle was situated at the point of production, and the dominant form of organization was the union. As the processes of deindustrialization and decentralization of factories first to the American South and then to the Global South progressed, the conditions of class struggle changed. New forms of class struggle are beginning to take place in Detroit and other deindustrialized cities in response to capital flight and accumulation by dispossession.

PRIVATIZATION AND ACCUMULATION
BY DISPOSSESSION

David Harvey describes "accumulation by dispossession" as one response to the chronic crisis of overaccumulation that capitalism has been experiencing since the 1970s. As the geographic expansion of global capitalism nears completion, the remaining public resources within capitalist countries are being privatized:

> Since privatization and liberalization of the market was the mantra of the neo-liberal movement, the effect was to make a new round of "enclosure of the commons" into an objective of state policies. Assets held by the state in common were released into the market where overaccumulating capital could invest in them, upgrade them, and speculate in them. (2003, p. 158)

Harvey describes privatization as one of the key practices of accumulation by dispossession. Privatization is an important element of neoliberal thought and has been actively encouraged by the policies of the World Bank and IMF. The privatization of public assets such as water, utilities, schools, hospitals, roads, and so on is increasing worldwide. A key tenet of neoliberal ideology is that private enterprise is more efficient than municipal services. The alleged savings, however, involved in privatization do not always materialize. The contracts that municipalities sign with water corporations often include financial guarantees on the part of the municipalities (Barlow and Clarke, 2002). These profit guarantees are standard practice in the industry, and are seemingly even more stringent as the water industry looks to cover its losses in the developing world. In the case of Atlanta, which privatized its water supply in 1999 to United Water Resources, a subsidiary of Suez, the savings to the city were less than half of what were promised (Hall, 2003a). Atlanta has since reestablished a municipal water service.

THE SOCIAL RESPONSE

Arundhati Roy describes privatization as

the transfer of productive public assets from the state to private companies. . . . These are the assets that the state holds in trust for the people it represents. . . . To snatch these away and sell them as stock to private companies is a process of barbaric dispossession on a scale that has no parallel in history. (2001, p. 43, quoted in Harvey, 2003, p. 161)

The early stages of privatization of water in Highland Park and Detroit are examples of this barbaric dispossession; using privatized armed security guards to shut off water for nonpayment, sealing shut off valves with cement, and seizing people's homes are all acts of forcible dispossession. These measures did not happen without a fight from the community. The very fact that the DWSD cemented shut the water valves demonstrates that people are illegally turning their water back on.

The Michigan Welfare Rights Organization (MWRO)—with roots dating back to the National Welfare Rights Movement of the 1960s discussed above—has become a leading organized expression of this opposition. The MWRO has built a broad coalition of local organizations called the Highland Park Human Rights Coalition. They have sponsored a wide array of tactics, all focused on uniting and organizing the low-income residents of Highland Park affected by the policies of dispossession and exposing the conditions that have resulted from these policies. Some of their activities have included organizing "water town hall meetings" where residents brought their water bills and exposed the situation in front of local television and radio broadcasters; and organizing a "State of the People Address" in Lansing by bringing large numbers of affected residents to lobby the governor and state congress. They have organized nonviolent civil disobedience in front of water departments. One protest was titled Protest the Death of Democracy and Water Rights in Highland Park.

HUMAN RIGHTS AND DEMOCRACY

The rhetorical strategies of the Highland Park Human Rights Coalition challenge the rollback of democracy and needed services that privatization demands. Their language focuses on the "death of democracy" and lack of human rights in Highland Park. The lack of democratic process is a major political vulnerability of the privatizers and makes a persuasive argument about the immorality of these policies. Maureen Taylor, codirector of the MWRO, states,

> Access to water, access to the means of survival is supposed to be
> one of the tenets that democracy is built [on]. When you have a
> class of people that are denied the ability to live, that is a straight-
> up democratic fight. Your children are under attack; your survival
> is under attack. All of our elected officials, 90% of them, look
> the other way. The Black politicians stand mute. This is the final
> frontier.

She continues, "Forty to forty-five thousand people turned off every year. . . . This is a human rights violation of enormous proportions" (interview, Chris Caruso, January 2007). The language of human rights is a powerful counter to the commodification of basic human needs like water. Although not without risks human rights are an internationally legitimated framework to make collective demands for human needs and to unite otherwise disparate, issue-based struggles.

This appeal to human rights has a long history in grassroots struggle. In 1947, W.E.B. Du Bois and the NAACP (National Association for the Advancement of Colored People) were the first to appeal to the Human Rights Commission at the United Nations about violations of economic human rights in the United States with a petition, "An Appeal to the World: A Statement on the Denial of Human Rights to Minorities in the Case of Citizens of Negro Descent in the United States of America and an Appeal to the United Nations for Redress" (Anderson, 2003). Less than twenty years later, both Malcolm X and Martin Luther King, Jr. also began to employ the human rights framework. (Malcolm X, 1964/1990, King, 1968). Struggles like the one in Detroit and Highland Park are renewing a bottom up human rights discourse in an age of neoliberal austerity and privatization.

COMMUNITY MEDIA

The hub of the wide array of tactics fighting water privatization was a live weekly call-in show hosted by members of the MWRO and broadcast on the local cable access station and radio. This was the primary way the latest information was shared and people were recruited. On a cable access program in January 2007, one caller expressed her indignation with the lack of respect that poor Detroiters receive from the city during eviction. She said,

> It's degrading and embarrassing that our mayor would want
> people that are being evicted's personal belongings put into a trash
> dumpster. Kids' school clothes, their groceries, everything into a
> dumpster? . . . They ought to help them, give them a place, go to
> a shelter, but instead they put all their personal belongings into a
> dumpster.

Marian Kramer, codirector of the MWRO and involved in welfare rights organizing in Detroit since the 1960s, responded on air that in the face of this indignity, the community should stand up and support one another:

> It becomes the duty of the community; it becomes the duty of all
> of us to begin to start stopping this from happening. They don't
> care about turning our water off. They don't care about turning
> us out into the street. We got to start caring and moving people
> back in, turning their water back on, turning their electricity back
> on. And letting these folks know that we are not just going to lay
> down and die.

POLITICAL AGENCY OF THE POOR

On May 24 and July 8, 2004, Highland Park City Council voted against the proposal from RWG to privatize their water department. They were shocked to learn that the city administrator had been negotiating in secret to privatize Highland Park's water. A copy of the contract was obtained by the MWRO, which then began to demand answers at City Council meetings. Marian Kramer explains, "There was a private company that was going to run the city of Highland Park's water department. Take public funds to do this, 20% of profits to city, 80% to them. We said look at this crap, and you don't know nothing about it. We demanded over and over. We wouldn't let them get to other business" (interview by Chris Caruso, January 2007).

The city administrator then stated in a letter to RWG that she would sign a 10-year contract with them for the management of the Highland Park Water Department. She claimed special powers because of Highland Park's financial situation and was willing to sign this over to RWG against the expressed will of the City Council. Met with mounting local pressure, she was replaced by the governor with a new administrator from the local community. Although water rates are still very high in Highland Park, the immediate threat of privatization was abated. The MWRO also worked with the Highland Park mayor and City Council and submitted a detailed alternate plan to resolve Highland Park's financial situation without cutting half the residents off from water.

MWRO has focused their efforts on the water affordability crisis taking place in Detroit as well. Maureen Taylor describes the process of putting together the "Water Affordability Plan":

When Michigan Welfare Rights first started negotiating with the water department around a new way to structure water rate charges, we contacted some groups of attorneys we knew. We had a number of meetings to pull together language that would be a systemic change in how water rates are charged. After many months, we found a legal expert out of Boston Mass[achusetts], specializing on developing language for afford-ability programs. We sent him packages of notes, this is what it should be, this is what it should say, and this is the outcomes, and he put something together and it is brilliant. We are very proud of it. We made copies and took it to members of city council, took it to the water department. People looked at it and scrutinized it, and couldn't find anything wrong with it. (inter-view, Chris Caruso, January 2007)

The MWRO, as an organization of poor people, has developed a practical policy solution to the Detroit water affordability crisis. They found the expertise and created a plan that could end the water shut-offs. The Detroit Water Board and City Council have both passed the MWRO's water affordability plan, but have refused to implement it. The implementation date was set for July 2006. The struggle then moved to pressure them to actually implement the solution. This fight over water privatization in Detroit has demonstrated the agency of the poor to create social change. The organization of the poor has become a leading force in efforts to challenge water privatization and other austerity programs. Their struggle is a school for us all.

REFERENCES

Anderson, C. (2003). *Eyes off the prize*. Cambridge: Cambridge University Press.

Angel, C. (2002, April 19). Official recommends bankruptcy for Highland Park, Mich. *Detroit Free Press*.

Babson, S. (1986). *Working Detroit*. Detroit: Wayne State University Press.

Baker, G. (2010). *Discussion with poverty scholars program at the U.S. social forum*. Retrieved January 20, 2011, from http://www.povertyinitiative.org/general-baker-ussf

Barlow, M., & Clarke, T. (2002). *Blue gold*. New York: The New Press.

Barlow, M., & Clarke, T. (2003). *The battle for water*. Retrieved January 20, 2005, from http://www.polarisinstitute.org/pubs/pubs_battle_for_water.html

Cronon, W. (1991). *Nature's metropolis*. New York & London: W.W. Norton.

Dillard, A. D. (2007). *Faith in the city*. Detroit: University of Michigan Press.

Finally Got the News. (1970). Bird, S., Lichtman R., & Gessner, P. [Directors]. 55 min. Icarus Films. New York.

Fine, S. (2000). Expanding the frontiers of civil rights: Michigan, 1948 to 1968. Detroit: Wayne State University Press.

Georgakas, D., & Surkin, M. (1998). *Detroit: I do mind dying*. Cambridge: South End Press.

Gilmore, R. (2007). *Golden gulag*. Berkeley: University of California Press.

Goldberg, D. (2010). Community control of construction, independent unionism, and the "short Black Power Movement" in Detroit. In D. Goldberg & T. Griffey (Eds.), *Black power at work*. Ithaca: Cornell University Press.

Hall, D. (2003a). *Water multinationals—No longer business as usual*. Retrieved January 20, 2005, from http://www.psiru.org/reports/2003-03-W-MNCs.doc

Hall, D. (2003b). *Water multinationals in retreat—Suez withdraws investment*. Retrieved January 20, 2005, from http://www.psiru.org/reports/2003-01-W-Suez.doc

Harvey, D. (1990). *The condition of postmodernity*. Oxford: Blackwell.

Harvey, D. (2003). *The new imperialism*. Oxford: Oxford University Press.

Kelly, R. (1996). *Race rebels*. Detroit: Free Press.

King, Jr., M. L. (1968). *Trumpet of conscience*. Boston: Beacon Press.

Lords, E. (2003, February 7). Water rates create flood of protests in Detroit area. *Detroit Free Press*.

Litowich, L. (2004, February 7). Coalition warns of possible water riots in Detroit. *Michigan Independent Media Center*.

Marx, K. (1990). *Capital, volume 1*. London & New York: Penguin Classics. (Original work published 1867)

Michigan Welfare Rights Organization. (2004). *Refusing to back down*. Retrieved January 20, 2005, from http://publiccitizen.org/print_article.cfm?ID=10795

Nadasen, P. (2004). *Welfare warriors*. New York: Routledge.

Piven, F. F., & Cloward, R. A. (1979). *Poor people's movements*. New York: Vintage Books.

Public Citizen. (2003). *Who are the major water companies?* Retrieved January 20, 2005, from http://www.citizen.org/cmep/Water/general/majorwater/index.cfm

Rothfeder, J. (2001). *Every drop for sale*. New York: Jeremy P. Tarcher/Putnam.

Roy, A. (2001). *Power politics*. Cambridge: South End Press.

Seelye, K. (2011, March 22). Detroit census confirms a desertion like no other. *The New York Times*.

Smith, S. E. (2001). *Dancing in the street*. Boston: Harvard University Press.

Sugrue, T. J. (1996). *The origins of the urban crisis*. Princeton: Princeton University Press.

Sweetwater Alliance. (2004). *Sweetwater Alliance condemns water privatization scheme in Highland Park, Michigan*. Retrieved January 20, 2005, from http://www.publiccitizen.org/print_article?ID=11974

Theoharis, J., & Woodard, K., Eds. (2003). *Freedom north*. New York: Palgrave.

Thompson, H. A. (2004). *Whose Detroit?*. Ithaca: Cornell University Press.

Tully, S. (2002, May 15). Water, water everywhere. *Fortune*.

Varghese, S. (2007). *Privatizing U.S. water*. Minneapolis: Institute for Agriculture and Trade Policy.

Ward, S. (2006). The Third World Women's Alliance: Black feminist radicalism and Black Power politics. in P. Joseph (Ed.), *The Black Power Movement*. New York: Routledge.

West, G. (1981). *The National Welfare Rights Movement*. Westport, CT: Praeger Publishers.

X, Malcolm. (1990). The ballot or the bullet. In G. Breitman (Ed.), *Malcolm X speaks* (pp. 23–44). New York: Grove Weidenfeld. (Original work published in 1964)

Willie Baptist at Bushville, a poor and homeless tent city in Philadelphia, PA, in 2000.

(L to R) Adam Barnes, Willie Baptist, Jan Rehmann, and Derrick McQueen at the Highlander Research and Education Center in New Market, TN, during Poverty Initiative's 2007 Appalachia Immersion.

Union Theological Seminary students, Columbia School of Social Work students, and leaders from Poverty Scholar organizations visit the Phillipi, WV, Head Start during Poverty Initiative's 2007 Appalachia Immersion.

Plenary session during the Poverty Scholars Program 2009 Leadership School in Charleston, WV.

Poverty Scholars visit Kayford Mountain with Keeper of the Mountains Foundation to learn about mountaintop removal coal mining during the 2009 Leadership School.

Willie Baptist lecturing at Evergreen State College.

Jan Rehmann lecturing at Union Theological Seminary as part of orientation for Poverty Initiative's 2007 Appalachia Immersion.

Willie Baptist and Liz Theoharis share the story of the 1995-96 church takeover by homeless families at the former St. Edward's site in Philadelphia, PA, with Union Theological Seminary students, Poverty Scholars, and Philadelphia Student Union leaders during Poverty Initiative's 2010 Northeast Immersion.

CHAPTER 7

Interview with Willie Baptist (IV): Lessons from the National Union of the Homeless: A Debate on Organizing

Jan Rehmann: From 1986 to 1991, you worked in the National Union of the Homeless, which became one of the largest networks of poor and homeless people in the United States at the time. That must have been a crucial experience for your development as an organizer of poor people.

Willie Baptist: Yes, it was a crucial experience. We were able to pull off these tremendous mobilizations of homeless people. By the 1980s, homelessness was no longer a skid row affair; it was structural. The shelter system was growing all over the country and was filled with dislocated families. We've come to accept the fact that every city has a shelter system, but that hasn't always been the case. Before this structural homelessness it was more of a transient affair, the skid row. But it has turned into a situation where today there are more homeless children than any other segment of the homeless population.

My involvement started in organizing against the workfare program I was on. In this context, I met some of the mothers who had been part of the old National Welfare Rights Organization but with its ending were now beginning to organize around workfare. These mothers, Marian Kramer, Annie Chambers, Annie Smart, Maureen Taylor, and others, taught me a whole lot about organizing among the poor. I also met Chris Sprowal, a homeless organizer in Philadelphia who was thinking about launching a nationwide organizing drive of homeless people. He was the lead organizer and eventually became the first president of the National Union of the Homeless. He was much older than me and had accumulated tremendous experience as part of the civil rights movement. He had led the Downtown CORE (Congress for Racial Equality) here in New York, led an election campaign in Long Island, ran the McGovern presidential campaign in Michigan, and

101

even ran for office himself. So he had accumulated a tremendous amount of tactical experience. I learned from him what it meant to organize among people who were dispossessed. No one can take away the huge contribution he made in the organizing of poor and homeless people. I had the great fortune and honor to learn from this well-experienced and extraordinary leader. My family and I lived with him and his family during this period.

At its height the Homeless Union had organized 25 local union chapters in 25 states with estimates as high as 15,000 homeless members of all races and genders. We had over 1,000 delegates from Los Angeles organized to form the L.A. chapter of the Union of the Homeless. In the Chicago-Gary (Indiana) area we had over 900 delegates. In 1987, we organized 1,200 homeless delegates representing all the shelters throughout the area to assemble at Riverside Church in New York City. That has to go down as the largest political gathering of homeless people in the United States thus far. We didn't know it at the time, but that was the same church, 20 years earlier in 1967, where Martin Luther King, Jr. first spoke out publicly against the Vietnam War, where he described the disproportionate deployment of the poor to the frontlines as a "cruel manipulation of the poor." I had heard the speech, but I didn't connect its important message with the founding convention of the New York Homeless Union.

That gathering was a tremendous experience. The mainstream press and large parts of academia at the time were talking about a "black underclass," saying that these miserable and demoralized folks were inept and incapable of doing anything. But here we were, a bunch of people who didn't have anything, successfully organizing ourselves. I played an educational role and also functioned as an outrider who would go into cities before the organizing team would arrive. Since I had developed connections with people from all over the country at workfare conferences held in Detroit and Chicago, I could connect up with these previous relationships and set up a support team ready to hit the ground running when the national team arrived. This effort would culminate in founding conventions like we had here in New York. It was a tremendous experience, but it was unprecedented, and we were very inexperienced in terms of dealing with an effort on that scale with that section of the population.

JR: But after the network's rise came the demise. In the early 1990s, the National Union of the Homeless collapsed and closed its doors. What happened?

WB: We were able to accomplish a lot when we reached a certain critical mass. We forced city councils in DC and Philadelphia to give homeless people the right to vote. No matter if you had a house or not, if you could identify a corner or a shelter, you could vote. In a number of cities we won the right to shelter. We did all kinds of stuff that built up our sense of ourselves, our self-worth. The head, Chris Sprowal, was named in *USA Today* in 1987 as one of the top 10 leaders to watch for in that year.

But what happened was that our growth took place at the same time that the impoverished communities, starting with African American communities, were being inundated with crack cocaine. The drug epidemic took us in. It served like a chemical warfare waged against us. I literally cried when I would get phone calls in the national office and could hear the internal fights that people were having, people stealing from each other. Chapter after chapter just broke down.

We also had cases where people carried out actions like civil disobedience when they hadn't taken their arrest records into account. We lost key leaders that way. There are homeless organizers who are still in prison serving as much as 25-year terms.

The Union of the Homeless was also devastated by a certain amount of co-optation. We were able to achieve victories in a number of cities. For instance, we were able to establish the Dignity Housing Programs in Philadelphia. It was a multimillion-dollar homeless program run by homeless people. We were able to take advantage of Mayor Goode's political liability after he took responsibility for the MOVE bombing in May 1985, which ended in eleven deaths, including five children, because it happened on his watch. It was the only time I think when an American city bombed itself. Exploiting that situation, we expanded the housing takeovers and insisted on a housing program. He conceded it to us and, as a fig leaf to brush up his political reputation, supported us in developing this multi-million-dollar housing program run by homeless people. Then the local chapter of the Union of the Homeless copied that program in Oakland, Minneapolis, and other cities.

But certain people who were assigned to run the programs became more closely tied to the housing department than to the Union of the Homeless. Then the housing department began to make demands on our structure that weakened the relationship of the Union of the Homeless to those programs. At first, we were using it as a resource base. When a homeless person really did a lot of work and made a large commitment, we would make sure that person got a house through the process. They cut that out. We had been able to get jobs, too. The Dignity Housing program was divided up into property management, social work, and peer counseling. Peer counseling was another name for organizing. We would give our homeless members those jobs. As the Homeless Union went into decline and Dignity Housing became more of an adjunct to the housing department, they began to cut those parts out of the whole picture. That weakened our relationship to it and we lost a number of leaders as a result of that development. It was a very devastating experience for me, having gone through that kind of militancy in getting actions and people to respond and then to losing it through drugs, prisons, and co-optation.

JR: It's a recurring phenomenon in social movements that when you finally achieve something in terms of concessions and certain electoral gains, these successes are often utilized by powers-that-be to destroy the movement. This is a painstaking dialectics. Is there no way out?

WB: Underneath all that, the main lesson for building an organization or a movement is that at its initial stage the question of finding committed leaders and developing their clarity and competence is key. We just didn't know that. We were inexperienced and couldn't deal with it. Not having a core of experienced and clear leaders left us unprepared to deal with the maneuvers of the powers-that-be and the all-around assault of the drug epidemic and then one chapter folded after another. The key lesson we learned from this was to focus on developing leaders so the movement doesn't have to be compromised by any individual who gets compromised.

JR: Wouldn't this experience of co-optation and demise validate the argument of Frances Fox Piven and Richard Cloward, who came out explicitly against any mass organization of the poor, because such an organization would necessarily end up as one of the usual bureaucratic lobby organizations in Washington? They proposed instead a national network of "cadre organizations" composed of clergy, students, civil rights activists, antipoverty workers, et cetera, that mobilize the poor to demand relief on a mass scale and thereby set off a fiscal crisis. Their argument was basically that the poor should disrupt the welfare system, but they should not organize themselves. Doing so would mean they would become caught in the system of co-optation. I suppose this is not the conclusion you would draw from your experience at the Union of the Homeless.

WB: Fox Piven and Cloward were influential figures in the National Welfare Rights Organization, which was formed in 1966. But there were two strands of thought. On the one side, you had the welfare recipients who were arguing that they themselves should assume leadership of this process—determining the allocation of money, targets, tactics, and so on. They argued that those decisions should come from the women who were facing the problems and were directly affected. This was the position of Johnnie Tillman, the first president of the National Welfare Rights Organization.

She had been part of a group of welfare recipients—poor mothers—who came together and organized themselves out of the Watts uprising to form the Anonymous Mothers of Watts.

On the other side, Cloward and Fox Piven argued that the poor were too poor to organize. Poor people's organizations could never get the clout necessary to offer economic benefits for their members, like the unions. To devote their energies and meager resources for organizing efforts was to forfeit energies that should have gone into disruption. In my reading of them, Cloward and Fox Piven relegated the poor, for the most part, to the role and function of disrupters, while the leadership of that process would be passed on to the middle-class intellectuals through which the interests of the upper class and their two-party system would dominate.

I know a number of those leaders who were welfare recipients that would later form the National Welfare Rights Union, in 1987, almost the same name as the older group, except with *union* instead of *organization*. I became a member of the board of the National Welfare Rights Union. They were definitely opposed to Fox Piven and Cloward's position. I think, if you look at history, you can see that Fox Piven and Cloward's equation of organizing and co-optation is overly simplistic. Look, for example, at the struggle of the runaway slaves. The Underground Railroad was largely the efforts of slaves and freed slaves who organized themselves and were able to have an impact on the situation. And certainly you can't get any poorer than slaves. How can Fox Piven and Cloward establish such a general assumption about the detrimental consequences of organizing without taking into account the freedom struggles of slaves? They construe an abstract dichotomy of mobilization and organization and overlook the reality that an organization can also be supportive for creative movements from below. Rosa Parks was not just a seamstress in a local department store, but she was a secretary in the NAACP (National Association for the Advancement of Colored People). Her allegedly spontaneous act of resistance on the bus was carefully prepared in this organization. The history I've studied and my own experience refute the position that the poor have no agency, and that they can't exhibit the qualities of leadership or sustain in a movement. It all depends on what kind of organization you build up.

For instance, Cloward and Fox Piven developed their argument largely against Saul Alinsky's type of "poor people's organization," which limited the agency of the poor to that of local community concerns (Fig. 7.1). It precluded the organizing of the poor as a leading social force in a broader mass movement to end poverty in the country. So both sides of this argument were predicated ultimately on the same basic assumption—that the poor cannot be a leading force in relation to all of society.

Figure 7.1. Mobilizing Versus Organizing?

We argued against the traditional organizing notion that poor people can become an effective political force by coming together in mass-based organizations. We did not think the political system would be responsive to such organizations, even if large numbers of the poor could be involved on a continuing basis. . . . To mobilize a crisis, we thought it would be necessary to develop a national network of cadre organizations rather than a national federation of welfare recipients. *This organization of organizers*—composed of students, churchmen, civil rights activists, antipoverty workers, and militant AFDC recipients—would in turn seek to energize a broad, loosely coordinated movement of variegated groups to arouse hundreds of thousands of poor people to demand aid. Rather than build organizational membership rolls, the purpose would be to build the welfare rolls. . . . Our emphasis on mass mobilization with cadre organizations as the vehicle struck organizers as exceedingly manipulative.

Source: Frances Fox Piven and Richard A. Cloward, *Poor People's Movements: Why They Succeed, How They Fail* (New York: Vintage Books, 1977), pp. 278–279, 284.

JR: This reminds me of the young Marx at the age of 26, when he first used the concept of the *proletariat* and defined it as a class "with radical chains," which has a universalist character because its sufferings are universal. It can only redeem itself by a total redemption of humanity. He uses here the original meaning of *proletariat*, derived from the Latin word *proles*, meaning "offspring," more specifically those who have no wealth other than their offspring. But most people only know Marx's later remarks on the "lumpenproletariat" as the "dead weight" of the working class, which has often been used by trade unionists to pit the industrial working class and its organizations against the poor. In my view, this is contradicted by the more substantial parts of Marx's class analysis, where he clearly shows that the proletariat is composed of different sections, comprising those employed and those permanently or intermittently thrown into unemployment. You have certainly struggled a lot with this kind of derogatory attitude toward poor people's movements.

WB: In both my studies and in my organizing experience among the homeless and the poor we've always encountered this argument from different kinds of leftists who instrumentalized Marx against the poor. I could also observe how the notion of a "lumpenproletariat" merged with or morphed into the notion of the "underclass" that was then used by neoliberal politicians to cut welfare programs. All those concepts and the reference to Marx's notion of lumpenproletariat serve to stigmatize the poor. Those people who were laid off and trying to grapple with the circumstances somehow were put into a definition that says that they were criminals, they were inert, they were lazy, and that they were incapable of exhibiting any kind of leadership in the process.

Marx's theory was worked out during the period of the steam engine. Later on you had a second industrial revolution that involved the massive assembly lines with the massive application of electricity. Today you've got a kind of transnational high-tech capitalism that, through the introduction of computer technologies, creates systemic unemployment and underemployment on a global scale. The point I want to convey is that when you're in a new day, you gotta do things in a new way. The first thing you have to determine is whether what you're dealing with is new or old, because if you try to apply old solutions to new problems you're always going to fail. The poor today is not the poor of yesterday. It's not the traditional agrarian poor, not the slave poor, and not the pauper of the classic industrial age. It is a poor that has a global character, that is being pushed increasingly outside the core production process, and that is currently involved in underemployment, taking on three or four SLJs (shitty little jobs) to barely make ends meet. Making this new analysis is very important.

Those who keep on using the notions of "lumpenproletariat" or "underclass" show that they have very little, if any, appreciation of the new social consequences of the unfolding tremendous technological revolution and globalization process that is presently transforming the world. The abilities of this growing segment of the population are being neglected like industrial waste, but represent a tremendous resource of intellectual genius. You can't talk about the problems of poverty—the pain of it, the daily struggles to survive, the plight, the fight, and the insight—without involving the newly emerging leaders from the growing ranks of the poor.

CHAPTER 8

The Relevance of Gramsci's Theory of Hegemony for Social Justice Movements

Jan Rehmann

> The popular element "feels" but does not always
>   know or understand;
> the intellectual element "knows" but does not
>   always understand
> and in particular does not always feel.
> The two extremes are therefore pedantry
> and philistinism on the one hand
> and blind passion and sectarianism on the other.
>   —(Gramsci, SPN, p. 418; Q 11, §67)[1]

In Willie's interview as well as in several of our class discussions, we have touched upon difficult strategic questions in terms of how to build sustainable social movements against poverty. Remember our debates on the Watts uprisings (Chapter 3) or Willie's critical comments on Fox-Piven and Cloward's approach (Chapter 7): Are poor people to be "mobilized" or can they develop the capacity to organize themselves? How can the usual split in social movements, namely, either to be marginalized or co-opted be avoided? In search of a theoretical base to discuss these issues, I would like to turn to one of the most interesting philosophers and social theorists of the 20th century, Antonio Gramsci. In the following introduction, I will try to demonstrate how his reflections on "hegemony," "common sense," and "organic intellectuals" helped overcome some major weaknesses of contemporary Marxist theories and how they could perhaps help us to find some useful orientations for today's social movements, in particular those against poverty. Let me start with some biographical information.[2]

WHO WAS GRAMSCI?

Born in 1891 in the province of Cagliari in Sardinia, the fourth of seven children, Antonio Gramsci grew up in modest conditions that turned dire when his father was suspended and imprisoned for 5 years for alleged administrative abuses. After his graduation from secondary school in 1911, Gramsci won a scholarship and moved to northern Italy to study humanities, social sciences, and linguistics at the University of Turin, in the industrial center of the country, where the famous car company Fiat had its headquarters. Coming from the countryside, he was suddenly exposed to the most advanced workers' struggles in Europe and became one of the leading figures of the factory councils of the auto workers in Turin. These councils were democratically elected by all workers in a plant, unionized or not, and were meant to be institutions capable of unifying and educating the working class. Their main difference from trade unions was, according to Gramsci, that the councils should help the workers to become aware of themselves as *producers* and *organizers* of production instead of being just wage earners who fight for wage raises and thereby remain within the rules of capitalism. Gramsci was first engaged in the Italian Socialist Party (PSI); in 1919, he founded the weekly review for Socialist culture *L'Ordine Nuovo*—together with Palmiro Togliatti, the future general secretary of the Italian Communist Party (PCI) and other future leaders like Angelo Tasca and Umberto Terracini. When the Socialist Party split at the Livorno Congress in January 1921, he became a member of the PCI's Central Committee and, from 1924 to 1926, the party's general secretary. His main theoretical contribution during these years was his analysis of *The Southern Question*, where he challenged the racialized images of the Italian South as "the ball and chain that prevents a more rapid process in the civil development of Italy" and laid out a strategy for a political alliance between northern workers and southern peasants (1995b, pp. 17, 20). It was first and foremost this concern that determined Gramsci's position in the internal struggles of the PCI and the Communist International, where he became one of the most articulate supporters of a worker-peasant alliance and a broad "united front" against fascism.[3]

Like other socialist movements after World War I, the factory council movement in Turin was soon defeated. Already in October 1922, the Italian fascists under Benito Mussolini organized their March to Rome and seized power. In 1926, Gramsci was arrested by the fascist government and sentenced to 20 years. When the verdict was announced, the chief prosecutor famously stated, "For twenty years we must stop this brain from functioning." It did not turn out this way, because it was during this prison time that Gramsci (1975) wrote his most important theoretical work, the *Prison Notebooks*, in which he developed his key concepts like hegemony, civil society, war of position, common sense, and organic intellectuals. His critical and self-critical reflections made him one of the most innovative socialist thinkers, not only for Italy and western Europe, but worldwide, not least in Paolo Freire's *Pedagogy of the Oppressed*, in liberation theology, and in antipoverty movements like the Brazilian Landless Worker Movement (Movimento dos Trabalhadores Rurais Sem Terra [MST]).

From his childhood on, Gramsci suffered from a hunched back and stunted growth as well as other conditions. During his 11-year imprisonment, his health deteriorated more and more, and his writing efforts turned into a race against time.[4] He was finally transferred to a hospital in Rome, where he spent the last 2 years under police guard. He died in 1937 at the age of 46 from a cerebral hemorrhage. The PCI started publishing some selections of his prison notebooks after World War II, but it took until 1975 for a complete and critical four-volume edition of the *Quaderni del carcere* to be published.

CIVIL SOCIETY, HEGEMONY, AND INTEGRAL STATE

I think the best way of getting a handle on Gramsci's theory is to understand the historical and political context that made a new assessment of the situation and a new strategy necessary. It was above all the devastating defeat of socialist movements after World War I that provoked Gramsci's reflections. Every attempt at a revolution in Western Europe failed and was cruelly crushed. In Italy, the Fascist movement had come to power already in 1922, that is, only two years after the spectacular occupations of auto factories by the worker's council movement in Turin (October 1920) in which Gramsci played a crucial role. In Germany, the leaders of the new Communist Party, Karl Liebknecht and Rosa Luxemburg, were assassinated by right-wing militias and thrown into the river. The split between social-democratic and communist parties deepened, which weakened not only the struggle for workers' economic rights, but also the legitimacy of the new democracy. About 20 years later most of Europe was fascist, either under the direct occupation by the Nazis or in the form of collaborating allies of Nazi Germany.

Why did this happen, Gramsci asked himself, and his response went beyond the usual accusations of "betrayal" of reformist leaders. Not that such a betrayal did not exist, but its denouncement did not explain the mass support for reformist strategies of co-optation. Gramsci formulated a serious self-critique instead: The revolutionaries had thought they could conquer state power in a similar way to that of the Bolsheviks in Russia, by armed insurgency, by frontal attack on the power centers, by a strategy that Gramsci describes in military terms as a "war of maneuver." By applying this strategy, they underestimated the sturdy structure of "civil society" in Western capitalism and therefore the inner stability of bourgeois hegemony:

> In Russia the State was everything, civil society was primordial and gelatinous;
> in the West, there was a proper relation between State and civil society, and
> when the State trembled a sturdy structure of civil society was at once revealed.
> The State was only an outer ditch, behind which there stood a powerful system
> of fortresses and earthworks. (SPN, p. 238; Q 7, §16)

We can see in this quote that Gramsci differentiates between the "State"
as an "outer ditch" and "civil society" as its sturdy system of "fortresses"
and "earthworks." We can also observe that his concepts of "civil society"
and "hegemony" are intimately linked. In the most developed capitalist
countries, the political system is maintained in two complementary ways:
by the state in the narrow sense, that is, the predominantly repressive apparatuses like the army, the police, the judiciary system, and the prison system,
which control mainly through force and laws. This system that Gramsci
calls "political society" (*società politica*) is usually highly centralized and
hierarchical, and it enforces its state power primarily by coercion. It is com-
plemented by a "civil society" (*società civile*) that consists of institutions
like schools, churches, and associations down to sport clubs and rifle associations, which are usually not controlled by the government but formally
independent.

It is in and by these institutions or associations that the dominant
classes produce a sort of consent, usually without resorting to force,
but not without contestation from other social forces. Gramsci calls
this (contradictory and always contested) production of consent *hegemony*, and the different institutions, by and in which this hegemony is
constructed, *hegemonic apparatuses* (SPN, pp. 365–366; Q 10.II, §12).[5]
The distinction between "direct domination" through the repressive
agencies of the state and "hegemony" through civil society is certainly
not to be understood as an absolute one—as if there were no coercion or
violence in schools and churches or no consent building in the military
or the police—but rather as an analytical tool to distinguish different
functions or dimensions.

To understand the importance of this analytical distinction, one should
have in mind that traditional Marxist approaches at the time tended to reduce the state to a repressive instrument of the ruling class that must be conquered in a frontal attack, in a "war of maneuver." Against such a narrow
understanding of the state, Gramsci proposed the concept of an "integral
state": "the state = political society + civil society, in other words hegemony
protected by the armor of coercion" (SPN, p. 263). This led him to an important conclusion: Once you include the relatively independent hegemonic
apparatuses in your concept of an "integral state," you have to modify your
oppositional strategy, in particular in terms of the relationship between "reform" and "revolution."

FROM "WAR OF MANEUVER" TO "WAR OF POSITION"

Let us go back to the socialist defeat after World War I—what went wrong in terms of hegemony? According to Gramsci, the attempts of conquering the state in a war of maneuver necessarily failed because the revolutionaries had no understanding about how the system was able to produce a hegemony, a consent that reached far beyond the elites that benefited from it. It included large sections of the middle classes, the peasants, and the working class who might otherwise have been inclined to revolt against the ruling order. The socialists had developed an ultraradical rhetoric of overthrowing the system, but without having the force and support to actually do it. They hadn't studied the hegemonic fabric of the society and were unable to intervene in it. They frightened large parts of the population that could have become their allies—for example, the peasants of the south, the lower middle classes—and this facilitated in Italy the victory of fascism.

When Gramsci proposes the concept of a "war of position" instead, one has to keep in mind that he uses the military term as a metaphor: "Comparisons between military art and politics, if made, should always be taken *cum grano salis* (with a pinch of salt)—in other words, as stimuli to thought"—in politics, the concept of "war of position" refers to the concept of hegemony (SPN, p. 231; Q 1, §133; Q 8, §52.). It means to intervene in civil society; to take positions within its "trenches," namely, its hegemonic apparatuses; and to fight there for support. Whereas many Marxists at the time assumed that winning the consensus of the majority of the people would take place *after* the seizure of state power, Gramsci insists that we need a political hegemony and "intellectual and moral leadership" *before* the advent of power (SPN, pp. 57–59; Q 1, §44).[6] According to him, Vladimir Lenin's formula of a "United Front" demonstrates that he understood the necessity of transitioning from a "war of maneuver" to a "war of position," but had no time to develop the concept further (SPN, pp. 237–238). Gramsci's historical examples also include Mohandas Gandhi's strategy of nonviolent resistance and boycotts: To confront such a flexible "war of position," the English colonial authorities sometimes tried to "*provoke* a premature outbreak of the Indian fighting forces, in order to identify them and decapitate the general movement" (SPN, pp. 229–230).

"Wars of position" usually take place under the predominance of the ruling power bloc, which determines to a large degree their limits and forms. Gramsci describes this determining aspect as "passive revolution." He develops this concept with the example of the formation of nation states in continental Europe as a reaction to the French Revolution: They emerged "by successive small waves of reform rather than by revolutionary explosions like the original French ones"; the old feudal classes were not expropriated but just "demoted from their dominant position to a 'governing' one," so that they became a "'caste' with specific cultural and psychological characteristics, but no longer with predominant economic functions" (SPN, pp. 115, 119; Q 1, §150; Q 10.II, §61). Looking for a contemporary example, Gramsci asks whether the new industrial system of Fordism (particularly in the United States) can be understood as a "passive revolution" that reacts to the "planned economy" of the USSR and adopts some elements of it in its Keynesian economic politics, without changing the fundamental power relations of capitalism (SPN, pp. 279–280). "Passive revolution" also defined the relations of force in which both Gandhism and early Christianity had to develop their strategies in confrontation with the respective superpowers of their time, the Roman and the British Empire (SPN, p. 107). In general, the concept can be defined as a modernization from above that takes place in periods characterized by a "lack of popular initiative," which enables it to absorb progressive elements from below: The development proceeds as a "reaction of the dominant classes to the sporadic, elementary and nonorganic rebelliousness of the popular masses," as a "restoration" that accepts a "certain part of the demands expressed from below" (Q 10.II, §41.XIV).

I think this description is to a large degree still valid for today's struggles: As long as the popular resistance is still sporadic, unorganized, fragmented, and dispersed into innumerable "identity movements," the dominant power bloc controls the outcome, and history proceeds in the form of a passive revolution that preempts any possible opposition. The ideological apparatuses pick up some of the most popular demands, cut them off from the more radical ones, and integrate them into their own agenda. They also try to co-opt the leaders of the movement, even those who seemed irreconcilably hostile at the beginning: "The absorption of the enemies' élites means their decapitation, and annihilation often for a very long time" (SPN, p. 59). Gramsci distinguishes two varieties of co-optation (he uses the term "transformism"), one referring to individual political figures, the other to "entire groups of leftists who pass over to the moderate camp" (SPN, p. 58, n. 8; Q 8, §36). The absorption of the oppositional forces can be organized by a "Caesarist" regime with an authoritarian leader figure on top (after the model of Caesar or Napoleon) or by more subtle forms "without a Caesar, without any great 'heroic' and representative personality," by parliamentary and trade unionist coalitions and compromise solutions (AGR, p. 270). In this regard, Fordism can be analyzed as a historic alliance between industrial capital and relevant parts of the upper strata of the (mostly white) working class with their "moderate" labor parties and conformist trade unions.

Against this backdrop, it becomes possible to try a tentative reformulation of the relationship between "reformism" and "revolution." The difference is obviously not about whether "reforms" as such are to be supported or rejected, but about the question of whether the respective reforms are convincingly embedded in a wider perspective of transcending the current system or not. In order to describe the difficult task of connecting near goals and far goals, Rosa Luxemburg has coined the (paradoxical) concept of a "revolutionary Realpolitik" (1970, p. 373). It helps to avoid both a sectarian rhetoric and an adaptation to the mainstream. From the perspectives of a Gramscian theory of hegemony, a "reformist" politics can be identified as a strategy that in the name of incremental reforms participates at a "passive revolution" from above and supports—willingly or unwillingly—the co-optation of oppositional social movements (or elements of them) by the ruling power bloc. A "revolutionary politics" (not in the sense of some hyperradical rhetoric of sectarians, but of Luxemburg's dialectical concept of revolutionary Realpolitik) has to determine whether specific reforms help transform the existing power structures, contribute to an alternative network of social forces from below, and open up perspectives that go beyond the existing system.

OVERCOMING ECONOMISM AND DETERMINISM

Gramsci applies his metaphors of "war of maneuver" and "war of position" to another area that seems to be far-fetched at first: the economy and the economic crisis in particular. From a war-of-maneuver perspective, "the immediate economic element (crises, etc.) is seen as the field artillery, which in war opens a breach in the enemy's defences—a breach sufficient for one's own troops to rush in and obtain a definitive . . . victory." Gramsci targets the widespread expectation among Marxists that economic crises would nearly automatically lead to a collapse of capitalism and criticizes it as a "form of iron economic determinism" and therefore "historical mysticism, the awaiting of a sort of miraculous illumination" (SPN, p. 233; Q 7, §10). The reason for this harsh criticism is the sober-minded analysis that in modern capitalism civil society has become a complex structure "which is resistant to the catastrophic 'incursions' of the immediate economic element," so that economic crises cannot by themselves produce fundamental historical events but only "create a terrain more favorable to the dissemination of certain modes of thought" (SPN, pp. 235, 184).

Gramsci's critique of "economism" and "determinism" is indeed a major frontline throughout the *Prison Notebooks*. With reference to Marx's political texts (e.g., *The 18th Brumaire, Civil War in France,* and *Class Struggles in France*), he wants to show that the "claim . . . that every fluctuation of politics and ideology can be presented and expounded as an immediate expression of the structure, must be contested in theory as primitive infantilism" (SPN, p. 407; Q 13, §18).

Against the prevailing position of contemporary Marxists that ideologies are just mental reflections of economic class positions, Gramsci insists on the institutional and therefore relatively autonomous character of ideologies: They "are anything but illusions and appearance," but are, rather, an "objective and effective reality," the terrain of the "superstructures" (SPN, pp. 376–377).[7] By focusing on the institutional reality of ideologies, Gramsci anticipates what later will be considered as the "new" paradigm of ideology theories in the 1970s: Being an integral part of the "superstructures," the ideological is to be investigated in its own "materiality"—as a set of ideological apparatuses, intellectuals (organic and traditional), ideological rituals, texts, and discourses.[8]

Such a critique of "economism" (i.e., of economic reductionism) is not to be confused with postmodernist tendencies to dissolve the economy into a set of discourses and cultural patterns. When Gramsci analyzes the different levels of "relations of force" in society, he starts out with the force relations that are "closely linked to the economic structure." The development of productive forces provides "a basis for the emergence of social classes" and constitutes "a refractory reality" that helps to check the degree of realism of ideologies: "Nobody can alter the number of firms or their employees, the number of cities or the given urban population" (SPN, pp. 180–181). To overlook or marginalize these basic structures of society is for Gramsci an example of "ideologism": While economism overvalues mechanical causes, ideologism "is fixated on the great individual personalities and absolutizes the 'voluntaristic and individual element'" (Q 13, §17; Q 19, §5).

But the analysis of economic relations is only a first step that does not explain the whole. The relations of political forces refer to the degree of self-awareness and organization of the different social classes and contain different sublevels, namely, (a) unity on an "economic-corporate" level, restricted to a professional group; (b) solidarity of interests among a social class, but only in the economic field and "within the existing fundamental structures"; and (c) intellectual and moral unity that "transcend[s] the corporate limits of the purely economic class" and is able to articulate the common interests of other subordinate groups "on a 'universal' plane" (SPN, pp. 181–182).[9] By "corporatism," Gramsci means the limitation to immediate economic goals, cut off from the wider perspective of socialist transformation. Historical background is, for example, the narrow-mindedness of industrial workers in northern Italy who despise the poor migrants from the rural South and thereby reveal themselves still incapable of building larger class alliances.[10] To organize the passage from the corporatist to an "ethico-political" level is the main difficulty and therefore the main task for leftist politics. To demonstrate the importance of this passage, Gramsci describes it as a moment of "catharsis" (purification), that is, a sort of turning point that liberates the movement from its egoistical-corporatist restrictions and thereby helps the subaltern class to transition from "objective to subjective" (meaning from being a passive "object" of social conditions to becoming an active historical "subject"), from "necessity to freedom." "To establish the 'cathartic' moment becomes therefore . . . the starting-point for all the philosophy of praxis" (SPN, p. 367).[11] On the level of practical activity, the main task is to patiently form a "permanently organized and long-prepared force, which can be put into the field when it is judged that a situation is favorable" (SPN, p. 185).

ORGANIC INTELLECTUALS, COMMON SENSE, AND GOOD SENSE

To understand how a ruling class maintains its hegemony or how a subaltern class might be able to challenge this hegemony one needs to study the functions of the respective intellectuals, of whom Gramsci distinguishes mainly two types: on the one hand, those who are closely linked to a fundamental social class that "creates together with itself, organically, one or more strata of intellectuals, which give it homogeneity and an awareness of its own function, not only in the economic but also in the social and political fields" and, on the other hand, traditional intellectual strata that have emerged out of a preceding social order and in connection to earlier social classes that have lost their predominant position in the meanwhile. Examples for "organic intellectuals" (of the capitalist entrepreneur) are, for instance, industrial technicians, specialists in political economy, and organizers of a new legal system; the most prominent example of "traditional intellectuals" are the ecclesiastics who had been organically bound to the landed aristocracy and therefore seem to be more independent from class positions in modern society (SPN, pp. 5–7).[12]

Every class that tries to gain (or to maintain) hegemony therefore needs to accomplish at least two tasks: to develop its own "organic intellectuals" and to "assimilate and to conquer 'ideologically' the traditional intellectuals" (SPN, pp. 10, 15). This double effort is also necessary for the (now) subaltern classes and their movements. Gramsci is very critical of the separation between "intellectuals" and "simple folks" and proposes a consequent grassroots approach: *All* people are intellectuals; even if not all "have in society the function of intellectuals," everyone is a "philosopher" and an artist, that is, "participates in a particular conception of the world" and "bring[s] into being new modes of thought" (SPN, p. 9). It is therefore not about a pedagogy in which the "true" and "enlightened" intellectuals teach the "nonintellectuals" what to believe or to do, "because non-intellectuals do not exist." "The problem of creating a new stratum of intellectuals consists therefore in the critical elaboration of the intellectual activity that exists in everyone" (SPN, p. 9).

Gramsci's perspective of "critically elaborating" an already existing intellectual activity is closely linked to his concept of "common sense" (*senso comune*). It is defined by its inner contradictions that people are usually unaware of. Gramsci introduces the concept with the statement that "we are all conformists of some conformism or other, always man-in-the-mass"; the question is, therefore, to *what* kind of mass humanity one belongs. This might sound provocative for anyone who believes in the "singularity" of each individual, but I would turn the argument around and argue (with Pierre Bourdieu) that the individualistic distinction from others (by taste, good education, etc.) is itself a widespread social pattern and as such a highly conformist attitude. Gramsci goes on: "When one's conception of the world is not critical and coherent but disjointed and episodic, one belongs simultaneously to a multiplicity of mass human groups. The personality is strangely composite: it contains Stone Age elements and principles of a more advanced science, prejudices from all past phases of history . . . and intuitions of a future philosophy, which will be that of a human race united the world over" (SPN, p. 324; Q 11, §12). From this perspective, common sense looks like a quarry consisting of several levels of different geographical periods. The incoherence shows itself also in the discrepancy between words and deeds, "intellectual choice" and "real activity," between a consciousness implicit in one's activity and one "inherited from the past and uncritically absorbed"—a contradiction that might lead to "moral and political passivity" (SPN, pp. 326, 333). For Gramsci, contemporary Marxism is not immune to such incoherence, in particular when it combined itself with "mechanical determinism": The active will of the subaltern classes is hidden "in a veiled and, as it were, shamefaced manner" behind a kind of secularized predestination dogma (the tide of history is working for me in the long term), which functions like a sort of "ideological 'aroma'" or opiate of the Marxist labor movement (SPN, pp. 336–337).[13]

At first glance, Gramsci's dealing with common sense's multiplicity seems to have some resemblance with postmodernist and postcolonial theories that depict such multiple compositions as "play of differences" or "hybridities." It is certainly no coincidence that Gramsci's influence on these theories has been a subject of much debate.[14] But there is a specificity in Gramsci's approach that has been virtually lost in postmodernist concepts: He focuses on the aspect of a "disjointed" and uncritically adopted incoherence that risks restricting or paralyzing people's capacity to act and therefore needs to be criticized and transformed into a higher degree of coherence. It is a critique that is far from any degradation:

[Philosophy of praxis] must be a criticism of "common sense," basing itself initially, however, on common sense in order to demonstrate that "everyone" is a philosopher and that it is not a question of introducing from scratch a scientific form of thought into everyone's individual life, but of renovating and making "critical" an already existing activity. (SPN, pp. 330–331)

Let us reflect a bit on the apparently paradoxical notion of a critique *of* common sense *based on* common sense. Obviously it takes its distance from an instruction from the outside, by intellectuals who convey the "truth" to "unenlightened" simple folks. Such a top-down enlightenment model had already been challenged by Marx, when he wrote in his "Theses on Feuerbach" that the educators are to be educated as well (MECW 5, p. 7). Criticizing common sense means for Gramsci "to make it a coherent unity," on the base of a critical "consciousness of what one really is" (SPN, p. 324). The stronghold for this critical "working coherent" can be found in what he calls "good sense" (*buon senso*). It is common sense's "healthy nucleus," characterized by a sense of "experimentalism" and of direct observation of reality, a practical reason that (unlike common sense) did not blame the plague on people's poisoning the wells and that after a while even discovers the superficiality of "brilliant" speeches that seemed fascinating at first. Gramsci concludes that, in this sense, the philosophy of praxis "coincides with 'good sense' that is opposed to common sense" (SPN, pp. 328, 348; Q 10.II, § 48; Q 11, § 56, Q 16, § 21; Q 12, §12, 1378).

Gramsci basically criticizes that the Left after World War I had not studied the contradictory composition of people's common sense and was therefore unable to communicate with it effectively. The fascists, however, were indeed able to exploit common sense's incoherence and to become a hegemonic force attractive not only to the middle classes, but also to poor peasants and workers. This experience is the background for Gramsci's project of educating and forming a new type of organic intellectuals, "which arise directly out of the masses, but remain in contact with them" (SPN, p. 340; Q 11, §12.). These intellectuals are "organic" only to the extent to which they are capable to work *on* and *in* the common sense of the people, listening to their stories, perceiving and acknowledging their multiplicities, but also intervening into their inconsistencies, and looking for "good-sense" strongholds starting from which it is possible to develop a greater level of coherence and capacity of act. At the same time, they need to build alliances with "traditional intellectuals" of different areas. The goal is "to construct an intellectual-moral bloc" that achieves "the intellectual progress of the mass and not only of small intellectual groups" (SPN, p. 332–333). "Philosophy" in this context becomes "a cultural battle to transform the popular 'mentality'" that requires particularly the "diffusion in a critical form of truths already discovered, their 'socialization' as it were" (SPN, pp. 348,

325): "For a mass of people to be led to think coherently and in the same coherent fashion about the real present world, is a 'philosophical' event far more important and 'original' than the discovery by some philosophical 'genius' of a truth, which remains the property of small groups of intellectuals" (SPN, p. 325).

GRAMSCI'S RELEVANCE FOR TODAY'S STRUGGLES

Much has changed since Gramsci jotted down his notes in his prison cell. He was one of the first thinkers to reflect on the new period of Fordism emerging in the United States (he actually coined the term), but he could obviously not anticipate the high-tech revolution and its effects on the working classes from the 1970s onward. He developed his theory of hegemony in the context of strong labor parties and trade unions that are now gone, in particular in the United States, so that the notion of developing organic intellectuals must be rethought in a more network like fashion. In spite of fundamental changes in the economic, political, and ideological constellation I think that there are still many lessons to be learned for today's struggles, of which I select only a few.

We dealt with the recomposition of the working class enforced by high-tech capitalism and neoliberal politics with contingent work as its most dynamic part (cf. Chapter 4). One of the fundamental problems of traditional class theories is the gap between structural meanings of class as an objective *class in itself* and processual meanings of class as a *class for itself*, that is, in the sense that "class happens" when people share a set of experiences that define their life in class terms and make them act accordingly. If one identifies a class in a matrix of objective positions, one does not yet know how this group of people will experience such a position and whether they identify and articulate such experiences in class terms. Fascism in Europe, trade unions' white racism in the United States, and other disastrous developments have taught the labor movement (and the Left in general) the painful lesson that there is no necessary link between structural class positions and specific political orientations. This applies as well to the process of precarization and impoverishment. There is no "guarantee" whatsoever that those sliding "objectively" into deep poverty develop "subjectively" a collective agency that confronts the structural injustice that is creating the misery. Poverty in itself does not prevent poor people from becoming the foot soldiers for racist demagogues and fundamentalist preachers. "Even within a single city, slum populations can support a bewildering variety of responses to structural neglect and deprivation, ranging from charismatic churches and prophetic cults to ethnic militias, street gangs, neoliberal

NGOs, and revolutionary social movements," observes Mike Davis (2006, pp. 201–202). The direction they take depends on the process of what some social theorists have called "class formation," in the course of which "class capacities," namely, forms of cooperation, social networks, independent organizations, leadership development, alliances, and so on are actually being shaped—or not.[15] Whether class formations are weak or strong, fragmented or coherent depends on the relations of force, not only at the workplace but also in the institutions of civil society and in public opinion. It is at this point that the research on class formation touches upon and is in need of Gramsci's theory of hegemony, which focuses on the capabilities of subaltern classes to overcome their subordination to the predominant ideological framework. In Gramscian terms, *class formation* can be described as the passage of a class movement from the corporatist to an "ethico-political" level. It requires that the class develops its own "organic intellectuals," elaborates a coherent "philosophy of praxis," and becomes capable of forging large class alliances.

The history of social movements is continually marked by two pitfalls that complement each other: One part of the movement is regularly co-opted into the political and ideological fabric; the other part is marginalized so that ordinary people turn away from these "lunatic" radicals. In order to overcome this vicious circle, we can learn from Gramsci the importance of building a movement from below that is not sectarian and narrow minded but stays connected to people's common sense and is capable of forging broad alliances. To build up a broad movement does not necessarily mean to adapt to the mainstream, but is to be done in a way to actively transform it by developing one's own hegemonic structures.

For a movement to be independent it has to build up its own "hegemonic apparatuses" and organic intellectuals who help it develop coherence and awareness of itself; for it to gain hegemonic traction it has to combine forces with intellectuals of different areas. Both components are closely connected. One can see some elements of the combined two-prong strategy when the Poverty Initiative at Union Theological Seminary prepares the specific Poverty Scholars Program to educate leaders and organizers *and* also involves progressive pastors, teachers, and professors in supporting their cause, struggles, and demands.

In this process, Gramsci's theory of intellectuals is very valuable in that it helps to avoid any academic elitism: *All* are intellectuals in the sense that they try to make sense of their social and individual lives. A philosophy of praxis does not import an (alleged) truth from the outside, but works on and within the common sense of the people. To strengthen its coherence means to elaborate further the practical, intellectual, and ethical good-sense capacities that already exist. Only by such a bottom-up approach can it perhaps be possible to overcome the gulf described in the Gramsci passage (quoted at the beginning of this chapter), namely, between simple folks who "feel" without "knowing" and pedantic ivory tower intellectuals who "know" but do not "understand" or "feel" (SPN, p. 418).

Any serious attempt at changing society must study the way the given social and political order produces its hegemony. This is a question not only of "ideas," but also of how civil society is actually structured. What are the most powerful "hegemonic apparatuses" in our society, and how do they function? What kinds of intellectuals are predominant in organizing the consent of large masses so that they tolerate or even actively support a system that damages them? How is the dominant ideology transformed into a common sense that seems perfectly "natural"? But also, and this is one of the main differences between Gramsci's theory of hegemony and Adorno/Horkheimer's more monolithic concept of a overall manipulating "culture industry": Where are the social struggles within the hegemonic apparatuses that could be used by social movements from below? What are the contradictions in common sense that could provoke its crisis and productive transformation? Social movements (and parties) against social injustice need a think tank network to map out the hegemonic landscape—maps not only of the ruling classes' strongholds, but also markers for contested issues, social struggles, and possible points of intervention.

NOTES

1. Following the internationally established standard, I will use the Italian edition of the *Quaderni del carcere* with the abbreviation Q, followed by notebook number and note; for example, Q 11, § 67 indicates notebook 11, note 67. In addition, the following abbreviations are used: *Selections from the Prison Notebooks* (SPN), *Further Selections from the Prison Notebooks* (FSPN), and *Antonio Gramsci Reader* (AGR). Similarly, the *Marx Engels Collected Works* will be abbreviated (MECW) in citations.

2. For a detailed and reliable biography available in English, see the classic study of Giuseppe Fiori (1990) and the introduction to the *Selections from the Prison Notebooks* (SPN) by the editors Quintin Hoare and G. N. Smith. A short chronological outline can be found in the *Antonio Gramsci Reader* (AGR), pp. 17–25.

3. During his time in prison, Gramsci raised fundamental objections against the Comintern's "left turn" politics from 1928 onward that led to a devastating forced collectivization of agriculture in the USSR and on the international level to an abandoning of any alliance with social-democratic parties, a politics that contradicted the earlier strategy of a "united front." Cf. the reports of Antonio's brother Gennaro Gramsci, of Athos Lisa, and of others on Gramsci's opposition in Fiori, 1990, pp. 252–258 and in the Introduction of the SPN (pp. xc–xcii).

4. "His years in prison were literally an eleven-year death-agony. His teeth fell out, his digestive system collapsed . . . , his chronic insomnia became permanent . . . ; he suffered from headaches so violent that he beat his head against the walls of his cell" (SPN, p. xcii).

5. The terminology has later been taken up and modified by the French philosopher Louis Althusser, who uses the terms "Repressive State Apparatus" (for "political" society) and "Ideological State Apparatuses" (for the hegemonic apparatuses of civil society); cf. Althusser, 2001, pp. 95–106.

6. Cf. Sassoon, 1980, pp. 130–132.

7. Cf. Gramsci, 1995a (FSPN), p. 413; Q 4, §15; Q 10.II, §41.I. Referring to Marx's description of "ideological forms," in which people become conscious of the conflict (between productive forces and relations of production) and "fight it out" (MECW 29, pp. 263), Gramsci emphasizes that this statement must be developed "with the entire ensemble of the philosophical doctrine of the meaning of the superstructures" (Q 11, §64). "Ideological forms" are therefore not only forms of thought, but also institutional forms (religion, politics, the judicial system, the media, etc.).

8. Cf. Rehmann, 2008, pp. 12 et seq., 82–104, 153 et seq.

9. Gramsci then goes on to analyze the relations of military forces (SPN, p. 183).

10. Gramsci had challenged this "northern" corporatism already in The Southern Question: "The proletariat, in order to be able to govern as a class, has to shed every residue of corporatism, every syndicalist prejudice or incrustation." This means to overcome not only distinctions between different trades, but also prejudices against the southern peasants and "some semi-proletarian categories within the cities" (1995b, p. 27).

11. Contrary to a widespread interpretation, "philosophy of praxis" is more than a code word for "Marxism," which is caused by the fascist censorship in prison: the term "was deliberately chosen in order to specify a particular tendency within Marx's legacy, which Gramsci's intervention proposed to strengthen, elaborate, and, ultimately, make hegemonic within the organized working class movement" (Thomas, 2009, p. 106). The term referred back to Marx's emphasis on "sensuous human activity," "subjective praxis," in the first "Thesis on Feuerbach" (MECW 5, p. 3) and opposed the prevailing tendencies of "objectivism" and reductionism at the time. In fact, Gramsci starts his writing in prison by translating the "Theses on Feuerbach" into Italian (Q, pp. 2355–2357).

12. See also Gramsci's analysis of the "intellectual bloc" of the South that mediates and holds together the "agrarian bloc," preventing its "cracks . . . from becoming too dangerous and causing a landslide," in The Southern Question (1995b, pp. 36–38, 42, 47).

13. "Predestination" refers to the Calvinist doctrine according to which God has preordained one part of humanity to eternal salvation, the other to eternal damnation.

14. See, e.g., Said, 1983, pp. 168–172; Holub, 1992, pp. 14, 20–21, 171–172, 180–182, 199–200; Laclau and Mouffe, 2001, pp. 65–71, 134–145.

15. O. Wright introduced the concept of "class formation" to bridge the gap between structural and processual definitions of class: "'Class formation' is thus a descriptive category which encompasses a wide range of potential variations. For any given class or group of class locations one can speak of 'strong' or 'weak' class formations; unitary or fragmented class formations; revolutionary, counterrevolutionary or reformist class formations" (1997, p. 380).

REFERENCES

Althusser, L. (2001). Ideology and ideological state apparatuses: Notes towards an investigation (1971). In *Lenin and philosophy and other essays*. London: Monthly Review Press.

Davis, M. (2006). *Planet of slums*. London & New York: Verso.

Fiori, G. (1990). *Antonio Gramsci: Life of a revolutionary*. London & New York: Verso.

Gramsci A. (1971). *Selections from the prison notebooks of Antonio Gramsci* (SPN) (Q. Hoare & G. N. Smith, Eds. & Trans.). New York: International.

Gramsci, A. (1975). *Quaderni del carcere. Four volumes, critical edition of the Gramsci Institute* (Q) (V. Gerratana, Ed.). Torino: Gramsci Institute.

Gramsci, A. (1995a). *Further selections from the prison notebooks* (FSPN) (D. Boothman, Ed. & Trans.). London: Lawrence & Wishart.

Gramsci, A. (1995b). *The southern question* (Pasquale Verdicchio, Trans.). West Lafayette, IN: Bordighera.

Gramsci, A. (2000). *The Antonio Gramsci reader: Selected writings, 1916–1935* (AGR) (D. Forgacs, Ed.). New York: New York University Press.

Holub, R. (1992). *Antonio Gramsci: Beyond Marxism and postmodernism*. London & New York: Routledge.

Laclau, E., & C. Mouffe (2001). *Hegemony and socialist strategy: Towards a radical democratic politics*. London & New York: Verso.

Luxemburg, R. (1970). *Gesammelte Werke* (Vol. I/1) (Institute for Marxism-Leninism at the Central Comittee of the Sozialistische Einheitspartei Deutschlands [SED], Ed.). Berlin/DDR: Dietz Verlag.

Marx, K., & F. Engels (1975–2005). *Collected works* (MECW). London: Lawrence & Wishart.

Rehmann, J. (2008). *Einführung in die Ideologietheorie*. Hamburg: Argument-Verlag.

Said, E. W. (1983). *The world, the text, and the critic*. Cambridge, MA: Harvard University Press.

Sassoon, A. S. (1980). *Gramsci's politics*. London: Croom Helm.

Thomas, P. (2009). *The Gramscian moment: Philosophy, hegemony, and Marxism.* Leiden & Boston: Brill.

Wright, E. O. (1997). *Class counts: Comparative studies in class analysis.* Cambridge, UK: Cambridge University Press.

CHAPTER 8 SUPPLEMENT

Gramsci, Martin Luther King, Jr., and the Watts Uprising: A Conversation with Willie Baptist

John Wessel-McCoy

What counts as scholarship and who gets to claim the title *scholar*? The concepts Gramsci contributed (hegemony, common sense, and organic intellectual, among others) have made their mark, especially among academics who identify as progressive. Gramsci was a formidable intellectual whose theoretical concepts were the product of rigorous intellectual labor. Yet he did not produce his ideas as a traditional academic scholar.

Gramsci emerged as a leader in the midst of the worker-led factory takeovers in Turin in 1918. He produced his famous notebooks as a political prisoner under the Fascists. Gramsci's insights were those of a leader in a social movement. As a youth in Sardinia, he was attracted to the position of Sardinian nationalists (who used the slogan "Throw the mainlanders into the sea!") (Fiori, 1990). After moving to Turin in the industrial north of Italy, Gramsci wrestled with how to build a movement that linked the peasants of the south to the industrial workers of the north. By the time he was arrested by the Fascists, Gramsci was an Italian leader connected to an international movement of the proletariat. As Gramsci's intellectual development deepened, his concept of the world in which he lived expanded—a world that he fought to improve. From narrow nationalism to a class conception that transcended borders, Gramsci exemplified the type of leadership he wrote about in his notebooks.

When Willie Baptist says he is still a student of Watts, it reminds me of where Gramsci's political development started and where it ended. It is striking when one considers Willie's journey from his experience coming out of Watts to the present day—from the days when he identified with black nationalism and "black power" to his ultimate commitment to building a broad social movement to end poverty led by poor people united across all lines, including color, that keep the poor pitted against one another. Just as with Gramsci, Willie's concept of who he's fighting for has expanded. Ultimately, as both Willie and Gramsci's political conceptions show, a social movement is for all of society.

Willie first came in contact with Gramsci's concepts during what he describes as a time of quiescence—when the movements of the 1960s gave way to the reaction of the 1970s and 1980s. Herein lies another fundamental commonality between Willie and Gramsci, which in essence reflects a movement from the particular to the universal. Just as Gramsci wrote the notebooks as a way to make sense of why the movement to which he had committed himself did not develop the hegemonic capacity to take power, Willie was struggling to understand what had happened in light of the defeat of the Watts uprising and the political formations that followed. This interview offers some of Willie's reflections on what Gramsci has to say to leaders building social movements today.[1] Gramsci's intellectual labor was dedicated to the service of movement-building long after he was gone. In that vein, this interview is intended for future leaders and future social movements.

John Wessel-McCoy (JW): You've studied the *Notebooks* and wrestled with Gramsci's concepts. In essence, what is Gramsci struggling to understand?

Willie Baptist (WB): Gramsci was dealing with fundamental relationships in society. He was trying to consider, "How do you take power?" This is what is often lost in discussions about Gramsci—the movement of the dispossessed was toward a common ownership of the means of production, and they needed power to accomplish that. That is what he was fighting for. He was asking certain questions. How are you going to take on the tremendous accumulation of wealth and power represented by a certain section of the population, which had tremendous influence on the rest of the population through their tremendous wealth? How do you challenge their ideological hegemony and then their power, and establish something else in its place? How do you concentrate a critical mass that would be powerful enough to take power? These are the questions Gramsci is dealing with when he develops concepts like hegemony and common sense. Some academics have taken up these Gramscian concepts but devoid of that content. When we are organizing to end poverty, we therefore have to investigate what groupings have an economic need and interest in maintaining poverty and what groupings don't. Who are they objectively, even though they might not know it?

JW: How have your experiences in political struggle shaped your understanding of some of Gramsci's concepts like organic intellectual, hegemony, or common sense?

WB: Well, the thing that keeps resounding in my thinking is the need, in any resistance against the status quo, to have in its leadership an intellectual core of connected, committed, clear, and competent leaders. If you don't have that, it is very difficult to deal with the complexities of the time. And if your assessment of the problem is not reflective of the reality, you're going to be vulnerable to manipulation by a ruling class—or a dominant social group—that has access to information and analysis and thinking that can reduce you to a pawn in their power game.

Again, I was involved in this resistance coming out of the 60s, and not knowing all these other forces and not having the kind of leadership development or any kind of intellectual force among us to anticipate these things reduced us to pawns. And I think the notion of Gramsci's *organic intellectual* represents a need for movements of the dispossessed to have leaders who can understand the economic and political forces arrayed against them and who can develop a level of sophistication that supports a certain independence from the influence of these powerful forces.

JW: You speak of the importance of having an analysis that is reflective of reality. And that analysis would not just be a matter of people being "correct" in terms of their assessment, but it would somehow translate into action. For example, the Watts rebellion, even if it did a lot to get people like you engaged politically, it also ended up becoming a tool used by the ruling class against poor people and the society at large. So how would the presence of organic intellectuals have made a difference there?

WB: Well, out of that resistance there emerged many formations. And they were heavily influenced by the slogans of black power or black resistance, which precluded relationships with other social groupings that had the same economic interest as the dispossessed strata of blacks. This is especially true in terms of the dispossessed mass of poor whites who were turned against this notion of a black criminal "underclass." I think if you had an intellectual force that was developed and prepared to take up the whole struggle in such a way, they would have been able to lead a powerful movement.

For example, during the Watts rebellion, there were white workers from the longshoremen in the San Pedro area, which is the port just south of South Central L.A., who went door to door in their community. They collected food, clothes, all kinds of stuff, and put it in the back of a truck to deliver it to the black resisters in Watts. They came there specifically to do that. Now if there was an intellectual force that was at play, they would have utilized that moment and strengthened those relationships. But as it is, only a few people know this part of the story.

At the same time, in Southgate, which borders Watts, you had the response of some of the mothers—white mothers—who collected food and came to the place where the police had set up barricades. The LAPD had cordoned off Watts. And these white working-class women came there with the idea of giving food because with the uprising the supermarkets were burned out. The people had no food, so a section of the white and Latino populations that bordered the area showed concern. Some of them even participated in the rebellion.

I'm looking back at the Watts uprising and the South Central uprising in 1992, and I'm trying to learn those lessons and then trying to share them in terms of developing other people—other intellectuals—having a sense of what we're dealing with and what lessons from history we need to learn.

JW: Some of the parallels are interesting. Starting in 1929, Gramsci was writing in prison after the revolutionary moment had passed—the fascists had triumphed. You, like so many people who had been active in the 60s, were in this similar position of feeling like there was something happening in the 60s that's not happening in the 70s and 80s. The moment had passed. Both Gramsci and you were asking similar questions: What happened? What failed to happen?

WB: For me, the Watts uprising and the general ghetto uprisings that followed showed that unless you can have a sophisticated intellectual development independent of the influences that supported and defended the status quo, you're not going to be able to withstand the efforts of the powers-that-be to manipulate the oppressed classes. And unless the oppressed classes can have this intellectual formation at its leadership, there's no way that they're going to succeed. So over and over again, the defeats that I've been a part of—the ghetto uprisings of the 60s as well as the Homeless Union movement—all served to emphasize the need for the development of organic intellectuals, who can understand the complex relationships of economic and political forces that you are going to have to contend with. On a strategic and tactical level, how you maneuver, how you influence, and how you keep from being manipulated, take a tremendous amount of mental labor and development that was missing in these struggles.

I think Gramsci saw that his responsibility was to sum up the lessons from his experience for what he saw as the emerging, future revolutionaries in Italy. And he was largely trying to get future movements to not repeat history. That's my responsibility. I've been through these experiences. Why should you have to bump your head against the same wall that I bumped my head against? Gramsci engaged in a fairly deep and wide analysis as best he could under the circumstances in which he was writing. He was thinking about future leaders and future social movements.

When I encounter the progressive "public intellectuals" of today, I want to ask, "Where is the formation you are helping to build?" "Where is the organization that you're developing?" If indeed there needs to be some appreciation of what we're dealing with, where's the formation of leaders that's at least comparable to what we're up against? How are we contributing to that process? Every leader should be measured by that. Are we forming organic intellectuals who think through the problems of the oppressed and impoverished classes? In order to outmaneuver the ruling classes, you have got to have an intellectual development that is *at least* comparable to their organic intellectuals. The oppressed classes—the dispossessed—have to have their organic intellectuals. They've got to have their "generals." Can you imagine an army going into battle without its generals or its officer corps? Well, that's what we have. We have a worldwide but disjointed "army" of the dispossessed that has no officer corps! It has no general staff.

And you know Gramsci makes a very important statement in regard to this. He said,

> One speaks of generals without an army, but in reality it is easier to form an army than to form generals. So much is this true that an already existing army is destroyed if it loses its generals, while the existence of a united group of generals who agree among themselves and have common aims soon creates an army even where none exists. (SPN, pp. 152–153)

So in this discussion of creating a core of organic intellectuals, the "organic" suggests the content. The leadership is organic in the sense of being connected to the dispossessed class. It's not just some isolated group of people who are smart or something. They are carrying out the interest of a whole section of society whose interest works itself out in different stages in different ways.

Martin Luther King, Jr. began to appreciate this when he prepared for the Poor People's Campaign. He began to tie his allegiance and his commitment to the most dispossessed. His shifting allegiance came out of an appreciation of where all the major contradictions of society, including the contradiction of foreign policy in the Vietnam War and the contradiction of race relationships combine in the position of the most dispossessed. The problem that he posed to the powers-that-be was that he threatened to link this tremendous force that was coming out of poor communities with the antiwar movement and with the tremendous apparatus developed out of the civil rights movement. That was the problem that the ruling classes had to solve, and that's why they mobilized their organic intellectuals inside the civil rights movements to say to King, "Hey, you should stick to civil rights! And you shouldn't oppose President Johnson." What they were really saying is that he should continue along the strategic line that he had already maintained, which was in concert with a larger strategic position. The wanted him to maintain his position as an "organic intellectual" of those powerful hegemonic forces.

The powers-that-be make sure they get the best thinkers to develop their ideology. In the United States, you've got elite Ivy League colleges and think tanks that produce their strategists and ideologists. And their strategies and ideologies come as a result of tremendous mental labor, study, and schooling. Gramsci understood this fact. He wrote about the intellectual development of intellectuals. He recognized that everybody has the capacity to be a philosopher or an intellectual. The function of a leader is the function of an intellectual. That means they've undergone a certain study and training. And to get beneath the surface of effects and events, in order to understand analytically the underlying causes, one must apply a certain amount of mental labor. This understanding doesn't come out of the plants or factories by itself. It doesn't come out of spontaneous rebellion alone.

I mean, the only thing you learn about police brutality, without studying it, is that that club is hard and it hurts. But you don't automatically understand the police system or the political system that gives rise to it, or the economic system that necessitates it, unless you study it. And that intellectual development is something that has to be organized around. And that was precluded for all kinds of reasons in terms of Martin Luther King, Jr.'s formation as an intellectual, especially the shift in his development toward the dispossessed.

JW: Could you delve further into King's development toward the Poor People's Campaign applying some of the concepts Gramsci laid out?

WB: Well, I think a good way to look at it is to see the Poor People's Campaign—the conceptualization of it—coming out of the struggle of the civil rights movement. What happened? What were the points of continuity and what were the points of departure? People like Martin Luther King, Jr., in terms of their intellectual formation, were heavily influenced by the major values and strategic concepts that were dominating the times. You've got to study the dissolution of the Communist Party in the South and the weakening and dissolution of the Negro Labor Councils that followed. Another important factor to look at is the weakening of the position of the black veterans coming out of the Second World War—a position that was quite radical. At the same time, there was the development of a new leadership coming out of the Negro colleges including many black preachers and other civil rights leaders.

Jim Crow labor policy in the South was blocking the full industrial exploitation of southern labor. This was the period when the mechanical cotton picker was releasing masses of workers into the labor market—both black and white. Jim Crow was an obstruction to potential profits. There was a point when Wall Street's interests *coincided* with the African American masses in getting rid of Jim Crow. And I think that's important because if you're going to look at intellectual formation and organic intellectualism, what's crucial in that formation is the content of it. What is its direction? Not just to say, "We're smart," but what are the goals? And much of the intellectual and ideological development that came to form the SCLC (Southern Christian Leadership Conference) was not in contradiction to the major powers-that-be.

JW: How do you understand the fallout from King's "Beyond Vietnam" speech—the way people talked about King afterward, saying he had set back "his cause"? But King said, "Injustice anywhere is a threat to justice everywhere."[2]

WB: This is where he's departing from the position of the powers-that-be. He was breaking from a strategy that relied on the upper classes to lead the fight for civil rights. Ultimately, he began to see the effect of this strategy was such that only the upper classes of the blacks were integrated into the capitalist system while the rest of the people still suffered from poverty. And he also saw economic transformations affecting not just certain sections of blacks but *also* whites. He saw the mechanization of coal mining displacing tremendous sections of workers out of Appalachia. He began to talk about the "Power for Poor People" as opposed to "black power."

JW: He argued against black power advocates that it would be better to say "Power for Poor People."[3]

WB: Well, what he was essentially arguing about with black power advocates was that the issue of class and economic exploitation was basic to the problem that the masses of blacks were facing, and that to project a position that isolated blacks from the rest of the folks who were having the same experiences is to weaken any real effort to get power. Many black power advocates were very militant in their comments, but the question is, "Are you going to move a critical mass that's going to undercut and weaken the position of the powers-that-be?" Ultimately, Martin Luther King, Jr. represented a threat; those advocating for black power did not.

JW: I was thinking we could talk about the Poverty Initiative and the Poverty Scholars Program parallel to what Gramsci was trying to figure out.

WB: The Poverty Scholars Program and the Poverty Initiative have the same mission, which is to end poverty by building a massive movement led by the needs and the demands of the poor. And for such a movement to succeed, we must have a leadership that understands these needs and demands—a leadership from the ranks of the poor and from other strata. This leadership is comprised of those who see that, in order to change society, you've got to embrace the section of society whose social position compels them ultimately to change all of society.

In our mission statement, we talk about community leaders and religious leaders, but we also talk about the leadership of the poor. And sometimes people reduce the concept of leadership of the poor down to *individual* leaders of the poor—as if to say, "Let's just find a poor person and put him out front." That is not what history would suggest is the full meaning. Gramsci's notion of hegemony involves a kind of leadership of a social group and the ideological positions that support that group's interests. And when we talk about the "leadership of the poor," it corresponds with Gramsci's effort to resolve this problem of hegemony. The other problem of leadership is the training and development of intellectuals—of religious and community leaders—as stated in the mission. These are two different but related concepts. One concept provides the content for the other.

When we look closely at the efforts of Martin Luther King, Jr. toward the end of his life, these two problems of hegemony and leadership development as organic intellectual development were both preempted. After King's murder, it immediately became clear that there was no corps of connected, clear, committed, and competent leadership to move forward the position King had taken. The struggle for hegemony was precluded because, in the 60s, the United States economy dominated the world economy, and the American people were enjoying the highest standard of living in the world. The mass of the population—the so-called middle class—was moving in a direction toward the rulers, the richest elements. And even though you had a certain level of automation and certain oppression that was affecting the poor across color lines, in terms of a greater struggle, King's ability to influence the middle section was made more difficult.

I think there was a possibility of influencing the middle section with regard to its attitude toward policies in Vietnam, and this presented a threat to the ruling class, but in that period, the middle strata of American society were like the peasantry in Italy during Gramsci's time in the sense that it was a large grouping of people who had to be won over to the interests of the dispossessed. If any movement from the bottom was going to take power, they needed a big enough critical mass. Our problem today is this big middle. This big middle, for a good period, was moving in its ideology and also in terms of its income toward the position of the upper class. Today, society is moving in the opposite direction. And so, unlike the 60s, the efforts to unite the poor today have more of a capability of winning—establishing a social hegemony, in other words—over the mass of the American people, as this mass is being dislocated economically and socially by the turn of economic events.

The development of the Poverty Scholars Program is an effort to develop leaders. We're starting with those who have had some experience among the ranks of the poor, or working in organizations that are trying to unite the poor around their struggles. We're starting with these leaders, but leadership development doesn't stop there. We're talking about everyone who sees the need to change society from whatever walk of life. The point is to have an expanding corps of leaders who have this kind of social hegemony in mind—that is the leadership of the poor.

JW: What is the significance of working out of a Christian seminary?

WB: For me, it comes from experience of working in the homeless movement and in the movements of the dispossessed for the past 40 years. It comes from my study of American history. And, I think, Gramsci's concept of "common sense" gets at this insight. So much of what influences how people understand things comes from values that have national-historical origins, and the American people are very religious—Judeo-Christian, largely. What you find is that religion is a common language of the most dispossessed, regardless of their color. For a lot of the so-called progressives, their intellectualism hasn't informed them of this reality. What good is it to try to get across certain concepts if you're speaking German to someone who only speaks Japanese? This bottom stratum that has very little stake in the status quo speaks not in terms of progressivism, not even in terms of trade unionism. Their language is often one of religion. And if we're going to develop an organic connection to this segment of the population so as to influence the greater population, we've got to talk the same language. And what I've learned through my experiences is that that language is heavily influenced by—or described in—religious terms. Martin Luther King, Jr. understood this.

From elementary school onward we are taught to pledge allegiance to the flag. This raises these concepts of freedom that are connected to notions of rights that are described very clearly in the founding creed of the nation: "We hold these truths to be self-evident . . . [that] everyone is created equal . . . and is endowed with certain and unalienable rights." The Creator gives them these God-given rights "to life, liberty, and the pursuit of happiness." You have in this fundamental document, at once, the concept of religion and the concept of rights, and those are the things that influence how people see things. If you're going to change people's thinking, you've got to understand those kinds of influences.

In one of his last sermons, in the National Cathedral in March 1968, King stated: "We are coming to demand that the government address itself to the problem of poverty. We read one day, 'We hold these truths to be self-evident, that all men are created equal, that they are endowed by their Creator with certain inalienable Rights, that among these are Life, Liberty, and the pursuit of Happiness.' But if a man doesn't have a job or an income, he has neither life nor liberty nor the possibility for the pursuit of happiness. He merely exists" (King, 1998).

And in his last speech, King, referring to the First Amendment in light of the injunctions in Memphis, stated, "All we say to America is, 'Be true to what you said on paper.'"

Because of the fact that we are not trying to end poverty on Mars but here in the United States, it's incumbent upon us to grasp profoundly those factors that influence the value formation of the people we're working with.

NOTES

1. A longer version of this text was submitted February 28, 2009, as part of the course requirements for Reading Gramsci, taught by Dr. Kate Crehan at the Graduate Center, City University of New York.

2. Originally attributed to him in his Letter from a Birmingham Jail, but used in this rhetoric in many other places.

3. King lays out much of this argument in *Where Do We Go from Here? Chaos or Community* (1968, p 50).

REFERENCES

Fiori, G. (1990). *Antonio Gramsci: Life of a revolutionary*. London & New York: Verso.

Gramsci, A. (1971). *Selections from the Prison Notebooks of Antonio Gramsci* (SPN) (Q. Hoare & G. N. Smith, Eds. & Trans.). New York: International .

King, M. (1968). *Where do we go from here: Chaos or community?* Boston: Beacon Press.

King, M. (1998). Remaining awake through a great revolution. In C. Carson & P. Holloran (Eds.), *A knock at midnight: Inspiration from the great sermons of Reverend Martin Luther King, Jr.* New York: Warner Books.

Marx, K. (1991) *Capital, volume III*. London: Penguin.

CHAPTER 9

Interview with Willie Baptist (V):
Evaluating Today's Struggles—
Stories from the Movement to End Poverty

Jan Rehmann (JR): For 10 years of your life you served as the education director of the Kensington Welfare Rights Union (KWRU). Our class has had the opportunity to read sections of David Zucchino's bestseller, *Myth of the Welfare Queen*, about the devastating social situation in Kensington, the poorest neighborhood in Pennsylvania, and about some of the courageous actions you folks organized, including the tent city in Kensington, that moved then to the historic Square Mile at the Liberty Bell for a few days, before being evicted (Fig. 9.1). Can you tell us about your experiences?

Figure 9.1. Homeless Families Build a Tent City in Front of the Liberty Bell

[When the tent was set up, Dennis Reidenbach, the park's chief ranger, approached Cheri Honkala, the "mayor" of the tent city.] Reidenbach said it appeared to him, from the tent that was going up, that the group intended to do more than exercise its free speech rights. It looked to him as if they were planning to camp out on the mall. "There's a prohibition against camping," he told Cheri. "They're not camping," Cheri said. "They're going to be living here. They don't have any place else to go." "Well, they can't live here, either," Reichenbach said. "There's a prohibition against that, too. If you want to exercise your First Amendment rights, we'll provide the proper location." "What's wrong with right here?" Cheri asked. "What better place to exercise your First Amendment rights than the Liberty Bell, the symbol of America?"

Source: David Zucchino, *Myth of the Welfare Queen* (New York: Scribner, 1997), p. 95.

Willie Baptist (WB): Kensington, in addition to being the poorest community in the entire state of Pennsylvania, is also multiracial—about one-third poor whites, one-third poor Latinos, and one-third poor blacks. In Kensington, poverty didn't discriminate. And I came to find out through further organizing that there are these proliferations of Kensingtons throughout the country. This was the first time I organized on a sustained level with poor whites that were just as committed and just as willing to fight as I was. All of us who led that struggle had gone to jail and committed civil disobedience. We had to confront all kinds of situations, like the time I was arrested by three groupings of police and they all put guns at my head. We were fighting for our kids and for our families, and we were determined to bring attention to the issue of poverty and homelessness.

The demographics of Kensington are such that east Kensington was mostly poor white, middle Kensington was mostly poor Latino, west Kensington was mostly poor blacks, and then there were pockets where there were mixtures of all of these people. Since KWRU was organizing everybody who was homeless and everybody who was poor, we didn't discriminate, and the composition of our membership and leadership reflected that. In the early period we entered this saga where we couldn't get an office because if we set it up in the black community, the white members wouldn't come and if we set it up in the white community, the black members wouldn't come. We tried several different locations for our office, but ended up in the Puerto Rican community, where all members would come.

The racial fears that beset the Kensington community found organized expression in the homeowners and real estate organizations, especially in the northeastern part of the neighborhood. When we'd set up the KWRU office in areas monitored by these hate groups—organized in the form of real estate associations—our multiracial makeup would attract attention and they would harass us. At one point, we set up our headquarters in the house of one of our members and a number of death threats were delivered to our office and to our executive director. We didn't learn who was actually orchestrating these death threats—that they were actually going to bomb our offices—until we recruited Cathy and Anthony. They were part of the Juniata Association, one of these real estate groups, and they themselves had become homeless. The Juniata Association was organized, and they used the race card—keeping blacks out—to try to maintain the property values in the community. It was not organized to deal with its members having a housing crisis or becoming homeless. So when you become homeless, who are you going to call? You call KWRU. So Cathy and Anthony, a white couple, came to KWRU, joined our organization, and began to tell us all the machinations and organizing of the Juniata Association. It turned out Cathy and Anthony themselves were part of the committee that had called KWRU with bombing and death threats. In KWRU, over time, they began to develop a relationship with everyone regardless of color in the fight against homelessness, and we became very close friends. Again, the lesson here is that this interrelationship of race and class defined our lives at that period, and we were able to overcome racial divisions through struggling around common class concerns of homelessness and poverty.

JR: Can you tell us about the Kensington 6 struggle?

WB: The first big action that we got involved in—Kensington 6—really put KWRU on the map. The case consisted of five mothers and my 17-year-old daughter, Alexis, who decided to do civil disobedience and as a result went to jail over this issue of a closed, abandoned welfare office right in the middle of the community. Upon discussion with other parents, they were particularly concerned that on the way to school their kids would have to pass by this abandoned building that had become a center for drug activity, gunrunning, and prostitution. They didn't want their kids to have to be exposed to that stuff. So the KWRU launched a campaign to turn the welfare office into a community center. At that time we didn't know the building was privately owned, because it had been a welfare office. With our housing-takeover campaigns we had a policy of only moving into publicly owned vacant buildings. But with deindustrialization and the decline of the population there were huge tracts of land in Kensington and the downtown area that were purchased by these speculator millionaires, including this particular building.

We took over the building, with the intention of turning it into a community center, and six of the leaders, all women, black and white, were arrested. Before they were arrested, the police were trying to convince the leaders to come out of the building and not get arrested so that they could avoid a media spectacle. But the women insisted on being there. Every city has a civil affairs–like group attached to the police department, like a local FBI, and they deal with political stuff, like protests, instead of criminal cases. The civil affairs approach was to come in and try to separate the whites from the blacks in our leadership, to pit them against each other as a way of getting them to come out. That was a real lesson for me in terms of how the color factor is manipulated. But having been through these struggles together, having been to jail together, our people were so committed to one another that they were prepared to stick and stay. The Kensington 6 even refused to walk to the police truck; the police had to carry them out. And we had one woman who had a lot of weight on her and she said, "They're going to have to carry me all the way to the place. I'm not going to walk." You could see the beads of sweat on those cops' foreheads when they carried her.

My daughter, Alexis, wasn't taken to jail, because she was a minor, but she was made to report to a youth study program and was told that she had to write a letter of apology to the multimillionaire that owned the vacant building. That's when we found out the building wasn't publicly owned. Her letter said this is not an apology, this is an appeal; this is an appeal to the owner and others to come to the assistance of the mothers and children of Kensington to end poverty and other life-threatening atrocities in their community.

JR: Why was this struggle a success?

WB: We were able to go to court and insisted on a judge and jury trial. The local justice department had trumped up the charges on these leaders, so they were facing upward of 10 years in prison for criminal trespassing on private property. It so happened that this particular speculator, Rappaport, was in collision with the other city fathers—the Greater Philadelphia First Corporation—a consortium of some of the largest corporations who were trying to renovate the downtown area. Rappaport was holding out, speculating, and trying to get the highest bid, which interrupted their renovation plans. We discovered this contradiction and used it as leverage. The Greater Philadelphia First Corporation chose to use our struggle as a way to give Rappaport a black eye and put public pressure on him. Because we were willing to go through a long jury trial with a long process of discussion and debate, we were covered on TV and the front page of the main local paper for a whole week. That put us on the map. We were local heroes after we won that battle. And we won with the power of our story. That's the thing I learned. All we wanted was for our kids not to have to deal with drugs and guns in our community. That building was sitting there not being used and we wanted a safe place for our kids. That's what we were doing. As a result of that story we had religious leaders come up and testify on our behalf. We had trade union leaders come in and testify on our behalf. Our story was so compelling that all 15 counts for all five mothers were dismissed. Afterward even members of the jury came to us and inquired about membership in the KWRU; they were trying to see how they could join. That's how moving our stories were.

JR: One could perhaps connect this to the debate we had in class about the possibilities or impossibilities for influencing media images. This seems to be an example of when under certain conditions, for example, when there's a split among the elites, a situation can be taken advantage of and a powerful story can be told. There was an opportunity for this story to be told of how organized poor people are not just victims—not just the preordained stereotypes. There was something that we could turn around.

WB: You've got to remember that we built on the successes and failures of the Homeless Union movement. We had a number of people, like myself, who had come out of the movement into the Kensington Welfare Rights Union, and we brought those experiences with us. We really emphasized the need for leadership development and education. We developed this principle of "teach as we fight, learn as we lead, talk as we walk, educate as we activate." That became a part of our process. As a result, we could look at the situation we faced and carry out a joint analysis of the holes and weak points of the people who were against us, enabling us to get the right issues out there and press for concessions.

JR: In 1998, the KWRU helped to found the Poor People's Economic Human Rights Campaign (PPEHRC) that evolved into a network of over a hundred grassroots organizations, community groups, and nonprofit organizations "committed to uniting the poor across color lines as the leadership base for a broad movement to abolish poverty." Could you tell us something about the importance of such a nationwide network?

WB: Clearly the poverty that we're dealing with today is different from the poverty that this country has been used to, and I think it's because of a number of objective factors. You have this real technological revolution and the consequence has been deindustrialization and the structural loss of jobs. Homelessness and poverty have become much more permanent and engulf increasing segments of the population, including the so-called middle class. So what we found when we were organizing the PPEHRC in a nationwide Freedom Bus Tour were, for example, farmers who were being dislocated in Kansas that had lived there for generations. They had owned the land and were losing it and going into crisis. We found a lot of Kensington-type communities across the country. We ran into people who had education, who had gotten degrees, but who were still experiencing poverty.

We were asked to do a training in Ohio and met a woman who had a support group made up of people who had PhDs, and the number one point on their agenda was how to expunge PhD from their portfolio so they could get a job. It became plain to me that the problems of poverty and homelessness are structural, and that people are not poor because they're stupid. They're poor because of specific economic structures that are based upon exploitation and social injustice. They're getting laid off because companies trying to ensure profits and dividends cut production costs. And with high technology they're able to deploy computers and robots to do the work that human beings used to do. The ATM—automatic teller machine—replaces human bank tellers. If you go to an auto plant today, there are complete processes of robotics in the assemblage of a car. Once there were herds of people. The main Dodge plant in the 1950s had upward of 100,000 workers that assembled cars. Today they have less than 10,000 workers that produce the same number of cars. That ripples to the rubber industry, the glass industry, et cetera, that feed into the auto industry. For that auto company to make a profit, all those feeder companies have to compete with other companies, and that means cutting production costs. And to cut production costs today means to employ the highest technology possible and to send the most labor-intensive processes over to China or to some other low-wage area. As a result, there is this huge dislocation of workers that makes up this population of the poor. The PPEHRC was gathering these kinds of forces. We had a number of successes, again drawing from the mistakes made and experiences gained through the prior work with the Homeless Union.

JR: You often invoke the development of "leadership" of the poor as the decisive factor. But how do you prepare such a leadership for the hegemonic crises that will certainly arise in one way or another? Is there any point of coalescence in sight where the different forces and energies could come together in a powerful way?

WB: What I learned through my experiences and study is, for the mass of the poor to exert a leading political and moral influence on the greater mass of public opinion in the U.S., they must be united and organized as a social force across color lines. To attain that unity, leaders must be identified, trained, and united. Gramsci called this unity of leaders "organic intellectuals," the people who are emerging from their ranks as leaders, the people who tend to see further and feel deeper. If you can unite the leaders and get them on the same page, you can unite a mass of poor folks who in turn move a greater mass of people. That's what happened with our organizing amongst the poor. Part of that unity is an educational process. It is a process where you learn to reflect on your experiences and see how best to move. We were able to accomplish things that for us were unthinkable.

I'll give you an example. In the Kensington Welfare Rights Union, we had an ex-Klansman in one of our tent cities, the tent city I lived in when I was homeless. He was homeless and had no other place to go, so he had to come into our tent city. We didn't know he was an ex-Klansman; we found that out later on. I don't know if we would have given him a chance, but there he was—this guy named Paul—and he had these kids and wouldn't let the black mothers or the Hispanic mothers deal with the kids. But over time that stuff broke down. He began to trust us, because we were the only people there and we were his family. We marched to the center of the state, to Harrisburg, and he contracted an illness and it was the black mothers who were very concerned, who kept going back to see him. They had this relationship. It just taught me that you have to have a leadership development that really approaches the nuances and specificity and complexity of a situation. You can't just paint with a broad brush. Paul's racism was not the same as elitist upper-class racism. His racism was interwoven with the fact that he didn't have a job; he was homeless. The underlying social dynamics are just different. If you paint with a broad brush you lose the opportunity to deal with the nuances that make a difference when you're in a concrete struggle and you have responsibilities to move a situation and try to impact peoples' lives.

I think this is what Gramsci had in mind when he said that organic intellectuals must be attentive to the contradictions in people's common sense. Instead of preaching from the outside, they must listen to the differences and work on their common problems. We were trying to create a critical mass. Whoever could come around, if they were prepared to take up what we were preparing to do, we were going to unite with them. So this question of leadership development from below and developing a core of leaders suggests a kind of intellectualism that we've focused on.

Every now and then we'd have some young progressive students come around and say they wanted to do an antiracism workshop and that we should join them. Then we'd laugh and tell them that we deal with racism every day. They acted like we don't deal with it and that's why we're all united. Obviously, they expected that if we had the courage to openly talk about the race issue we'd fall apart. We told them the stories of what we had to go through and they had to learn lessons from us.

That to me is critical and I think it should inform our study, because the problems that we're confronted with—we can't deal with them merely academically. We need to use the intellectual tools of academia to get to deeper understanding of social structures and to come to generalizations to further guide our analyses and actions, but then we have to go back home to reality.

JR: I hear you emphasizing that struggles of poor people need to develop an intellectualism that is organically connected with the reflection of their life practices. But if you look at the general intellectual landscape, you can see an unproductive polarization between a whole range of social theories in academia that have become aloof and disengaged and, on the other hand, social movements disconnected from advanced social theory. Is this a fair assessment, and if so, how can we overcome that polarization?

WB: Yes, this is a problem with which we have to come to terms. We have a culture that tends toward a pragmatic philosophical outlook, an antitheory approach. American culture puts a premium on "let's just do it" and not on stepping back and reflecting on the problem and deciphering its solution.

A lot of this anti-intellectualism comes from the intellectuals themselves. In fact, pragmatism was formulated mainly by three philosophers: Charles S. Peirce, William James, and John Dewey. All graduated from elite U.S. universities. Dewey attended Johns Hopkins University. Pierce and James attended Harvard University.

Pragmatism says that a theory is true because it works and not that it works because it is true, that is, an accurate reflection of objective reality. What matters for this way of thinking is only whether a theory, thought, or thing works in terms of immediate results; never mind the fundamental causes and long-term consequences.

Although the pragmatists often claim to unite theory and action, they on the contrary exhibit a narrow practicalism along with a tremendous impatience toward the development and use of theoretical truths or knowledge. Therefore practice is left blind without theoretical insight and guidance; practice is reduced to expediency in means and ends, impromptu trials and errors. To guide action, knowledge must reflect the way things exist and develop in the real world. It is this latter aspect which the pragmatists repudiate. This is a formula that destroys scientific theory as a guide to practical action.

I find that the people out there in the trenches of the practical struggles are very hungry for education and knowledge, hungry to figure out solutions to the problems they face. What I often see in academia is a disengaged intellectualism—an intellectualism that supports all the assumptions of American pragmatic philosophy, which is, in fact, anti-intellectual and antitheoretical in that it separates theory from practical movements. Our college and university system is producing very smart people, but it's like in the movie I, Robot when Will Smith is talking to this professional and says, "You're the dumbest smart person I ever met in my life." We have a lot of dumb smart people, especially in regard to one of the most deadly issues of our time: poverty. There's an intellectualism that's separated from the suffering and struggles that's going on, so the kind of solutions that can come from a thought-out analysis of the problem are blocked. That's why our interdisciplinary study is so important. By combining critical social theory and grassroots experience, it can help to overcome this blockade.

JR: Can you give us an example of the importance of analysis in social action directly?

WB: I can give you an example from 1993 during the homeless organizing. We had formed a Homeless Union in Houston, Texas. So we had some notoriety because we had done the kinds of things that we needed to do in terms of organizing from service programs like job programs to protests that brought attention to the issues. We were known for moving families in the dead of winter into empty HUD (U.S. Department of Housing and Urban Development) housing that was deteriorating. It was civil disobedience, basically, bringing attention to the conditions and trying to get some kind of response in terms of negotiations. So from time to time, groups would ask us to come in to help them organize.

A group in Austin, Texas, asked us to come in to deal with a situation where there were no programs to deal with people who had been laid off and then were evicted because they couldn't pay their rent. Austin had massive numbers of homeless families living in the downtown area in vacant lots, in alleyways, and in structures no bigger than doghouses. We saw it when we walked the streets. They were trying to figure out what to do, so we exchanged experiences, sharing what we had done in other cities to bring attention to the issue and break our isolation. Then we divided up into research groups. Homeless people became researchers, looking at different areas of the city to find out the extent of the problem, the city's priorities, how that found expression, and so on.

One of the research groups went to the city council and got a hold of the budget. They looked at every item on the budget and found that there was nothing being allocated to assist people who were being evicted—no housing programs. What they did find, though, was a curious item on the budget—monies allocated for the purchase of Canadian geese to the tune of $800 per goose. The geese that you see downtown—the ones that the yuppies and buppies do lunch with and throw bread at—they pay for those bad boys. I didn't know that. That was one of the reports on Austin's budget priorities.

Based on that analysis and research we came up with an action plan. Every city has a historic district where someone important did something important—some famous personality came down and used the bathroom or something and they now have a historical marker. We identified this historic district in downtown Austin with these mansions where important people resided, and they have tours where you can come and visit these mansions.

So based on our research, we decided to move into one of the mansions. The idea was to bring attention to the issue, so we called the police and the media to tell them about it. The news vans and the police cars raced to the scene. With the news cameras rolling, the police jump out of the cars with their guns out, knocking on the door and yelling, "Come out, we know you're in there, open the door, come out of there." For a moment there was complete silence. Finally, the door slowly opened and you see a brother and sister holding one of the geese at knifepoint, saying, "If you come one step closer, this goose is cooked."

You know, they held the media attention for 2 weeks discussing what kind of priorities we have when we don't put human lives and human beings first. Out of that struggle they were able to build connections with the trade union leaders, religious leaders, and students. They were able to solve the problem of their isolation and expand their network based on their research, analysis, and leadership.

JR: In our interviews so far, we covered the different periods of your antipoverty work up to 2004, when you came to Union Theological Seminary (Union). How did you end up as Poverty Scholar in Residence at Union?

WB: First of all, I want to say that I don't think I would have come here to Union if not for the requirements and needs of the work that I was doing organizing a movement, organizing poor folks as a leading force of this movement to end homelessness and poverty. That's really why I came. I didn't come here because it's a nice thing or I wanted a degree. Although I believe all this is important; rigorous intellectual work is important, but I came here to build the movement. I saw in this institution, with its social justice tradition, a great potential to contribute to the building of this movement, making the movement a very effective and legitimate force to be reckoned with in this country. That's what motivated me.

For most of my 40 years of organizing in impoverished communities my division of labor was in the area of education. I always gravitated toward the educational task, dealing with pedagogy and how that connected to our organizing effort. My experiences as the KWRU's education director and then as co-coordinator of the University of the Poor made me appreciate the potential of an institution like Union Theological Seminary. I first became acquainted with Union when we had the founding convention of the New York Union of the Homeless in 1987, held next door at Riverside Church. Then in October 1999 the Poor People's Economic Human Rights Campaign, which consisted at that time of about 67 poor people's organizations, held its March of the Americas where we marched from Washington, D.C., to the United Nations headquarters in New York City, raising the question of poverty as a violation of human rights before the UN. On the way we met several people from Union who were important in later forming the Poverty Initiative, including President Joe Hough, when they hosted us on our way to the UN conference.

My coming to Union was connected to the founding of the Poverty Initiative—a comprehensive antipoverty project that came out of the work of several coinciding developments. One had to do with the work of Rev. Cathlin Baker, a Union alumna who became the special assistant to Union's president, Joe Hough, after we established the Poverty Initiative. She is now a pastor in Massachusetts. I met her in the Dignity Housing program in Philadelphia that came out of the Homeless Union's takeover struggle. Cathlin left there to attend Union and seek ordination, and she began to lay some of the groundwork—meeting people, talking about the homeless, and talking about our struggle. For a period she worked with Rev. James Forbes, minister at Riverside Church, in his Emancipation of Poverty project. Others who were very important in the creation of the Poverty Initiative included Paul Chapman, Professor Janet Walton, Rev. Amy Gopp, Jessica Chadwick, and Art Trotman.

Then another person who was central to the founding and development of the Poverty Initiative is Liz Theoharis. She was the assistant education director while I was the education director of the Kensington Welfare Rights Union. She came out of the University of Pennsylvania and was a member of the student group called Empty the Shelters and Fill the Homes, which grew alongside the Homeless Union. We eventually became cofounders and co-coordinators of the University of the Poor, which was at that time the educational arm of the Poor People's Economic Human Rights Campaign. Liz got the William Sloane Coffin Social Justice scholarship to attend Union because of her efforts and sought ordination in the Presbyterian Church. She is now the coordinator of the Poverty Initiative. She built on the work that Cathlin had initiated, and began to have meetings here to talk about the question of poverty with the faculty, administration, and student body. As a field education student at Union, Liz also drew from a survey of over 40 seminaries that found that even though there was some efforts dealing with poverty, it was spotty and spasmodic, not matching the severity of the problem. It was these findings, her discussion with students and faculty, and President Hough's commitment to address issues of the poor, that led to a conference in 2004, where leaders from poor organizations, like Picture the Homeless, came together to talk about the need for an effort to develop the religious leadership that could respond to the issues of poverty. From our experience we knew that if we were going to deal with poverty we had to include leaders from the ranks of the poor. Not the stereotypical notion of the poor, but the leaders who were beginning to wage a fight against their plight and have some insight into the situation. We came to the conclusion that we needed a comprehensive antipoverty program based on and including the input of the poor who are organizing themselves, and out of that the Poverty Initiative developed.

CHAPTER 10

Ideology Theory and Antipoverty Movements

Jan Rehmann

As you were preparing Louis Althusser's essay "Ideology and Ideological State Apparatuses" for today's meeting, you might have asked yourself how this highly sophisticated and apparently abstract text is related to the experiences of poverty. What the heck has this kind of French "ideology theory" to do with the plight and the fight of the poor? But as you remember, that's exactly what our class is all about. We have the ambitious project to bring together social theories and social justice movements, and if the relationship is not evident at first, we have to break down the theory in a way that we are able to make a meaningful connection. The challenge is to find a way to break it down without dumbing it down.

There is a second challenge. Relating a theory to relevant issues of antipoverty movements does not mean to simply "apply" it. This would imply that it is basically the theory that contains the deeper insight or higher intelligence, and it shares some of this treasure by being "applied" to social praxis. But as soon as one construes the relationship as in such a one-way street manner, one ends up in a dead end. A meaningful interaction requires that one listen to both sides. That's why I would like to confront Althusser's ideology theory with a completely different kind of text, namely with a section from Ashwin Desai's book about community struggles in postapartheid South Africa: We Are the Poors (2002). After going through the main concepts of Althusser's theory of ideology, in particular his connection between ideology and the subject and his concept of "interpellation," both of which became very influential in postmodernist theories, I would like us to discuss to what extent his approach is capable of grasping the new resistance identity Desai is describing. Are there elements in this account that contradict Althusser's theory of ideological subjection and oblige us to reject or to modify it? The goal is to learn how to look at a social theory from the perspectives of a specific social movement. It is an experiment. I am curious to see how it works out.

Let me start with some background information about what theories of ideology are about. The term was coined in the 1970s and 1980s in order to designate a renewal of critical research on ideology that emerged almost simultaneously in several Western countries. In France, it was mainly connected to the school of Althusser, in the United Kingdom it was primarily associated with Stuart Hall and his Centre for Contemporary Cultural Studies at Birmingham University, and in Germany with Wolfgang Fritz Haug and his research project called Projekt Ideologietheorie (PIT), in which I had the chance to participate when I was a student. Despite some differences, the common concern of these theories is to explain why and how masses of people go along with an economic and political order that neglects their basic needs. Why do they subject themselves actively and voluntarily to systems that exploit and oppress them? This is what Althusser means when he starts out his essay with the question of how the power relations in a class society are being ideologically "reproduced." It's not only about certain professional and technical skills and competences that need to be acquired for that reproduction, but also certain "rules of good behavior," "rules of respect" for the division of labor, and ultimately the rules of the order established by class domination (Althusser, 2001, p. 89).

I am convinced that an understanding of these mechanisms is of importance for any social justice movement that organizes to change society. As we have seen, Gramsci had already realized in the 1920s and 1930s that one cannot explain the inner stability of Western capitalism by mere economic factors or by force and repression alone. Much depends on the capacity of a class to educate "organic intellectuals" and to produce consent in and through the hegemonic apparatuses of civil society (see Chapter 8). In many regards, Althusser's theory of ideology can be regarded as a follow-up to Gramsci's theory of hegemony. Both theorists pointed out that ideologies cannot be reduced to mere expressions of "the economy." While Gramsci differentiated between "civil society" and "political society" (hegemony protected by the "armor of coercion"), Althusser distinguishes between the "repressive state apparatus" (RSA) and the "ideological state apparatuses" (ISA), which do their work of ideological submission "behind the 'shield' provided by the repressive State apparatus" (2001, p. 101).[1] Whereas the RSA is usually highly centralized and functions predominantly by repression, the ISAs are usually "multiple, distinct, 'relatively autonomous'" (pp. 97, 100). An "empirical list" includes the religious ISA; the educational ISA (public and private schools); and the familial, juridical, political, trade union, cultural, and information ISAs (p. 96). Althusser's insight that the resistance of subaltern classes can gain a hearing in the ISAs by using the contradictions that exist there or by conquering "combat positions" (p. 99) takes up elements from Gramsci's considerations on the "war of position" about hegemony in civil society.

There are in my view two main characteristics that are typical for Althusser's approach. First, taking up an argument of Gramsci and pushing it further, Althusser insists that ideologies are not to be considered as ideas or as phenomena of consciousness, but rather to be studied in their own materiality. By this, he means that they work through material rituals, practices, and actions that are embedded in material ideological apparatuses. In order to explain this, he goes back to the religious philosopher Blaise Pascal (1623–1662), who in his work Pensées described the emergence of faith as follows: "Kneel down, move your lips in prayer, and you will believe" (1954, p. 114).[2] In Althusser's reading, this explanation inverts the usual ideological perception. Whereas the believers imagine their faith to be coming from the "inside," they are actually moved by a complex ideological system: "Ideology existing in a material ideological apparatus, prescribing material practices governed by a material ritual" (2001, p. 115). The methodological consequences can be summarized as follows: If you want to understand how ideologies work, look at the material arrangements and practices that move the subject from the outside and thereby create ideological effects on the inside. Those of you who are familiar with Michel Foucault's Discipline and Punish might observe a similarity in as far as Foucault focuses on the asymmetric spatial arrangements in prisons and other disciplining institutions and their effects on the subjects (cf. 1977, pp. 195 et seq.).

The second characteristics of Althusser's theory of ideology is the use of psychoanalytical categories with the help of which he tries to understand the ideological as a mainly unconscious, imaginary relationship. Against the reduction of ideology to false consciousness or manipulation, he emphasizes that it imposes itself as images and structures that are unconscious. Ideological rituals and practices do not affect just the minds and ideas of people but are effective by producing specific subjectivities, by creating ideological "subjects" by what he calls "ideological interpellations." Ideology is therefore about how subjects are constituted: "All ideology has the function (which defines it) of 'constituting' concrete individuals as subjects" (2001, p. 116). You might have come across similar expressions in other texts. That the subject is not something "given," but rather "socially constructed" (as well as his/her gender, race, sex, culture and what not) has almost become a commonplace in the humanities. The approach can usually be traced back to Althusser, even if he is not explicitly mentioned in the social theory literature in question.

But what does that actually mean? I think a good way to get a handle on Althusser's concept of subject construction is to start out from the term "subject" itself, which has in French as well as in English a double meaning: It means on the one hand a subjected being that submits to a higher authority (and could in this sense be defined by a lack of "freedom") and on the other hand the seemingly opposite, namely a self-confident and responsible author of one's actions, endowed with a free subjectivity, an intentional center of initiatives. According to Althusser, it is exactly through the combination of these two seemingly opposite meanings that ideology works. You submit to higher authorities, high moral values, and while doing this, you consider yourself as a free, independent person, guided merely by your inner impulses, convictions and beliefs.

Subjection and "freedom," the act of submitting oneself to higher authorities while having the subjective feeling of "freedom"—that's the main topic of Althusser's ideology theory. But how does ideology succeed in combining the two? That is where Althusser introduces the concept of "interpellation." If you look up the French verb interpeller in a dictionary, you find "to call out to, to shout out to, to hail"; in regard to the police, it can also mean "to take in someone for questioning." Althusser gives the example of hailing someone on the street: "Hey, you there!" And usually, the hailed individuals will turn around and respond, "Yes, it is me," because they recognize that it was really them to whom the hail was addressed (2001, p. 118). This is, for Althusser, the basic mechanism of ideology: By turning round and responding, the individuals recognize themselves as the ones being called upon; they recognize and accept their identity in that interpellation, and that is what transforms them into subjects.

This might sound a bit trivial. But that is exactly what Althusser is targeting. It is in this obviousness, this self-evident reaction of all of us (namely, that when called upon we turn around), that the ideological subjection has its foundation. Please look at the religious example that Althusser gives us on page 121 and relate it to Figure 10.1.

Figure 10.1. Althusser's Concept of Subjection by Interpellation

SUBJECT
(e.g., "God")
↓↓
interpellation
↓↓
↓↓
subject
(e.g., "Moses")

recognizes the call   turns around   responds

[no resistance, no negotiation]

The religious example is the famous thornbush story from the Hebrew Bible (Exodus 3). We find at the top of the arrangement an upper-
case SUBJECT, which is God, an unchallenged authority—"I am who I am"
(v. 14)—and at the bottom, we find Moses, who is frightened by the burning
bush that is not consumed. The interaction starts with the SUBJECT's interpellation: "God called to him out of the bush: 'Moses, Moses!' And Moses
turns around and responds "Here am I" (v. 4), or in Althusser's account:
"It's really I! I am Moses thy servant, speak and I shall listen!" (2001, p.
121). Recognizing that it is really him who is called by his name, Moses also
"recognizes that he is a subject, a subject of God, a subject subjected to God,
a subject through the Subject and subjected to the Subject. The proof: he
obeys him, and makes his people obey God's Commandments" (p. 121). We
are obviously dealing with a pretty one-sided interaction. That's why all the
arrows in the diagram point downward. The only activity of Moses seems to
be that he recognizes himself in the call and shows this in his response. But
this response is also a part of the interpellation itself.

To translate the biblical example into our times, we could imagine a
speech by our president, who addresses us in the name of the Almighty or
of our American values or of the great American path toward freedom. He
might call us to help the nation and the government in its "war on terror-
ism," which is framed as a struggle between "good" and "evil." The effec-
tiveness of such a speech is not merely determined by the extent to which
the president is telling the truth or lying (it might usually be something in
between: working with half-truths, quoting some "facts" and dissimulating
others, etc.), but by the way he is "interpellating" us as ideological subjects:
In the name of what ideological instances and values is he speaking to us?
The point is to analyze why and under what conditions we "turn around"
and "recognize" ourselves when we are called upon as members of a great
nation, as brave and law-abiding citizens, as fighters for freedom and justice
(maybe even in the name of Martin Luther King, Jr.'s civil rights movement).
Why do we respond: Yes, he is speaking to "us," that's what we really are
(or rather: want to be)?

Althusser describes this ideological mechanism as a "mirror structure": the subjects are subjected in a way that they can contemplate in
the big Subject their "own image (present and future)" so that they are
given "the guarantee that this really concerns them" (2001, p. 122).
The subjects can also recognize one another as being little subjects subjected to the same big Subject. By this "mutual recognition of subjects"
(p. 123), they might also recognize who does not belong, who does not
share the "American values" and the belief in America's greatness, for
example, the "barbarian" foreigner or the "underclass" that is cut off

from the American mainstream. This identification might still work even if the subjects have only poorly paid jobs that keep them in poverty (or no job at all).

I think it is fair to say that Althusser's perspective is rather pessimistic. This has often been attributed to his adoption of the psychoanalytic theory of Jacques Lacan, which describes human development from early childhood on as a permanent series of subjections to an alienating "symbolic order." I cannot discuss here the specifics of Lacan's psychoanalysis and its impact on Althusser's ideology theory.[3] But since Althusser sees our entire life in the perspective of being subjected to authorities—starting with the family as the first "Ideological State Apparatus" that imposes gender expectations on us even before birth—he can conclude that "an individual is always-already a subject," even before he or she is born (2001, p. 119). In this sense, ideology in general is an "omni-historical reality" for him, "eternal," like the unconscious according to Freud (pp. 108–109). Since we are permanently called upon from the start and have learned to turn around and to respond appropriately, our identity is built up through innumerable layers of interpellations, so that ideological subjection and subjectivity become one and the same.[4]

Althusser's ideological interpellations thus provide "the absolute guarantee" that the subjects function "'all by themselves,' i.e., by ideology," with the exception of some "'bad subjects' who on occasion provoke the intervention of one of the detachments of the (repressive) State apparatus" (2001, p. 123).

———————

These are the main characteristics of Althusser's theory of ideology. After our discussion, I will introduce you to some of the theoretical objections his critics have raised. But first, I would like to step out of his theoretical framework and look at Ashwin Desai's account of a concrete community struggle in South Africa. The historical context is that after the liberation from the apartheid regime, the African National Congress (ANC) government under President Thabo Mbeki adopted the doctrine of neoliberalism and pushed through an economic politics of privatization and deregulation that was directed against large parts of poor communities. Since the end of apartheid, only 3% of arable land had been redistributed and much of that small percentage had been given "to black commercial farmers and not to landless peasants" (2002, p. 11). The struggle Desai examines takes place between a local council of the ANC in Chatsworth that tries to push poor neighborhoods from their homes and the poor communities that defend themselves against water cutoffs and impending evictions. To understand the dynamics of the struggle it is important to point out that most of the people of this community are Indian. When the ANC City Council tries to evacuate the community it meets such a determined resistance in the form of demonstrations and squatting that it has to give up and withdraw. Furious about this defeat, a City Council member pulls the race card and begins castigating the crowd as "Indians" who seek to keep their ethnic privileges against the poor black majority of the district. But the crowd responds by shouting, "We are not Indians, we are the poors," and, from the ranks of the black constituencies: "We are not African, we are the poors" (p. 44). This response could not be co-opted. According to Desai, "Identities were being rethought in the context of struggle and the bearers of these identities were no respecters of authority" (p. 44).

Let's transition now to our discussion. I'd like to know your opinion of how this story can be related to Althusser's theory of ideology.

CHAPTER 10 SUPPLEMENT 1

Excerpts from the Ensuing In-Class Debate

Adam: Althusser is right when he points out that ideological interpellations are very powerful. And they are all over the place. He gives the everyday example of friends knocking at each other's door, asking, "Who's there?" "It's me"—or shaking hands on the street, thereby showing that they recognize each other. That's why he says that ideology recruits us all and transforms us all. It is impossible to find a stance outside interpellations. That is what Foucault has shown in terms of his "microphysics of power."

Vanessa: But for me this notion of ideology is too general. It is true, we are all dependant on being called upon. We need recognition in order to develop our self-esteem. The important question is, however, to which interpellations do we respond and which ones do we reject? This is where ideologies come into play.

Miriam: Desai's example shows the possibility of developing resistant subjectivities that Althusser does not account for. In his model, the interpellated subjects can only turn around and say, "Yes, here am I." But in reality, they can keep going their way or even say, "Sorry, it ain't me; I am someone different."

Jessica: But in general, Althusser has a point. In most cases, the ideological interpellations work—everyone wants to be a "good subject," wants to be recognized by the authorities of our society.

Onleilove: But maybe one should go a step further: Isn't there an inner desire to be called upon? Like an interpellation from within?

Willie: One has to have in mind that Althusser's theory is about the manufacturing of conformist subjectivities that comply with the dominant order. These subjectivities can certainly be found among the poor as well. But as poor people organize as part of a broader movement to end poverty, they begin to question the old subjectivities which make them open to the creation of new subjectivities.

Aaron: I want to point out that these "new subjectivities" are not completely new, at least not in the sense of being outside the general ideological framework. It is not that they were "Indians" before and now they are just "the poors." Identities are never homogeneous, but always multiple. Judith Butler argues in *Bodies That Matter* (1993) that even when you oppose and resist you cannot prevent that you draw your agency from the same power relations you are challenging.[5]

Anne: Would it be possible for an antipoverty movement to become a big SUBJECT? Couldn't it function as a powerful moral value that calls people toward something greater and better?

Jan: This might happen indeed when a resistance movement gains power and hegemony, but the transformation into a new SUBJECT, an unquestionable authority that is to be obeyed, is in my view a dangerous shift to an authoritarian regime. I'd rather prefer to commit to developing "horizontal" interpellations between subjects that recognize one another as equals in cooperation and solidarity, without being dependent on a SUBJECT "above" us.

Brian: That's how I understand what the poor in Desai's story are doing. They do not recognize one another by way of a big interpellating SUBJECT but rather as brothers and sisters living together in poverty. It is only by mutually recognizing one another in this way that they can resist the rule and divide strategies from above.

Anne: It is not that simple, though. The oppressed also need a strong Good to be able to resist the powers-that-be. Without a big SUBJECT you couldn't hold up the moral values that prevent you from being co-opted and corrupted.

Colleen: Althusser should have explored more closely what God was actually doing with Moses. God called him to take up a leadership role in the liberation from slavery.

Charlene: What is missing in Althusser's model is that he does not examine the real-life experiences that have a decisive impact on whether people accept a specific ideological interpellation or instead reject it. They might also take up the dominant ideological values and claim or reappropriate them for their own purpose.

CHAPTER 10 SUPPLEMENT 2

Some Theoretical Comments and Transition to the Next Session

Let me go over some of the elements of this substantial debate. You might be surprised that many of your observations can be found in the theoretical controversies around Althusser's concept of ideology, some of which you will read and evaluate for next week.

There is, for instance, a general consensus that Althusser is mostly interested in a general formal structure of ideological submission without looking at the specific contents of ideologies. Althusser himself is aware of that and admits that his definitions are still schematic and abstract (2001, pp. 124–125). I think one could argue that it is legitimate to think about how ideologies work "in general" without going immediately into the question of what concrete content the ideology in question might have. A social theory does not work in the same way as a specific description of empirical reality.

But it is another question whether Althusser's general model of ideological interpellation and subjection is wide and nuanced enough to allow for the different varieties that can be observed in the history of ideologies. For example, some of your objections are supported by Stuart Hall, who argues that Althusser gives "an *over-integrative* account" of the reproduction of a ruling ideology and does not account sufficiently for the contradictions and struggles that lead to its continuous production and transformation (1988, p. 48). In a similar way, cultural theorist Terry Eagleton objects that Althusser's model is "a good deal too monistic," because he "runs together the necessity of some 'general' identification with our submission to specific social roles" (1991, p. 145). In other words, the fact that we are all subjected to the "symbolic order" of a language is one thing, but whether we follow this or that orientation is another question. I think this points to a general problem in social theories: Monistic concepts, be they of "ideology" or of "discourse" or of "power," have only a limited value for social movements, because these movements need to differentiate and to specify *what kind of* discourses they must speak and *what kind* of collective power they must build up to be effective in their struggle against poverty and social injustice.

Eagleton adds another argument that corresponds with your observation that identities are always multiple: "There are, after all, many different ways in which we can be 'hailed,' and some cheery cries, whoops and whistles may strike us as more appealing than some others. Someone may be a mother, Methodist, house-worker and trade unionist all at the same time, and there is no reason to assume that these various forms of insertion into ideology will be mutually harmonious" (1991, p. 145). I think one could conclude that Althusser does not take into consideration that the ideological interpellations we are exposed to are not one and the same but may contradict one another, according to the different ideological apparatuses that call upon us and also according to the different relations of force within the different ideological apparatuses. But as soon as we are subjected to contradicting interpellations, we have some room of maneuver. We can or might even have to reject some interpellations and accept others.

I agree with the argument of some of the class that Desai shows a response to ideological interpellations that Althusser does not seem to be interested in. The poor that reject the interpellation "you are privileged Indians" break out of what Althusser describes as the "mirror structure" of ideology. They do not recognize themselves through the big SUBJECT but rather recognize one another as "equal" little subjects living in poverty and fighting together against their eviction. Althusser neglects the fundamental difference between "vertical" interpellations that come from above, from Ideological State Apparatuses, and more "horizontal" types of mutual recognition among equals. Asking "who's there?" when a friend knocks at my door is hardly the same as the big SUBJECT God calling upon Moses.

But even in this biblical example, the ideological dynamic is much more complicated than Althusser seems to notice. He should indeed have explored more closely the relationship between God and Moses.

If you look at the wider context of the thornbush story you can see that the actual superpower defining the power field is not God but the Egyptian state equipped with huge apparatuses, both repressive and ideological. If you include the real power relations, it becomes clear that God's interpellation of Moses is in itself part of a resistance movement. God calls upon Moses to be the leader of a slave revolt that leads the people out of Egypt. There is no doubt that he calls "from above" in an authoritarian way, but the ideological arrangement is much more complex: the big SUBJECT God interpellates the little subject Moses to *resist* another big SUBJECT, namely, the ruling powers, and to take on a leadership role in the process. This might not be the pure type of grassroots resistance that perhaps some of us would wish to develop. But we have to acknowledge that the real history of ideological struggles is replete with such contradictory combinations. I think a critical theory of ideology should be able to analyze both the efficacy of these contradictions and the enormous risks and dangers they contain.

I would like to introduce you to a possible alternative model that you will study more closely for next week, namely, Stuart Hall's famous essay "Encoding, Decoding" that has become a foundational text for critical cultural studies. Hall distinguishes between the "encoding" of a message by an ideological apparatus, for example, the cultural apparatus of a TV channel, and its "decoding" by the receiver, that is, by the TV watcher. He argues that the "encoding" does not "fully guarantee" the "decoding," which is a meaningful and therefore relatively autonomous activity of interpretation (1993, p. 508). He is not saying that the TV consumer and the producer are on an equal footing—this would be a naive illusion. According to him, the different mappings are "structured in dominance," but not closed (p. 514).

Against this background, he distinguishes three possible types of decoding: (1) In the "dominant-hegemonic" type, the decoding takes place within the dominant code; (2) in the "negotiated code," the viewers accept the dominant position only on a general or abstract level and redefine it differently in regard to their local conditions; and (3) in the "oppositional code," the viewer "decodes the message in a *globally* contrary way"; he or she "detotalizes" the hegemonic message in order to "retotalize" it in an alternative framework of reference (1993, p. 517).

This model might give us a more flexible framework that allows us to better explain the different possibilities to respond to ideological interpellations. It is obvious that the first "dominant-hegemonic" type of decoding corresponds to what Althusser describes as the "turning around" of the subject—the TV watchers accept and take over the "encoded" interpellations without questioning them; the third "oppositional code" describes what the poor communities of Desai's account are doing: They reject the encoded message ("We are not Indians") and "retotalize" it in an opposite framework, by affirming a counteridentity: "We are the poors!" The second type, the "negotiated" code, has become the favorite subject of postmodernist and postcolonialist theories that focus on the ambivalences and "hybridities" (Homi Bhabha) in discourses and power relations. The finding itself is not as new as it seems. Much of the ambivalences highlighted in these theories have already been captured by W. E. B. Du Bois's concept of "double consciousness" in 1897.[6] In terms of Althusser's ideology theory, the "negotiated" code covers different kinds of compromise and ambiguity toward ideological interpellations: restricting their meaning, applying them only halfway, mimicking them in a way that might slip into mockery or subversion, "resignifying" them by using the slippages of the message's signifiers, as Judith Butler would phrase it.[7]

At this point, we might want to use a piece of Gramsci's analysis. The different ways in which such "decodings" are being done depend on the hegemonic relations of force, both within the interpellating ideological powers and on the side of those exposed to these interpellations. To what extent are they dispersed and fragmented? Can they build up sustainable communities that stabilize resisting worldviews? Can they become a part of social movements that build up their own intellectual activities and interpretations?

Someone mentioned in the discussion that Althusser does not relate his concept of ideological interpellations to the real-life experiences of people. I think this is indeed a crucial point, namely, the danger of "totalizing" ideology. If we want to explain the possibility of different responses to ideologies, we need to presuppose that the subjects are not mere "effects" of ideological interpellations. They are not "constituted" merely by ideologies or by "discourses," as some postmodernist theorists assume, but have other levels of practice and experience as well. The point is not to argue that there is a "pure" standpoint "outside" of social constructions and meanings. Language and discourses are certainly always with us, but they are not the only factors that determine our lives. Without the lived experience of being poor and of sharing that situation across color lines, the communities in South Africa wouldn't have had the ground point from which to resist the dominant interpellations. They live in living bodies with real needs and try to survive in specific material conditions of life. Experiences like feeling hunger, sleeping in the cold, and getting sick can hardly be characterized as ideological interpellations or discourses, even if the interpretation of that hunger, cold, and sickness are heavily influenced by the predominant ideologies. Ideological interpellations are effective only when they succeed in appealing to lived experiences, and they can only be challenged or rejected when there are better and more convincing ways of making "good sense" (Gramsci) of our lives.

For next week, please read the chapter from Ashwin Desai's *We Are the Poors* and compare it with the selected readings from Judith Butler (1993), Du Bois (1995), Terry Eagleton (1991), and Stuart Hall (1988, 1993). I would like you to look at all the materials we've read so far and to prepare some reflections on the relationship between social movements and ideology theories.

NOTES

1. Althusser explicitly refers to Gramsci's argument that the state could not be reduced to the Repressive State Apparatus, "but included . . . a number of institutions from 'civil society': the Church, the Schools, the trade unions, etc." (2001, p. 95, note 7).

2. This is, however, not a literal quote by Pascal, who actually did not simply deduce the inner belief from outer practices, but rather reflected on how to connect the exterior of rituals to the interior of beliefs and attitudes (1954, p. 1219).

3. Cf., e.g., Dews, 1987, pp. 45–86, 87–108, 234–242; Eagleton, 1991, pp. 144–156; Rehmann, 2007, pp. 224–226; 2008, 112–117.

4. Judith Butler has taken up the identification of subjection and subjectivation: Since the I is produced through the accumulation and convergence of an endless chain of interpellating calls, the estrangement or division produced is both violating and enabling; it is what Spivac calls an "enabling violation" (Butler, 1993, p. 122).

5. "The 'I' who would oppose its construction is always in some sense drawing from that construction to articulate its opposition" (Butler, 1993, p. 122). It draws its agency in part from being implicated in the power relations that it seeks to oppose (p. 123).

6. W. E. B. Du Bois had developed the concept of "double consciousness" to describe the African American condition. He defines it as the "peculiar sensation . . . of always looking at one's self through the eyes of others, of measuring one's soul by the tape of a world that looks on in amused contempt and pity" (1995, p. 45).

7. Cf., e.g., Butler, 1993, pp. 122, 124, 137.

REFERENCES

Althusser, L. (2001). Ideology and ideological state apparatuses: Notes towards an investigation (1971). In *Lenin and philosophy and other essays* (pp. 85–126). New York: Monthly Review Press.

Butler, J. (1993). *Bodies that matter*. New York: Routledge.

Desai, A. (2002). *We are the poors: Community struggles in post-apartheid South Africa.* New York: Monthly Review Press.

Dews, P. (1987). *Logics of disintegration: Post-structuralist thought and the claims of critical theory.* New York: Verso.

Du Bois, W. E. B. (1995). *The souls of black folk.* New York: Signet Classic.

Eagleton, T. (1991). *Ideology: An Introduction.* London & New York: Verso.

Foucault, M. (1977). *Discipline and punish: The birth of the prison.* New York: Random House.

Hall, S. (1988). The toad in the garden: Thatcherism among the theorists. In C. Nelson & L. Grossberg (Eds.), *Marxism and the interpretation of culture* (pp. 35–55). Chicago: University of Illinois Press.

Hall, S. (1993). Encoding, decoding. In S. During (Ed.), *The cultural studies reader* (2nd ed., pp. 507–517). London & New York: Routledge.

Pascal, B. (1954). *Pensées* (1670). In *Oeuvres complètes.* Texte établi, présenté et annoté par Jacques Chevalier (pp. 1079–1345). Paris: Gallimard.

Rehmann, J. (2007). Ideology theory. *Historical Materialism 15*, 211–239.

Rehmann, J. (2008). *Einführung in die Ideologietheorie.* Argument-Verlag: Hamburg [English translation in preparation].

CHAPTER 11

Teach As We Fight, Learn as We Lead: Lessons in Pedagogy and the Poverty Initiative Model

Willie Baptist and Liz Theoharis

This book has focused on poverty as the defining issue of our time and theoretical and practical educational methods to address the root causes of poverty and build a social movement to eliminate it. The interview with Willie Baptist about his life in poverty and the lessons drawn from his over-40-year-long participation in social justice movements, as well as the other chapters, have been developed in classes taught by Jan and Willie titled "Poverty, Social Theories—Alternative Models?" and "Poverty and Poor People's Movements—Social Analysis and Ethical Reflection" at Union Theological Seminary. In addition to the lessons learned and shared in this extensive interview with Willie and the other topics taken up in these classes, the whole of the leadership development process that Willie has undergone through his life in the movement is an example of the leadership development necessary for these times and the kind of pedagogy that we wish to share in this book. The pedagogic specifics of these classes are also part of a larger pedagogical program of the Poverty Initiative and a wider network of organizations working to end poverty. That is why we conclude Pedagogy of the Poor with an attempt to lay out some other key concepts drawn from the poor organizing the poor on the importance of education and new methods of teaching and learning as part of a social movement.

Poverty with all its complexity requires practical engagement with the struggles of the poor as well as interdisciplinary scholarship to unravel its root causes and manifestations. For over 2 decades of organizing with the National Union of the Homeless, the National Welfare Rights Union/Kensington Welfare Rights Union, and now the Poverty Initiative, we have distilled lessons on the importance and role of education in our movement. We sum up some of these lessons here.

WHY EDUCATION?

In our work of building a social movement to end poverty, we have found that education is central. If we are serious about the work of ending poverty, we don't have to merely do more actions; we have to do smarter actions. We don't just have to be more active; we have to be more effective. We live in a very pragmatic society, and many of us think that if we just start one more program or effect one more policy change it will bring an end to poverty. But our experience has shown that poverty is more complex than that and it is going to take clarity, competence, and commitment to achieve real social change in this country. To outfight the forces arrayed against us, we must outsmart them. Nowhere in world history can anyone find where a dumb force rose up and defeated a smart force. Therefore, it is vitally important for anyone interested in ending poverty to develop an engaged intelligence that will outsmart, not only out organize, the current conditions that cause poverty and misery.

LEADERSHIP IS KEY IN THE FIRST STAGE OF DEVELOPMENT IN BUILDING A SOCIAL MOVEMENT

Before the elements of mass and velocity of a social movement are considered, its direction must be determined. This is what leadership of a social movement is all about. History teaches us that this leadership is twofold: (1) The unity of the leading social force for social change; that is, a unity on the basis of needs and demands incompatible with the status quo. And (2) systematically educated and trained core(s) of leaders sufficiently connected, clear, competent, and committed to enlighten and organize the leading social force. Today's society is defined by the problem of the ever-deepening polarity between wealth and poverty. Today the poor and dispossessed are the leading social force because they have the least or no stake in such a polarized society. Either they end this inhumane polarity or it will end them. In the last years of his life, the words and work of the Rev. Dr. Martin Luther King Jr. anticipated the present situation. His launching of the Poor People's Campaign in 1967–1968 inspires us today. The strategic concept introduced by this historic campaign was the need and possibility "to lift the load of poverty" through uniting the poor across color lines into "a new and unsettling force." The Poverty Initiative has taken up this mantle by working to reignite a new Poor People's Campaign in response to the present deepening economic and social crises. We believe that such a campaign adapted to today's economic and political situation is needed to build a broader social movement to end poverty. The first step and requirement in organizing and building this campaign and movement is the development of a united and sophisticated core of leaders capable of analyzing and putting forth solutions that address the scale and complexity of poverty today. It seeks to carry this mission out by helping establish a multiracial, multifaith, multi-issue network of grassroots community and religious leaders. Central to this process is the identification and development of leaders who are emerging out of the growing ranks and struggles of the dispossessed. Learning from the crippling effects of Dr. King's assassination, the Poverty Initiative is clear that there is a need to develop many Martin Luther Kings. Such leaders are not developed spontaneously, but instead must be systematically educated and trained.

We work with an analogy of building a house to understand the stages of development of building a social movement. Building a house has to be done in stages, and builders must have a blueprint or a strategic plan. No stage can be skipped, nor can we stop at any stage. Today with our remote control mentality we impatiently want to fast-forward to start with building the roof, to begin at the end. But before a building has a roof, it must have a strong foundation. Presently, we are at the foundation stage of building a massive movement to end poverty led by the poor as a united and organized force. This is the stage of building the large and expanding core of leaders who are connected, clear, competent, and committed. History teaches that every successful social movement has to begin with the development of such a core as its cadre base or foundation. The basic strategic content of this leadership is the recognition of the necessity of poverty being solved by the building of a massive movement led by the poor as a force united and organized across color lines. All our various activities, tactical as well as educational, must be coordinated as means toward accomplishing this task of the current initial stage of the construction of a movement to end poverty.

Organizing to unite the poor as the base of a broader movement to abolish poverty is necessarily founded on the concept of "commitment, not compensation." Commitment to build such a movement is the primary quality of leadership. This must be a commitment strengthened by clarity, competence, and connection to the emerging struggles of the poor and dispossessed. The other indispensable quality of leadership is the ability to learn and teach as well as to organize. This includes, most important for this initial stage, that the indispensable quality of a leader is the development of other leaders. "The more you know, the more you owe" sums up this quality. Therefore, the cornerstone of our general education plan must be "educating the educators, training the trainers."

ORGANIZING WITHOUT EDUCATING IS MOBILIZING

Without education, organization is reduced to mobilization. We cannot afford to just mobilize bodies—we must move minds. Without a deep understanding of the causes and conditions of poverty, it is difficult to develop the commitment necessary to endure the hardships and inevitable setbacks of a protracted struggle. Despite the fact that the Kensington Welfare Rights Union was able to house over 700 formerly homeless families over the course of a decade of organizing work, many of those families left the movement when they got their houses rather than staying committed to the fight to end homelessness for everyone. Simply mobilizing bodies, moving from one event to another, is not enough to counter the sophisticated and dangerous forces arrayed against us and to "stick and stay" the necessary course of ending human misery.

OUR APPROACH TO EDUCATION

We believe that popular conceptions about poverty are in most cases inaccurate, incomplete, and biased. Therefore, we have found that it is important to have education central in the struggle so people can acquire new information and understanding about poverty. Education is about teaching people that it is possible to end poverty. We have a saying in the Poverty Initiative: We have to first end poverty in our minds before we end poverty with our hands. We see the main playing field or battleground for a movement to end poverty as our minds.

Our basic pedagogical approach recognizes that the mind does not present itself as a blank tablet. The mental battlefield is littered with old and entrenched values and views. These values and views are held intact by emotion-laden myths and stereotypes. Our experiences, particularly in the work of the poor organizing the poor, have taught us that the process of education is at once one of uneducating and unlearning as well as one of educating and learning. "Plowing the field" of old ideas is indispensable to "planting seeds" of new ideas. The wrenching conditions of economic and social crises and the practical struggles in response to these conditions compel especially those embattled to question their deeply held beliefs and habits. This begins to clear the way for the introduction of new ideas, new consciousness, and the development of new leaders. The pedagogical principle of "plowing the fields and planting the seeds" is what is meant by the teachings that every action, protest, and campaign must be used as a school.

We have learned that, especially in an age of a profound information revolution, education is pivotal in developing leaders and organizing a broad movement to abolish poverty. Most of our work has been carried out in this new age in which people are rapidly and constantly bombarded with all sorts of information, all sorts of appeals to old ideas and images, and all sorts of miseducation and stereotypes. In such a period, leadership development in terms of imparting a true and effective epistemology (true and false), ethics (right and wrong), and expertise (capacity in strategy, tactics, and techniques) requires an educational process that focuses more on how we think than what we think, more on initiative than on imitation, more on commitment than on compensation.

In our work, we are repeatedly coming up against the strong influences of old American pragmatism. Being pragmatic is often interpreted as being practical. This is not what we are referring to here. We are talking about a worldview, a philosophical way of thinking, that is deeply embedded in American culture and that results in separating theory from practice, knowing from doing. Although it affects all of us, this philosophy is an anti-intellectualism created by intellectuals from elite universities. It promotes an impatience with and resistance to study, educational discipline, and social theory that provides vital lessons from history and political economy. While at times giving lip service to the "long term" or strategy, it is consumed with the immediate, with "what works for the moment for me." For this reason, it is a very eclectic and categorical way of seeing the world, seeing only the superficial separateness of things and not their substantial inner connections. The poor cannot afford this pragmatism. We need to fight for an intellectual rigor and theory to guide our actions.

"Teaching as we fight, learning as we lead, talking as we walk" is how we approach education. This pedagogy ensures that the fight teaches. Carrying out plans for using antipoverty campaigns, activities, and protests as schools has been effective in imparting transformative experiences that lead to a transformation of values. For example, the Homeless Union's nationwide housing takeovers (as discussed earlier) served as effective schools for developing leadership and membership. Other examples (also discussed in earlier chapters of this book) include bus tours and marches, which became traveling schools. These experiences have been effective in raising questions in participants, offering a space for mutual living and learning.

We have embraced the concept that "the struggle is a school" and that integrating education into daily actions and activities is a central way to raise consciousness among pragmatic people. One example of this was in October 1999, when organizations of the poor and homeless from across the Americas marched from Washington, DC, to the United Nations in New York City. We marched in protest of economic human rights violations caused by the U.S. government around the world. We marched 10 to 20 miles a day for 32 days, sleeping in community centers and churches throughout DC, Maryland, Delaware, Pennsylvania, New Jersey, and New York. Each day we held press conferences, educational presentations, events, rallies and protests, cultural presentations, and so on to show the world how poor people from the United States, Canada, and Latin America were coming together to build a movement to end poverty. More than anything this march was a traveling school for all participants, as groups and individuals were able to share what lessons they had learned from their communities with others.

We have also found that the use of civil disobedience actions and schooling in jail cells has proved to be a particularly effective means for values formation and the development of commitment. Civil disobedience helps to produce moments where participants question the things that govern behavior and form their core belief system. Being prepared to go to jail because you understand the current system/status quo is unjust is a huge step in the development of a commitment to ending poverty and human misery and standing up for something bigger than just yourself.

TEACHING METHODS, FORMS, AND ACTIVITIES

In order to end poverty in our minds, we have culled lessons from our years of organizing and educating. These lessons are in the form of specific methods and activities as well as content of the teaching and learning. Following is a select but important list of methods of teaching and learning that we have used to develop low-income and other leaders dedicated to ending poverty. We know this list is not complete but hope that educators, social movement practitioners, and other people of conscience find these methods and insights useful.

Collective study and self-study. Our educational process involves collective study, including classes, retreats, conferences, schools, and seminars, as well as ongoing self-study and research. Both are aided by a general and individual library system, including books, articles, videos, audio recordings, and photo documentation. We take advantage of every opportunity to teach and learn together. We prioritize small-group and one-on-one conversations because in these situations barriers of distrust and insecurity are more likely overcome so that real questions and concerns can be grappled with.

Teaching in dialogue. We can sum up a key teaching method with one phrase: less monologue, more dialogue. In addition to lectures and presentations, which are important for conveying large amounts of knowledge, seminars and a culture of dialogue are important methods to convey respect and mutual learning as well as to help participants engage the material and apply it to their own situations.

Buddy system. To reinforce an inquisitive and participatory method of teaching, we have found it is important to use the "buddy system" to pair up less experienced participants with veteran leaders and educators so each participant has an opportunity to get more specialized attention. In this case, the new leader follows the veteran organizer around and "runs with" them as they go though their day-to-day organizing work. This offers the new leaders an opportunity to have new experiences, get mentored by someone with different experiences from theirs and in general, ask questions. Depending on the educational style of each person, it is important to offer educational opportunities in small, personal settings, including pairing people up.

Use of art, music, videos, theater ... Use must be made of those arts and cultural forms most accessible to the poor for education purposes. Movies, street theater, music, pictures, and posters are among the most prominent fixtures in the lives of impoverished communities. Combining entertainment with education has proved to be a most effective way of engaging and elevating people's thinking. We have found that new views and values are more easily and effectively introduced by a song, theater piece, or work of art than through hours of lecture, and at the same time you can reach the heart and soul of a person.

We have written our own songs, including "All of Our Rights Now" and "Rich Man's House." To this end we have even formed choirs and have hosted memorial services and art exhibits.

Use of the Internet. The Internet is a useful educational tool both for doing research and for sharing our educational principles with others. In fact, the Internet is the largest library system in the world, and anyone who is serious about deepening knowledge of theory and history would see the importance of integrating the Internet into an educational system. New methods of communication make it possible for movement leaders and participants to learn from one another and to learn together using online instruments, including the World Wide Web and social networking tools.

To see how the Internet can be used to educate and organize, we wish to share the experience of one of our partner organizations, the Coalition of Immokalee Workers (CIW). The CIW has had an award-winning Web page for over 10 years, with YouTube videos, photo slideshows, editorials, press coverage, and member highlights. Hundreds of thousands of people in countries all over the world have followed the activities, boycotts, and campaigns of the CIW on the Web (http://www.ciw-online.org). Many of their successful organizing campaigns were waged both online and off-line. The CIW posts information and educational materials on their Web site, and thousands of students, religious allies, and other low-wage workers have made use of these materials to learn about the conditions of farm workers, be informed about the organizing campaigns of the CIW, and get involved. This is possible in part because of their use on the Internet. In their case and many others, the Internet has played a key role in education and organization toward social transformation.

Leadership schools. Leadership schools are intensive, weeklong training gatherings for organizers and educators involved in the movement to end poverty. The purpose of leadership schools is to bring together grassroots leaders from across the country to exchange and learn from one another's experiences, analyses, and lessons, drawn from struggles to secure economic justice in their home communities. To ensure that the flow of information is optimized in all directions, our leadership schools are guided by an understanding that teachers have the capacity both to teach and to learn, and that students have the capacity both to learn and to teach. This philosophy of equality among participants insures a maximum exchange of skills and information. These schools strive to create an environment of joy and fun, as well as a safe space for rigorous discussions and critique. Developed on a "train the trainer" model, leadership schools equip participants to further develop their own educational and leadership development programs within their local organizations. This groundbreaking effort is partly modeled on and inspired by the educational work of the Brazilian Landless Workers Movement (MST), the largest social movement in this hemisphere. The 90-day training sessions of the MST create the foundation for their expanding collection of leaders. Based on the MST experience, our leadership schools are an immersion, with both staff and students expected to participate in all aspects of community life, including food preparation, child care, and recreation.

Immersions. Poverty immersion experiences are hands-on and experience-based travel seminars conducted over a period of a week or 2 that serve to introduce participants to community organizations in different locales. Poverty Initiative immersions include dialogue with leaders of local and national poor people's organizations and local congregations engaged in mission work, human rights trainings and documentation in poor communities, Bible studies, video showings, and poverty reality tours. Significant time is spent discussing the theological implications of building a movement to end poverty, led by poor people and the role of religious communities in building a social movement. We have found that immersions affect participants on a holistic level, since they are intense experiences for all involved. Taking people out of their day-to-day environment and connecting them with other communities in struggle has a profound impact. (Please find a longer description of immersion courses below.)

Reality tours. We have used reality tours—activities in which leaders travel to historic sites as well as sites where significant organizing from within our movement has taken place—to study social movement history and reinforce shared values. These reality tours draw on at once multiple sense perceptions and the reflective capacities of people to think and feel. We have found that reality tours are important for both the tour guides and participants.

One example of a reality tour is the Poverty Initiative's Poverty Scholars Self-Guided Tour of Wall Street. This tour is both virtual and in person and dozens of grassroots organizers, students, and religious leaders have had the opportunity to learn about the connection between wealth and poverty and the relation of Wall Street to issues such as homelessness, low-wage work, and mountaintop removal through participation in this tour.

Personal maps. We have discovered the importance of doing personal maps or poverty life narratives in bringing to the forefront of our hearts and minds those life experiences that tend to reinforce poverty-ending values, self-confidence, and commitment to reestablishing the human dignity of all. In this activity, participants are asked to depict (through drawing, writing, imagining, and so on) their experiences and conceptions of poverty, in many instances in the form of how each person has come to be involved in the struggle to end poverty. This activity surfaces people's emotions and ideas about poverty and asks people to reflect deeply and personally. Many people come to see that they have personal connection to poverty and that they are not alone in their experiences. This connection to people's emotions is an important pedagogical tool for affecting the values as well as ideas of people. Connected to this, we have used biographies of important leaders (through videos and books) to teach history and especially the role of individuals in history.

Levels of education. Popular education forms have been very useful especially for orientation and introductory education for those just getting involved in organizing and advocacy work. However, our experience is that they must be applied with the view of advancing especially the prospective leaders to intermediate and more advanced educational forms. Paulo Freire exposed himself to higher levels of education, which he then used to creatively formulate and apply popular education approaches. The sophisticated leadership development of the cadre of the powers-that-be requires in our leadership development process more than simply popular education–level graduates. It requires nothing less than the training of many more Paulo Freires, which translates into higher levels of education development methods.

IMPORTANT THEORETICAL CONCEPTS IN OUR PEDAGOGY

In educating leaders for a movement to end poverty, we have found that the content of our education is as important as the methods used to educate. We have developed innovative ways and means to educate, including the use of participatory activities, in addition to teaching through conferences, schools, and public events. We have also focused on certain theoretical concepts that are central to our curriculum. These concepts include an investigation into an understanding of the leadership of the poor, of poverty as a moral issue, and the concept of rights, as detailed in the Declaration of Independence and the Universal Declaration of Human Rights. We explore these three concepts in what follows.

The Leadership of the Poor

The poor and dispossessed today differ from the poor and dispossessed of the past. They are compelled to fight under qualitatively new conditions and to creatively wield new weapons of struggle. In other words, the socioeconomic position of the low waged, laid-off, and locked out is not that of the industrial poor, the slave poor, or the colonial poor of yesterday. Today's new poor embody all the major issues and problems that affect the majority of other strata of the country's population. Its growing ranks are filled with people economically "downsized" and socially dislocated from every walk of life. Therefore, the massive uniting and organizing of the poor across color and all other lines has "a freedom and a power" to create the critical mass of the American people needed to move this country toward the abolition of all poverty. Dr. King called this leading social force the "non-violent Army or 'freedom church' of the poor."

Presently, we are experiencing the wholesale economic destruction of the "middle class" in this country. This is huge in terms of political power relations and of strategy and tactics. This "middle class" is beginning to question the economic status quo. The point here is not that the economic and social position of the poor is one to be pitied and guilt-tripped about, but that it indicates the direction in which this country is heading if nothing is done to change it. Poverty is devastating me today; it can hit you tomorrow.

If poverty is to be ended, the minds of the bulk of the nearly 300 million people who make up this country need to be changed. The united actions of the poor across color lines serve greatly to break down the stereotypes and unsettle the thinking of the mass of the people. We are building a big movement to solve a big problem, and we need a lot of leaders, coming from different social strata and bringing different social skills and resources to carry this out. Central to uniting and organizing the poor as a social force is identifying and training of massive numbers leaders from the ranks of the poor. This has to be our point of concentration at this initial stage of building a movement broad enough to end poverty. However, for this very reason we must challenge all people, including those coming from other important social ranks, to be trained as leaders committed to this movement as well. Only leaders can ensure the development of leaders. This is no easy task.

Here we must understand the strategic difference between leadership of the poor as a social group and leadership of individuals from the ranks of the poor as well as from other ranks. History and our hard-won experiences have taught us a lot in this regard. Leadership of the poor as a social group is secured primarily through united actions and organization. The development of individual leaders is secured primarily through political education and training. The content of this individual leadership development process includes acquiring the qualities of clarity, competence, commitment, and connectedness necessary to understatnd and fight for the leadership of the poor as a social group united around their immediate and basic human needs. For example, the Rev. Dr. Martin Luther King, Jr., who initiated the organizing of the historic Poor People's Campaign, was himself not poor. However, he was a highly insightful and trained leader committed to organizing the poor across color lines and giving his life to the struggle to end all poverty everywhere. His words and work contributed greatly to the development of both kinds of leadership, social and individual. A very important lesson for us today from his life, especially his last years, is that we can and must develop "many Martins," especially from the ranks of the poor.

Morality

Poverty in a land of abundance is a moral outrage, yet society, including our religious leaders and institutions, has learned to tolerate it. In fact, many people use the quote "The poor will always be with you" from the Bible as an excuse for why religious congregations and even society at large are doing very little in the face of growing poverty. This passage has been used to explain the "futility" of doing antipoverty work because poverty is "inevitable." Many people have been immobilized by the extent of poverty and their inability to imagine a way to address it. Too many have conceded that poverty simply cannot be ended. In fact, we have institutionalized this view with soup kitchens and charity programs focused on the alleviation, rather than the elimination, of poverty.

Society, including our social service agencies, is set up to administer antipoverty programs, not build a movement to end poverty. Many continue with Band-Aid solutions and charity programs because they are concrete actions that seem as though they are addressing the problem— when someone is hungry you give him or her some food. But statistics in metropolitan areas across the United States state that a person becomes homeless every 30 seconds. The severity of this problem means that the tremendous effort put into building a house (where one religious congregation mobilizes enormous resources to build a single house for a homeless family over 6 to 8 months) will never be enough to meet the ever-growing need.

Charity programs also often maintain a relationship in which there are "helpers" and "those who need help" and in fact set up institutions and agencies in which people's jobs rest on the continuation of poverty. For this kind of effort to promote justice, our social services and Band-Aid programs need to really meet the needs of poor people (rather than giving canned goods to a person with no place to open and cook them); they need to be available all the time in a holistic manner so that people's housing, health care, food, and education needs can be met (or at least in a network of other services where people can get what they need when they need it rather than limiting such programs to once a month or every 3 months), and they need to be viewed as a means rather than an ends (so that at the same time as people receive housing or food, legislation that will improve housing or health care options for poor people is being advocated for and community organizing and education to develop leadership for a social movement is taking place). Our work is showing us the need to develop a new morality. This morality promotes justice over charity and human needs over corporate greed. It asserts that poverty is immoral and a sin rather than seeing poor people as immoral and sinners. This morality is a new language and foundation for a social movement to end poverty, led by the poor as an organized and united force.

We can see the need for this new morality in the following example. Some years ago, there were three deaths that occurred in the New York transit depot in the period of a week: the death of a dog, the death of a maintenance worker, and the death of a homeless person. Within that week, nearly 100 calls came in concerning these deaths. Ninety-three of the calls came in for the dog, one call came in for the maintenance worker, and no calls came in for the homeless person. This story shows the moral direction this country is going in. This moral direction reflects an economic direction in which every day, more people are downsized, impoverished, and made homeless. The direction is morally and economically devaluing human lives. And in order to change this direction we need to win the hearts and minds of the American people to end poverty once and for all. Each of our educationals, each of our activities must keep in mind that we are building unity and organization among the poor in order to win the hearts and minds of the people to a vision of human worth and dignity.

Using a Human Rights Framework

In May 1967, the Rev. Dr. Martin Luther King Jr. said, "We have moved from an era of civil rights to the era of human rights, an era where we are called upon to raise certain basic questions about the whole society." Following this shift of Dr. King's, we have found that rights and especially human rights are important concepts in our educational process. Economic human rights offers a framework to unite poor and working people across color lines into a common struggle, appealing to certain core values of the U.S. tradition and culture. These core values are drawn from the historical struggles in this country to define and redefine the meaning of its founding creed. The tactic of using the demand "Economic human rights for all!" allows us to raise the basic question of why poverty exists in the richest country in the world, and to raise another basic question of the relation between the growth of poverty in the United States and its growth worldwide.

In underscoring two of the most important historical influences on the thinking of the American people, the poor white abolitionist John Brown once stated, "The two most sacred documents in the world are the Bible and the Declaration of the Independence." The U.S. Declaration of Independence anticipated and influenced the formulation of the UN's Universal Declaration of Human Rights. It states, "We hold these truths to be self-evident, that all [human beings] are created equal, that they are endowed by their creator with certain unalienable Rights, that among these are life, liberty, and the pursuit of happiness."

. History teaches that the success of any social struggle requires moral and political legitimacy, that is, a broad and deep public sentiment that the struggle is right and just. Today that legitimacy for the struggles of the poor is not going to come from the federal government or from any section of the powers-that-be, as has happened on certain occasions in the past. History and our recent experiences show that legitimacy can come from reference to the emerging international struggles of the impoverished world majority, from reference to those core values of the United States that affirm the basic human rights to life, and from reference to this moral affirmation in international documents such as the Universal Declaration of Human Rights, signed by all the member nations of the United Nations.

Economic human rights are therefore a powerful source of legitimacy for local and national antipoverty struggles and the urgent and basic issues that unite the poor as a social group. As a tactic, using the struggles of the poor along with human rights documentation to expose the fact that every issue of poverty in a time of plenty is a violation of human rights can be an effective means to awaken the consciousness of the "sleeping giant," the mass of the American people.

THE POVERTY INITIATIVE MODEL

Our pedagogical lessons from past decades of organizing and educating in poor communities have culminated in the work of the Poverty Initiative. In particular, both the Poverty Scholars Program and the poverty immersion courses (which are described at more length below) are attempts to sum up and integrate best educational practices for building a social movement to end poverty. They weave together the content, methods, and educational approaches summarized above.

The Poverty Initiative was founded in May 2004 with the goal of bridging poor people's organizations, religious leaders, and the academy in an attempt to build a national movement to end poverty. It began as a project of mainly students at Union Theological Seminary to connect religious communities and poor communities but has grown into a multifaceted program led by community leaders, religious leaders, and others across the United States. Since 2007, we have focused our efforts on reigniting the Poor People's Campaign and finishing the unfinished business of the Rev. Dr. Martin Luther King, Jr. In December 1967, King called upon all people of goodwill to "lift the load of poverty."

Over the years, we have worked to implement our vision for the role of religious communities in a movement to end poverty that brings together critical analysis and prophetic witness to the realities of poverty and oppression. Emphasizing the belief that the voices of those most affected by the problem must be in the forefront of a movement, our educational model seeks to establish and strengthen relationships between poor people's organizations and religious leaders, institutions, and communities so that they can be partners in efforts to end poverty.

The Poverty Initiative offers an antipoverty pedagogical paradigm different from models of other professional graduate schools by bringing students and faculty into direct contact with leaders of poor people's organizations in their homes and neighborhoods as well as in the classroom. It provides a multidisciplinary curriculum—integrating theoretical, theological, and experiential learning that incorporates the analysis, practice, scholarship, and faith that exists in poor communities with graduate-level seminary courses. This new pedagogical paradigm posits the people with lived experience of economic injustice as the intellectual and experiential leaders whose scholarship, when placed in dialogical conversation with the academy, creates solutions to systemic problems.

Since its inception, the Poverty Initiative has had both an educational and an organizing mandate. First, our signature events from 2005–2007 were three National Poverty Truth Commissions inspired by South African and Peruvian truth commissions. Here, low-income leaders testified to the economic human rights abuses (the lack of health care, housing, adequate food, education, or living-wage jobs) before an esteemed panel of religious, academic, and community leaders who served as commissioners. Dozens of testifiers from across New York State and the United States have been heard. Following this history of truth commissions and community meetings, the Poverty Initiative hosted a New York City Town Hall Meeting with Raquel Rolnik, the United Nations' Special Rapporteur on Adequate Housing, to discuss concerns about public housing, Section 8 availability, homelessness, and the foreclosure crises in New York City. The Poverty Initiative was an active part of a citywide coalition of groups charged with coordinating the visit (the first official U.S. Housing Mission from the UN in history) and links to grassroots voices.

Second, the Poverty Initiative has developed the pedagogical methodology of poverty immersion courses, leading a total of six courses since 2005, including to the Gulf Coast in the aftermath of Hurricane Katrina, Appalachia to explore the effects of welfare reform and resource extraction, the Mississippi Delta to commemorate the 40th anniversary of Martin Luther King's Poor People's Campaign, and New York, New Jersey, Maryland and Pennsylvania, visiting local low-wage worker, health care, and public school student organizations. Each immersion course enrolls Union students and Poverty Scholars (as many as 60 participants, depending on logistical capacity, funding, and interest) who investigate conditions of poverty, visit and form partnerships with local churches and social service agencies, and participate in trainings and biblical reflections. The short-term goals of the immersion experiences have been to develop the leadership capacity of low-income leaders; equip all participants to develop their own leadership and education program; and establish new partnerships, trainings, and collaborations among all those involved. The long-range goal is to help develop commitment on the part of these budding leaders (low-income, religious, social work, and so on) to a lifetime vocation of overcoming poverty and, toward this end, to build long-lasting relationships between impoverished people and communities we visit and the communities the participants represent. Upon their return from these trips, participants have time to reflect on the theological and practical implications of the visit and the course overall.

On campus at Union Theological Seminary, the Poverty Initiative has worked with Union faculty to develop and coteach nearly a dozen poverty-themed courses offered at Union to current students, alumni, and local Poverty Scholars; among these courses are Reading the Bible with the Poor, Women's Experience as a Resource for Worship, Poverty and Poor People's Movements: Social and Ethical Analysis, the Gospel of Paul: Poverty and Spirituality, and World Religions and Poverty.

Third, to further our mission, itself inspired by King's historical and strategic conclusions about the poor needing to unite across color lines into "a new and unsettling force," the Poverty Initiative launched our cornerstone Poverty Scholars Program, a leadership development training program and network for a leadership core of 250 grassroots low-income, religious, and community leaders from over 50 poor communities nationwide. The Poverty Scholars Program organizes Strategic Dialogues and Leadership Schools; themes and skills covered at program gatherings include a comprehensive study of the economic crisis and its impact on our communities; the history of Martin Luther King, Jr., the Poor People's Campaign, and the shift from civil rights to human rights for all; theories of impoverishment; using human rights to organize; history of past conditions of poverty and social movements in the United States and abroad; technical training on the use of communication tools such as the Internet, Flip cameras, and blogs, for human rights violation documentation; sharing campaigns and lessons learned from local organizations; and sharing of arts and cultural practices.

The program seeks to lift up the hidden genius of existing grassroots leaders most affected by poverty, while further developing their leadership voice, organizing skills, and capacity for intellectual engagement. Our program engages organizers with proven success in winning local-level campaigns on issues of unemployment, community revitalization, housing and homelessness, immigration, water privatization, ecological devastation, eviction and foreclosure, health care, hunger, low-wage workers' rights, organizing poor youth, public education reform, grassroots media production, and living wages. The Poverty Scholars Program seeks to make an impact at three levels: (1) to provide leadership development and skills training for each individual leader or Poverty Scholar; (2) to inform and sharpen existing and future local campaigns conducted by each partner organization; and (3) to nurture a national network that unites across lines of race, religion, geography, and issue-focused organizing into a social movement to end poverty.

The Poverty Initiative also provides technical support, ongoing training, and strategy development for garnering support from faith-based allies for poor people's organizations and their successful campaigns, including the Restaurant Opportunities Center—New York (prayer vigils and Fireman Hospitality Group lawsuit), Picture the Homeless (Potter's Field Campaign), Domestic Workers United (Domestic Workers Bill of Rights), the United Workers (Living Wages at Camden Yards Campaign), the Coalition of Immokalee Workers (Fair Food Campaign), and others.

Fourth, the Poverty Initiative serves as a clearinghouse and resource center and released our third book, titled *A New and Unsettling Force: Reigniting Rev. Dr. Martin Luther King Jr.'s Poor People's Campaign*. This book, which grew out of the Poverty Scholars Strategic Dialogues, immersion courses, and Poverty Initiative–sponsored seminary courses, features chapters on the history of the Poor People's Campaign of 1968, the role of religion, the importance of art and culture in the struggle to end poverty, and an interview of Bertha Burris (Queen of the Mule Train) and 16 essays submitted by organizations we call the modern-day sanitation workers' struggles. Two other Poverty Initiative publications that grew out of immersion experiences include *Katrina: Listening with Our Hearts* (2006) and *Appalachia: Listening with Our Hearts* (2007). Both contain reflections by immersion participants and photographs taken as we traveled. These publications drew from blogs that the Poverty Initiative set up as part of that pedagogical experience. These online spaces were integrated into the reflection on the immersion and served to deepen this reflection process for the students.

A survey conducted of 30 major U.S. seminaries found that very few offer courses in economic justice, despite our biblical and ecclesiological tradition that places major emphasis on justice for poor people. Therefore, since its inception, the Poverty Initiative has worked with faculty and students from other seminaries and universities to replicate the Poverty Initiative. The impact at other schools includes Poverty Truth Commissions, immersion programs, and participation in our Poverty Scholars Program. Through this work and the replication of our efforts, we hope to develop the leaders and methods for a social movement to end poverty. We invite all the readers of this book to join us.

Check out our website: www.povertyintiative.org.

Index

About the Authors and Contributors

Willie Baptist is a formerly homeless father who came out of the Watts uprisings and the black student movement, and worked as an organizer and shop steward with the United Steelworkers. He has 40 years of experience organizing the poor, including with the National Union of the Homeless, the Kensington Welfare Rights Union, the National Welfare Rights Union, the Poor People's Economic Human Rights Campaign, and many other networks. Willie serves as the Poverty Initiative Scholar-in-Residence and is the coordinator of the Poverty Scholars Program.

Chris Caruso has over 15 years experience training social movements, community organizations, NGOs, unions, and national and international foundations specializing in political education and information technology. He is a PhD candidate in Cultural Anthropology at the Graduate Center of The City University of New York and an instructional technology fellow for the Macaulay Honors College at City College. Chris researches poverty, social movements, and new media. He received his BA from the University of Pennsylvania.

Jan Rehmann, Dr. phil. habil, teaches philosophy and social theories at Union Theological Seminary and at the Free University in Berlin. He has published several books, including on theories of ideology, Nietzsche's influence on postmodernism, Max Weber, and the churches in Nazi Germany. Jan is also co-editor of the *Historical-Critical Dictionary of Marxism* (HKWM).

Liz Theoharis is the coordinator and cofounder of the Poverty Initiative. She has spent the past 15 years organizing the poor in the United States. Liz received her MDiv from Union Theological Seminary in 2004, where she was the first William Sloane Coffin Scholar. Currently, Liz is a PhD candidate and Henry Berg Scholar in New Testament and Christian Origins. Liz is certified for ordination to the Ministry of Word and Sacrament in the Presbyterian Church (USA).

Colleen Wessel-McCoy has been involved with the Poverty Initiative since 2004 and currently works as the Fellows Program Coordinator. She received her undergraduate degree from Agnes Scott College and worked for several years as a community organizer in Chicago before moving to New York to attend Union Theological Seminary, where she earned a MDiv in 2007. She is currently a PhD student in the field of Christian ethics.

John Wessel-McCoy is a project organizer at the Poverty Initiative. He is originally from Decatur, Illinois, and worked for several years as a union organizer. He earned an MA in 2009 from Union Theological Seminary.